THE WORKS OF
JOHN GALSWORTHY

FICTION

VILLA RUBEIN: AND OTHER STORIES
THE ISLAND PHARISEES
THE MAN OF PROPERTY
THE COUNTRY HOUSE
FRATERNITY
THE PATRICIAN
THE DARK FLOWER
THE FREELANDS
BEYOND
FIVE TALES
SAINT'S PROGRESS
TATTERDEMALION
IN CHANCERY
TO LET

———

THE FORSYTE SAGA

———

STUDIES

A COMMENTARY
A MOTLEY
THE INN OF TRANQUILLITY
THE LITTLE MAN
A SHEAF
ANOTHER SHEAF
ADDRESSES IN AMERICA, 1919

———

POEMS

MOODS, SONGS AND DOGGERELS

———

MEMORIES (ILLUSTRATED)
AWAKENING (ILLUSTRATED)

———

PLAYS

FIRST SERIES: THE SILVER BOX
              JOY
              STRIFE

SECOND SERIES: THE ELDEST SON
              THE LITTLE DREAM
              JUSTICE

THIRD SERIES: THE FUGITIVE
              THE PIGEON
              THE MOB

FOURTH SERIES: A BIT o' LOVE
              FOUNDATIONS
              THE SKIN GAME

FIFTH SERIES: A FAMILY MAN
              LOYALTIES
              WINDOWS

SIX SHORT PLAYS

THE SKIN GAME

(A TRAGI-COMEDY)

BY

JOHN GALSWORTHY

"Who touches pitch shall be defiled"

NEW YORK

CHARLES SCRIBNER'S SONS

1923

CHARACTERS

HILLCRIST	.	.	.	.	A Country Gentleman
AMY	.	.	.	.	His Wife
JILL	.	.	.	.	His Daughter
DAWKER	.	.	.	.	His Agent
HORNBLOWER	.	.	.		A man newly-rich
CHARLES	.	.	.	.	His Elder Son
CHLOE	.	.	.	.	Wife to Charles
ROLF	.	.	.	.	His Younger Son
FELLOWS	.	.	.	.	Hillcrist's Butler
ANNA	.	.	.	.	Chloe's Maid
THE JACKMANS	.	.	.		Man and Wife

AN AUCTIONEER
A SOLICITOR
TWO STRANGERS

ACT 1

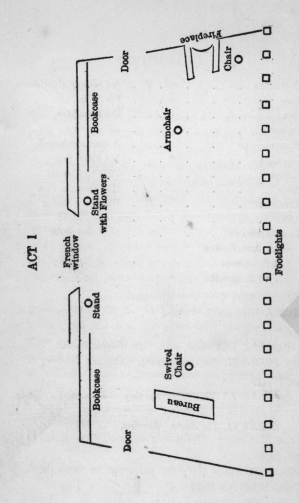

ACT I

HILLCRIST'S *study. A pleasant room, with books in calf bindings, and signs that the* HILLCRISTS *have travelled, such as a large photograph of the Taj Mahal, of Table Mountain, and the Pyramids of Egypt. A large bureau [stage Right], devoted to the business of a country estate. Two foxes' masks. Flowers in bowls. Deep armchairs. A large French window open [at Back], with a lovely view of a slight rise of fields and trees in August sunlight. A fine stone fireplace [stage Left]. A door [Left]. A door opposite [Right]. General colour effect—stone, and cigar-leaf brown, with spots of bright colour.*

[HILLCRIST *sits in a swivel chair at the bureau, busy with papers. He has gout, and his left foot is encased accordingly. He is a thin, dried-up man of about fifty-five, with a rather refined, rather kindly, and rather cranky countenance. Close to him stands his very upstanding nineteen-year-old daughter* JILL, *with clubbed hair round a pretty, manly face.*]

JILL. You know, Dodo, it's all pretty good rot in these days.

HILLCRIST. Cads are cads, Jill, even in these days.

JILL. What is a cad?

Copyright, 1920, by Charles Scribner's Sons

1

HILLCRIST. A self-assertive fellow, without a sense of other people.

JILL. Well, Old Hornblower I'll give you.

HILLCRIST. I wouldn't take him.

JILL. Well, you've got him. Now, Charlie—Chearlie —I say—the importance of not being Charlie——

HILLCRIST. Good heavens! do you know their Christian names?

JILL. My dear father, they've been here seven years.

HILLCRIST. In old days we only knew their Christian names from their tombstones.

JILL. Charlie Hornblower isn't really half a bad sport.

HILLCRIST. About a quarter of a bad sport—I've always thought out hunting.

JILL. [*Pulling his hair*] Now, his wife—Chloe——

HILLCRIST. [*Whimsical*] Gad! your mother'd have a fit if she knew you called her Chloe.

JILL. It's a ripping name.

HILLCRIST. Chloe! H'm! I had a spaniel once——

JILL. Dodo, you're narrow. Buck up, old darling, it won't do. Chloe has seen life, I'm pretty sure; *that's* attractive, anyway. No, mother's not in the room; don't turn your uneasy eyes.

HILLCRIST. Really, my dear, you are getting——

JILL. The limit. Now, Rolf——

HILLCRIST. What's Rolf? Another dog?

JILL. Rolf Hornblower's a topper; he really is a nice boy.

HILLCRIST. [*With a sharp look*] Oh! He's a nice boy?

JILL. Yes, darling. You know what a nice boy is, don't you?

HILLCRIST. Not in these days.

JILL. Well, I'll tell you. In the first place, he's not amorous——

HILLCRIST. What! Well, that's some comfort.

JILL. Just a jolly good companion.

HILLCRIST. To whom?

JILL. Well, to anyone—me.

HILLCRIST. Where?

JILL. Anywhere. You don't suppose I confine myself to the home paddocks, do you? I'm naturally rangey, Father.

HILLCRIST. [*Ironically*] You don't say so!

JILL. In the second place, he doesn't like discipline.

HILLCRIST. Jupiter! He does seem attractive.

JILL. In the third place, he bars his father.

HILLCRIST. Is that essential to nice *girls* too?

JILL. [*With a twirl of his hair*] Fish not! Fourthly, he's got ideas.

HILLCRIST. I knew it!

JILL. For instance, he thinks—as I do——

HILLCRIST. Ah! *Good* ideas.

JILL. [*Pulling gently*] Careful! He thinks old people run the show too much. He says they oughtn't to, because they're so damtouchy. Are you damtouchy, darling?

HILLCRIST. Well, I'm——! I don't know about touchy.

JILL. He says there'll be no world fit to live in till we get rid of the old. We must make them climb a tall tree, and shake them off it.

HILLCRIST. [*Drily*] Oh! he says that!

JILL. Otherwise, with the way they stand on each other's rights, they'll spoil the garden for the young.

HILLCRIST. Does his father agree?

JILL. Oh! Rolf doesn't talk to *him*, his mouth's too large. Have you ever seen it, Dodo?

HILLCRIST. Of course.

JILL. It's considerable, isn't it? Now yours is—reticent, darling. [*Rumpling his hair.*]

HILLCRIST. It won't be in a minute. Do you realise that I've got gout?

JILL. Poor ducky! How long have we been here, Dodo?

HILLCRIST. Since Elizabeth, anyway.

JILL. [*Looking at his foot*] It has its drawbacks. D'you think Hornblower had a father? I believe he was spontaneous. But, Dodo, why all this—this *attitude* to the Hornblowers?

> She purses her lips and makes a gesture as of
> pushing persons away.

HILLCRIST. Because they're pushing.

JILL. That's only because we *are*, as mother would say, and they're *not*—yet. But why not let them be?

HILLCRIST. You can't.

JILL. *Why?*

HILLCRIST. It takes generations to learn to live and let live, Jill. People like that take an ell when you give them an inch.

JILL. But if you gave them the ell, they wouldn't want the inch. Why should it all be such a skin game?

HILLCRIST. Skin game? Where *do* you get your lingo?

JILL. Keep to the point, Dodo.

HILLCRIST. Well, Jill, all life's a struggle between people at different stages of development, in different positions, with different amounts of social influence and property. And the only thing is to have rules of the game and keep them. New people like the Hornblowers haven't learnt those rules; *their* only rule is to get all they can.

JILL. Darling, don't prose. They're not half as bad as you think.

HILLCRIST. Well, when I sold Hornblower Longmeadow and the cottages, I certainly found him all right. All the same, he's got the cloven hoof. [*Warming up*] His influence in Deepwater is thoroughly bad; those potteries of his are demoralising—the whole atmosphere of the place is changing. It was a thousand pities he ever came here and discovered that clay. He's brought in the modern cutthroat spirit.

JILL. Cut *our* throat spirit, you mean. What's your definition of a gentleman, Dodo?

HILLCRIST. [*Uneasily*] Can't describe—only feel it.

JILL. Oh! Try!

HILLCRIST. Well—er—I suppose you might say—a

man who keeps his form and doesn't let life scupper him out of his standards.

JILL. But suppose his standards are low?

HILLCRIST. [*With some earnestness*] I assume, of course, that he's honest and tolerant, gentle to the weak, and not self-seeking.

JILL. Ah! self-seeking? But aren't we all, Dodo? *I* am.

HILLCRIST. [*With a smile*] You!

JILL. [*Scornfully*] Oh! yes—too young to know.

HILLCRIST. Nobody knows till they're under pretty heavy fire, Jill.

JILL. Except, of course, mother.

HILLCRIST. How do you mean—mother?

JILL. Mother reminds me of England according to herself—always right whatever she does.

HILLCRIST. Ye–es. Your mother *is* perhaps—the perfect woman——

JILL. That's what I was saying. Now, no one could call *you* perfect, Dodo. Besides, you've got gout.

HILLCRIST. Yes; and I want Fellows. Ring that bell.

JILL. [*Crossing to the bell*] Shall I tell you *my* definition of a gentleman? A man who gives the Hornblower his due. [*She rings the bell*] And I think mother ought to call on them. Rolf says old Hornblower resents it fearfully that she's never made a sign to Chloe the three years she's been here.

HILLCRIST. I don't interfere with your mother in

such matters.   She may go and call on the devil himself if she likes.

JILL. I know you're ever so much better than she is.

HILLCRIST. That's respectful.

JILL. You do keep your prejudices out of your phiz.
But mother literally looks down her nose.   And she
never forgives an "h."   They'd get the "hell" from
her if they took the "hinch."

HILLCRIST. Jill—your language!

JILL. Don't slime out of it, Dodo. I say, mother
ought to call on the Hornblowers.   [*No answer.*
Well?

HILLCRIST. My dear, I always let people have the
last word. It makes them—feel funny. Ugh! My
foot!   [*Enter* FELLOWS, *Left.*
Fellows, send into the village and get another bottle
of this stuff.

JILL. I'll go, darling.

          [*She blows him a kiss, and goes out at the window.*

HILLCRIST. And tell cook I've got to go on slops.
This foot's worse.

FELLOWS. [*Sympathetic*] Indeed, sir.

HILLCRIST. My third go this year, Fellows.

FELLOWS. Very annoying, sir.

HILLCRIST. Ye—es. Ever had it?

FELLOWS. I fancy I have had a twinge, sir.

HILLCRIST. [*Brightening*] Have you? Where?

FELLOWS. In my cork wrist, sir.

HILLCRIST. Your what?

FELLOWS. The wrist I draw corks with.

HILLCRIST. [*With a cackle*] You'd have had more than a twinge if you'd lived with my father. H'm!

FELLOWS. Excuse me, sir—Vichy water corks, in my experience, are worse than any wine.

HILLCRIST. [*Ironically*] Ah! The country's not what it was, is it, Fellows?

FELLOWS. Getting very new, sir.

HILLCRIST. [*Feelingly*] You're right. Has Dawker come?

FELLOWS. Not yet, sir. The Jackmans would like to see you, sir.

HILLCRIST. What about?

FELLOWS. I don't know, sir.

HILLCRIST. Well, show them in.

FELLOWS. [*Going*] Yes, sir.

> HILLCRIST *turns his swivel chair round. The* JACKMANS *come in. He, a big fellow about fifty, in a labourer's dress, with eyes which have more in them than his tongue can express ; she, a little woman with a worn face, a bright, quick glance, and a tongue to match.*

HILLCRIST. Good morning, Mrs. Jackman! Morning, Jackman! Haven't seen you for a long time. What can I do?

> [*He draws in foot, and breath, with a sharp hiss.*

JACKMAN. [*In a down-hearted voice*] We've had notice to quit, sir.

HILLCRIST. [*With emphasis*] What!

JACKMAN. Got to be out this week.

MRS. J. Yes, sir, indeed.

HILLCRIST. Well, but when I sold Longmeadow and the cottages, it was on the express understanding that there was to be no disturbance of tenancies.

MRS. J. Yes, sir; but we've all got to go. Mrs. 'Arvey, and the Drews, an' us, and there isn't another cottage to be had anywhere in Deepwater.

HILLCRIST. I know; I want one for my cowman. This won't do at all. Where do you get it from?

JACKMAN. Mr. 'Ornblower, 'imself, sir. Just an hour ago. He come round and said: "I'm sorry; I want the cottages, and you've got to clear."

MRS. J. [*Bitterly*] He's no gentleman, sir; he put it so brisk. We been there thirty years, and now we don't know what to do. So I hope you'll excuse us coming round, sir.

HILLCRIST. I should think so, indeed! H'm! [*He rises and limps across to the fireplace on his stick. To himself*] The cloven hoof. By George! this is a breach of faith. I'll write to him, Jackman. Confound it! I'd certainly never have sold if I'd known he was going to do this.

MRS. J. No, sir, I'm sure, sir. They do say it's to do with the potteries. He wants the cottages for his workmen.

HILLCRIST. [*Sharply*] That's all very well, but he shouldn't have led me to suppose that he would make no change.

JACKMAN. [*Heavily*] They talk about his havin' bought the Centry to put up more chimneys there, and that's why he wants the cottages.

HILLCRIST. The Centry! Impossible!

MRS. J. Yes, sir; it's such a pretty spot—looks beautiful from here. [*She looks out through the window*] Loveliest spot in all Deepwater, I always say. And your father owned it, and his father before 'im. It's a pity they ever sold it, sir, beggin' your pardon.

HILLCRIST. The Centry!   [*He rings the bell.*

MRS. J. [*Who has brightened up*] I'm glad you're goin' to stop it, sir. It does put us about. We don't know where to go. I said to Mr. Hornblower, I said, "I'm sure Mr. Hillcrist would never 'ave turned us out." An' 'e said: "Mr. Hillcrist be ——" beggin' your pardon, sir. "Make no mistake," 'e said, "you must go, missis." He don't even know our name; an' to come it like this over us! He's a dreadful new man, I think, with his overridin' notions. And sich a heavy-footed man, to look at. [*With a sort of indulgent contempt*] But he's from the North, they say.

[FELLOWS *has entered, Left.*

HILLCRIST. Ask Mrs. Hillcrist if she'll come.

FELLOWS. Very good, sir.

HILLCRIST. Is Dawker here?

FELLOWS. Not yet, sir.

HILLCRIST. I want to see him at once.

[FELLOWS *retires.*

JACKMAN. Mr. Hornblower said he was comin' on to see you, sir. So we thought we'd step along first.

HILLCRIST. Quite right, Jackman.

MRS. J. I said to Jackman: "Mr. Hillcrist'll stand up for us, I know. He's a gentleman," I said. "This man," I said, "don't care for the neighbourhood, or the people; he don't care for anything so long as he makes his money, and has his importance. You can't expect it, I suppose," I said; [*Bitterly*] "havin' got rich so sudden." The gentry don't do things like that.

HILLCRIST. [*Abstracted*] Quite, Mrs. Jackman, quite! [*To himself*] The Centry! No!

> MRS. HILLCRIST *enters. A well-dressed woman, with a firm, clear-cut face.*

Oh! Amy! Mr. and Mrs. Jackman turned out of their cottage, and Mrs. Harvey, and the Drews. When I sold to Hornblower, I stipulated that they shouldn't be.

MRS. J. Our week's up on Saturday, ma'am, and I'm sure I don't know where we shall turn, because of course Jackman must be near his work, and I shall lose me washin' if we have to go far.

HILLCRIST. [*With decision*] You leave it to me, Mrs. Jackman. Good morning! Morning, Jackman! Sorry I can't move with this gout.

MRS. J. [*For them both*] I'm sure we're very sorry, sir. Good morning, sir. Good morning, ma'am; and thank you kindly. [*They go out.*

HILLCRIST. Turning people out that have been there thirty years. I won't have it. It's a breach of faith.

MRS. H. Do you suppose this Hornblower will care two straws about that Jack?

HILLCRIST. He must, when it's put to him, if he's got any decent feeling.

MRS. H. He hasn't.

HILLCRIST. [*Suddenly*] The Jackmans talk of his having bought the Centry to put up more chimneys.

MRS. H. Never! [*At the window, looking out*] Impossible! It would ruin the place utterly, besides cutting us off from the Duke's. Oh, no! Miss Mullins would never sell behind our backs.

HILLCRIST. Anyway I must stop his turning these people out.

MRS. H. [*With a little smile, almost contemptuous*] You might have known he'd do something of the sort. You will imagine people are like yourself, Jack. You always ought to make Dawker have things in black and white.

HILLCRIST. I said quite distinctly: "Of course you won't want to disturb the tenancies; there's a great shortage of cottages." Hornblower told me as distinctly that he wouldn't. What more do you want?

MRS. H. A man like that thinks of nothing but the short cut to his own way. [*Looking out of the window towards the rise*] If he buys the Centry and puts up chimneys, we simply couldn't stop here.

HILLCRIST. My father would turn in his grave.

MRS. H. It would have been more useful if he'd not dipped the estate, and sold the Centry. This Hornblower hates us; he thinks we turn up our noses at him.

HILLCRIST. As we do, Amy.

MRS. H. Who wouldn't? A man without traditions, who believes in nothing but money and push.

HILLCRIST. Suppose he won't budge, can we do anything for the Jackmans?

MRS. H. There are the two rooms Beaver used to have, over the stables.   [FELLOWS *enters.*

FELLOWS. Mr. Dawker, sir.

> DAWKER *is a short, square, rather red-faced terrier of a man, in riding clothes and gaiters.*

HILLCRIST. Ah! Dawker, I've got gout again.

DAWKER. Very sorry, sir.   How de do, ma'am?

HILLCRIST. Did you meet the Jackmans?

DAWKER. Yeh.

> [*He hardly ever quite finishes a word, seeming to snap off their tails.*

HILLCRIST. Then you heard?

DAWKER. [*Nodding*] Smart man, Hornblower; never lets grass grow.

HILLCRIST. Smart?

DAWKER. [*Grinning*] Don't do to underrate your neighbours.

MRS. H. A cad—I call him.

DAWKER. That's it, ma'am—got all the advantage.

HILLCRIST. Heard anything about the Centry, Dawker?

DAWKER. Hornblower wants to buy.

HILLCRIST. Miss Mullins would never sell, would she?

DAWKER. She wants to.

HILLCRIST. The deuce she does!

DAWKER. He won't stick at the price either.

MRS. H. What's it worth, Dawker?

DAWKER. Depends on what you want it for.

MRS. H. He wants it for spite; we want it for sentiment.

DAWKER. [*Grinning*] Worth what you like to give, then; but he's a rich man.

MRS. H. Intolerable!

DAWKER. [*To* HILLCRIST] Give me your figure, sir. I'll try the old lady before he gets at her.

HILLCRIST. [*Pondering*] I don't want to buy, unless there's nothing else for it. I should have to raise the money on the estate; it won't stand much more. I can't believe the fellow would be such a barbarian. Chimneys within three hundred yards, right in front of this house! It's a nightmare.

MRS. H. You'd much better let Dawker make sure, Jack.

HILLCRIST. [*Uncomfortable*] Jackman says Hornblower's coming round to see me. I shall put it to him.

DAWKER. Make him keener than ever. Better get in first.

HILLCRIST. Ape his methods!—Ugh! Confound this gout! [*He gets back to his chair with difficulty*] Look here, Dawker, I wanted to see you about gates——

FELLOWS [*Entering*] Mr. Hornblower.

> HORNBLOWER *enters—a man of medium height, thoroughly broadened, blown out, as it were, by success. He has thick, coarse, dark hair, just grizzled, very bushy eyebrows, a wide mouth. He wears quite ordinary clothes, as if that department were in charge of someone*

> *who knew about such things. He has a small*
> *rose in his buttonhole, and carries a Hom-*
> *burg hat, which one suspects will look too*
> *small on his head.*

HORNBLOWER. Good morning! good morning! How are ye, Dawker? Fine morning! Lovely weather!

> *His voice has a curious blend in its tone of*
> *brass and oil, and an accent not quite Scotch*
> *nor quite North country.*

Haven't seen ye for a long time, Hillcrist.

HILLCRIST. [*Who has risen*] Not since I sold you Longmeadow and those cottages, I believe.

HORNBLOWER. Dear me, now! that's what I came about.

HILLCRIST. [*Subsiding again into his chair*] Forgive me! Won't you sit down?

HORNBLOWER. [*Not sitting*] Have ye got gout? That's unfortunate. I never get it. I've no disposition that way. Had no ancestors, you see. Just me own drinkin' to answer for.

HILLCRIST. You're lucky.

HORNBLOWER. I wonder if Mrs. Hillcrist thinks that! Am I lucky to have no past, ma'am? Just the future?

MRS. H. You're sure you have the future, Mr. Hornblower?

HORNBLOWER. [*With a laugh*] That's your aristocratic rapier thrust. You aristocrats are very hard people underneath your manners. Ye love to lay a body out. But I've got the future all right.

HILLCRIST. [*Meaningly*] I've had the Jackmans here, Mr. Hornblower.

HORNBLOWER. Who are they—man with the little spitfire wife?

HILLCRIST. They're very excellent, good people, and they've been in that cottage quietly thirty years.

HORNBLOWER. [*Throwing out his forefinger—a favourite gesture*] Ah! ye've wanted me to stir ye up a bit. Deepwater needs a bit o' go put into it. There's generally some go where I am. I daresay you wish there'd been no "come." [*He laughs*].

MRS. H. We certainly like people to keep their word, Mr. Hornblower.

HILLCRIST. Amy!

HORNBLOWER. Never mind, Hillcrist; takes more than that to upset me.

> MRS. HILLCRIST *exchanges a look with* DAWKER, *who slips out unobserved.*

HILLCRIST. You promised me, you know, not to change the tenancies.

HORNBLOWER. Well, I've come to tell ye that I have. I wasn't expecting to have the need when I bought. Thought the Duke would sell me a bit down there; but devil a bit he will; and now I must have those cottages for my workmen. I've got important works, ye know.

HILLCRIST. [*Getting heated*] The Jackmans have their importance too, sir. Their heart's in that cottage.

HORNBLOWER. Have a sense of proportion, man. My works supply thousands of people, and *my* heart's in *them*. What's more, they make my fortune. I've got ambitions—I'm a serious man. Suppose I were to consider this and that, and every little potty objection—where should I get to?—nowhere!

HILLCRIST. All the same, this sort of thing isn't done, you know.

HORNBLOWER. Not by you because ye've got no need to do it. Here ye are, quite content on what your fathers made for ye. Ye've no ambitions; and ye want other people to have none. How d'ye think your fathers got your land?

HILLCRIST. [*Who has risen*] Not by breaking their word.

HORNBLOWER. [*Throwing out his finger*] Don't ye believe it. They got it by breaking their word and turnin' out Jackmans, if that's their name, all over the place.

MRS. H. That's an insult, Mr. Hornblower.

HORNBLOWER. No; it's a repartee. If ye think so much of these Jackmans, build them a cottage yourselves; ye've got the space.

HILLCRIST. That's beside the point. You promised me, and I sold on that understanding.

HORNBLOWER. And I bought on the understandin' that I'd get some more land from the Duke.

HILLCRIST. That's nothing to do with me.

HORNBLOWER. Ye'll find it has; because I'm going to have those cottages.

HILLCRIST. Well, I call it simply—

[*He checks himself.*

HORNBLOWER. Look here, Hillcrist, ye've not had occasion to understand men like me. I've got the guts, and I've got the money, and I don't sit still on it. I'm going ahead because I believe in meself. I've no use for sentiment and that sort of thing. Forty of your Jackmans aren't worth me little finger.

HILLCRIST. [*Angry*] Of all the blatant things I ever heard said!——

HORNBLOWER. Well, as we're speaking plainly, I've been thinkin'. Ye want the village run your old-fashioned way, and I want it run mine. I fancy there's not room for the two of us here.

MRS. H. When are you going?

HORNBLOWER. Never fear, *I'm* not going.

HILLCRIST. Look here, Mr. Hornblower—this infernal gout makes me irritable—puts me at a disadvantage. But I should be glad if you'd kindly explain yourself.

HORNBLOWER. [*With a great smile*] Ca' canny; I'm fra' the North.

HILLCRIST. I'm told you wish to buy the Centry and put more of your chimneys up there, regardless of the fact [*He points through the window*] that it would utterly ruin the house we've had for generations, and all our pleasure here.

HORNBLOWER. How the man talks! Why! Ye'd think he owned the sky, because his fathers built him a house with a pretty view, where he's nothing to do but live. It's sheer want of something to do that gives ye your fine sentiments, Hillcrist.

HILLCRIST. Have the goodness not to charge me with idleness. Dawker—where is he?—[*He shows the bureau*] When you do the drudgery of your works as thoroughly as I do that of my estate—— Is it true about the Centry?

HORNBLOWER. Gospel true. If ye want to know, my son Chearlie is buyin' it this very minute.

MRS. H. [*Turning with a start*] What do you say?

HORNBLOWER. Ay, he's with the old lady; she wants to sell, an' she'll get her price, whatever it is.

HILLCRIST. [*With deep anger*] If that isn't a skin game, Mr. Hornblower, I don't know what is.

HORNBLOWER. Ah! Ye've got a very nice expression there. "Skin game!" Well, bad words break no bones, an' they're wonderful for hardenin' the heart. If it wasn't for a lady's presence, I could give ye a specimen or two.

MRS. H. Oh! Mr. Hornblower, that need not stop you, I'm sure.

HORNBLOWER. Well, and I don't know that it need. Ye're an obstruction—the like of you—ye're in my path. And anyone in my path doesn't stay there long; or, if he does, he stays there on my terms. And my terms are chimneys in the Centry where I need 'em. It'll do ye a power of good, too, to know that ye're not almighty.

HILLCRIST. And that's being neighbourly!

HORNBLOWER. And how have ye tried bein' neighbourly to me? If I haven't a wife, I've got a daughter-in-law. Have ye called on her, ma'am? I'm new,

and ye're an old family. Ye don't like me, ye think
I'm a pushin' man. I go to chapel, an' ye don't like
that. I make things and I sell them, and ye don't
like that. I buy land, and ye don't like that. It
threatens the view from your windies. Well, I don't
like you, and I'm not goin' to put up with your attitude. Ye've had things your own way too long, and
now ye're not going to have them any longer.

HILLCRIST. Will you hold to your word over those
cottages?

HORNBLOWER. I'm goin' to have the cottages. I
need them, and more besides, now I'm to put up me
new works.

HILLCRIST. That's a declaration of war.

HORNBLOWER. Ye never said a truer word. It's
one or the other of us, and I rather think it's goin' to
be me. I'm the risin' and you're the settin' sun, as
the poet says.

HILLCRIST. [*Touching the bell*] We shall see if you
can ride rough-shod like this. We used to have decent
ways of going about things here. You want to change
all that. Well, we shall do our damnedest to stop
you. [*To* FELLOWS *at the door*] Are the Jackmans still
in the house? Ask them to be good enough to come in.

HORNBLOWER. [*With the first sign of uneasiness*] I've
seen these people. I've nothing more to say to them.
I told 'em I'd give 'em five pounds to cover their
moving.

HILLCRIST. It doesn't occur to you that people,
however humble, like to have some say in their own
fate?

HORNBLOWER. I never had any say in mine till I had the brass, and nobody ever will. It's all hypocrisy. You county folk are fair awful hypocrites. Ye talk about good form and all that sort o' thing. It's just the comfortable doctrine of the man in the saddle; sentimental varnish. Ye're every bit as hard as I am, underneath.

MRS. H. [*Who had been standing very still all this time*] You flatter us.

HORNBLOWER. Not at all. God helps those who 'elp themselves—that's at the bottom of all religion. I'm goin' to help meself, and God's going to help me.

MRS. H. I admire your knowledge.

HILLCRIST. We are in the right, and God helps——

HORNBLOWER. Don't ye believe it; ye 'aven't got the energy.

MRS. H. Nor perhaps the conceit.

HORNBLOWER. [*Throwing out his forefinger*] No, no; 'tisn't conceit to believe in yourself when ye've got reason to.   [*The* JACKMANS *have entered.*

HILLCRIST. I'm very sorry, Mrs. Jackman, but I just wanted you to realise that I've done my best with this gentleman.

MRS. J. [*Doubtfully*] Yes, sir. I thought if you spoke for us, he'd feel different-like.

HORNBLOWER. One cottage is the same as another, missis. I made ye a fair offer of five pounds for the moving.

JACKMAN. [*Slowly*] We wouldn't take fifty to go out of that 'ouse. We brought up three children there, an' buried two from it.

MRS. J. [*To* MRS. HILLCRIST] We're attached to it like, ma'am.

HILLCRIST. [*To* HORNBLOWER] How would you like being turned out of a place you were fond of?

HORNBLOWER. Not a bit. But little considerations have to give way to big ones. Now, missis, I'll make it ten pounds, and I'll send a wagon to shift your things. If that isn't fair—! Ye'd better accept, I shan't keep it open.

> The JACKMANS *look at each other ; their faces show deep anger—and the question they ask each other is which will speak.*

MRS. J. We won't take it; eh, George?

JACKMAN. Not a farden. We come there when we was married.

HORNBLOWER. [*Throwing out his finger*] Ye're very improvident folk.

HILLCRIST. Don't lecture them, Mr. Hornblower; they come out of this miles above you.

HORNBLOWER. [*Angry*] Well, I *was* going to give ye another week, but ye'll go out next Saturday; and take care ye're not late, or your things'll be put out—in the rain.

MRS. H. [*To* MRS. JACKMAN] We'll send down for your things, and you can come to us for the time being.

> MRS. JACKMAN *drops a curtsey ; her eyes stab* HORNBLOWER.

JACKMAN. [*Heavily, clenching his fists*] You're no gentleman! Don't put temptation in my way, that's all.

HILLCRIST. [*In a low voice*] Jackman!

HORNBLOWER. [*Triumphantly*] Ye hear that? That's your protegee! Keep out o' *my* way, me man, or I'll put the police on to ye for utterin' threats.

HILLCRIST. You'd better go now, Jackman.

[*The* JACKMANS *move to the door.*

MRS. J. [*Turning*] Maybe you'll repent it some day, sir. [*They go out,* MRS. HILLCRIST *following.*

HORNBLOWER. We—ell, I'm sorry they're such unreasonable folk. I never met people with less notion of which side their bread was buttered.

HILLCRIST. And I never met anyone so pachydermatous.

HORNBLOWER. What's that, in Heaven's name? Ye needn' wrap it up in long words now your good lady's gone.

HILLCRIST. [*With dignity*] I'm not going in for a slanging match. I resent your conduct much too deeply.

HORNBLOWER. Look here, Hillcrist, I don't object to you personally; ye seem to me a poor creature that's bound to get left with your gout and your dignity; but of course ye can make yourself very disagreeable before ye're done. Now I want to be the movin' spirit here. I'm full of plans. I'm goin' to stand for Parliament; I'm goin' to make this a prosperous place. I'm a good-natured man if you'll treat me as such. Now, you take me on as a neighbour and all that, and I'll manage without chimneys on the Centry. Is it a bargain? [*He holds out his hand.*

HILLCRIST. [*Ignoring it*] I thought you said you didn't keep your word when it suited you to break it?

HORNBLOWER. Now, don't get on the high horse. You and me could be very good friends; but I can be a very nasty enemy. The chimneys will not look nice from that windie, ye know.

HILLCRIST. [*Deeply angry*] Mr. Hornblower, if you think I'll take your hand after this Jackman business, you're greatly mistaken. You are proposing that I shall stand in with you while you tyrannise over the neighbourhood. Please realise that unless you leave those tenancies undisturbed as you said you would, we don't know each other.

HORNBLOWER. Well, that won't trouble me much. Now, ye'd better think it over; ye've got gout and that makes ye hasty. I tell ye again: I'm not the man to make an enemy of. Unless ye're friendly, sure as I stand here I'll ruin the look of your place.

[*The toot of a car is heard.*

There's my car. I sent Chearlie and his wife in it to buy the Centry. And make no mistake—he's got it in his pocket. It's your last chance, Hillcrist. I'm not averse to you as a man; I think ye're the best of the fossils round here; at least, I think ye can do me the most harm socially. Come now!

[*He holds out his hand again.*

HILLCRIST. Not if you'd bought the Centry ten times over. Your ways are not mine, and I'll have nothing to do with you.

HORNBLOWER. [*Very angry*] Really! Is that so? Very well. Now ye're goin' to learn something, an' it's time ye did. D'ye realise that I'm very nearly round ye? [*He draws a circle slowly in the air*] I'm at Uphill, the works are here, here's Longmeadow, here's the Centry that I've just bought, there's only the Common left to give ye touch with the world. Now between you and the Common there's the high road. I come out on the high road here to your north, and I shall come out on it there to your west. When I've got me new works up on the Centry, I shall be makin' a trolley track between the works up to the road at both ends, so my goods will be running right round ye. How'll ye like that for a country place?

> *For answer* HILLCRIST, *who is angry beyond the power of speech, walks, forgetting to use his stick, up to the French window. While he stands there, with his back to* HORN-BLOWER, *the door L. is flung open, and* JILL *enters, preceding* CHARLES, *his wife* CHLOE, *and* ROLF. CHARLES *is a goodish-looking, moustached young man of about twenty-eight, with a white rim to the collar of his waistcoat, and spats. He has his hand behind* CHLOE'S *back, as if to prevent her turning tail. She is rather a handsome young woman, with dark eyes, full red lips, and a suspicion of powder, a little under-dressed for the country.* ROLF, *who brings up the rear, is about twenty, with an open face and stiffish butter-coloured hair.* JILL *runs over to her father at the window. She has a bottle.*

JILL. [*Sotto voce*] Look, Dodo, I've brought the lot!

Isn't it a treat, dear Papa? And here's the stuff. Hallo!

> *The exclamation is induced by the apprehension that there has been a row. HILLCRIST gives a stiff little bow, remaining where he is in the window. JILL stays close to him, staring from one to the other, then blocks him off and engages him in conversation. CHARLES has gone up to his father, who has remained maliciously still, where he delivered his last speech. CHLOE and ROLF stand awkwardly waiting between the fireplace and the door.*

HORNBLOWER. Well, Chearlie?

CHARLES. Not got it.

HORNBLOWER. *Not!*

CHARLES. I'd practically got her to say she'd sell at three thousand five hundred, when that fellow Dawker turned up.

HORNBLOWER. That bull-terrier of a chap! Why, he was *here* a while ago. Oh—ho! So that's it!

CHARLES. I heard him gallop up. He came straight for the old lady, and got her away. What he said I don't know; but she came back looking wiser than an owl; said she'd think it over, thought she had other views.

HORNBLOWER. Did ye tell her she might have her price?

CHARLES. Practically I did.

HORNBLOWER. Well?

CHARLES. She thought it would be fairer to put it

up to auction. There were other enquiries. Oh! She's a leery old bird—reminds me of one of those pictures of Fate, don't you know.

HORNBLOWER. Auction! Well, if it's not gone we'll get it yet. That damned little Dawker! I've had a row with Hillcrist.

CHARLES. I thought so.

> *They are turning cautiously to look at* HILL-CRIST, *when* JILL *steps forward.*

JILL. [*Flushed and determined*] That's not a bit sporting of you, Mr. Hornblower.

> [*At her words* ROLF *comes forward too.*

HORNBLOWER. Ye should hear both sides before ye say that, missy.

JILL. There isn't another side to turning out the Jackmans after you'd promised.

HORNBLOWER. Oh! dear me, yes. They don't matter a row of gingerbread to the schemes I've got for betterin' this neighbourhood.

JILL. I *had* been standing up for you; now I won't.

HORNBLOWER. Dear, dear! What'll become of me?

JILL. I won't say anything about the other thing because I think it's beneath dignity to notice it. But to turn poor people out of their cottages is a shame.

HORNBLOWER. Hoity me!

ROLF. [*Suddenly*] You haven't been doing that, father?

CHARLES. Shut up, Rolf!

HORNBLOWER. [*Turning on* ROLF] Ha! Here's a league o' youth! My young whipper-snapper, keep your mouth shut and leave it to your elders to know what's right.

> *Under the weight of this rejoinder* ROLF *stands biting his lips.   Then he throws his head up.*

ROLF. I hate it!

HORNBLOWER. [*With real venom*] Oh! Ye hate it? Ye can get out of my house, then.

JILL. Free speech, Mr. Hornblower; don't be violent.

HORNBLOWER. Ye're right, young lady. Ye can stay in my house, Rolf, and learn manners. Come, Chearlie!

JILL. [*Quite softly*] Mr. Hornblower!

HILLCRIST. [*From the window*] Jill!

JILL. [*Impatiently*] Well, what's the good of it? Life's too short for rows, and too jolly!

ROLF. Bravo!

HORNBLOWER. [*Who has shown a sign of weakening*] Now, look here! I will not have revolt in my family. Ye'll just have to learn that a man who's worked as I have, who's risen as I have, and who knows the world, is the proper judge of what's right and wrong. I'll answer to God for me actions, and not to you young people.

JILL. Poor God!

HORNBLOWER. [*Genuinely shocked*] Ye blasphemous young thing! [*To* ROLF] And ye're just as bad, ye young freethinker. I won't have it.

HILLCRIST. [*Who has come down, Right*] Jill, I wish you would kindly not talk.

JILL. I can't help it.

CHARLES. [*Putting his arm through* HORNBLOWER'S] Come along, father! Deeds, not words.

HORNBLOWER. Ay! Deeds!

> MRS. HILLCRIST *and* DAWKER *have entered by the French window.*

MRS. H. Quite right!

> [*They all turn and look at her.*

HORNBLOWER. Ah! So ye put your dog on to it. [*He throws out his finger at* DAWKER] Very smart, that —I give ye credit.

MRS. H. [*Pointing to* CHLOE, *who has stood by herself, forgotten and uncomfortable throughout the scene*] May I ask who this lady is?

> CHLOE *turns round startled, and her vanity bag slips down her dress to the floor.*

HORNBLOWER. No, ma'am, ye may not, for ye know perfectly well.

JILL. *I* brought her in, mother [*She moves to* CHLOE'S *side*].

MRS. H. Will you take her out again, then.

HILLCRIST. Amy, have the goodness to remember——

MRS. H. That this is my house so far as ladies are concerned.

JILL. Mother!

> *She looks astonished at* CHLOE, *who, about to speak, does not, passing her eyes, with a queer, half-scared expression, from* MRS. HILLCRIST *to* DAWKER.

[*To* CHLOE] I'm awfully sorry. Come on!

> [*They go out, Left.* ROLF *hurries after them.*

CHARLES. You've insulted my wife. Why? What
do you mean by it?

> [MRS. HILLCRIST *simply smiles.*

HILLCRIST. I apologise. I regret extremely. There
is no reason why the ladies of your family or of mine
should be involved in our quarrel. For Heaven's sake,
let's fight like gentlemen.

HORNBLOWER. Catchwords—sneers! No; we'll play
what ye call a skin game, Hillcrist, without gloves on;
we won't spare each other. Ye look out for yourselves,
for, begod, after this morning I mean business. And
as for you, Dawker, ye sly dog, ye think yourself very
clever; but I'll have the Centry yet. Come, Chearlie!

> *They go out, passing* JILL, *who is coming in
> again, in the doorway.*

HILLCRIST. Well, Dawker?

DAWKER. [*Grinning*] Safe for the moment. The old
lady'll put it up to auction. Couldn't get her to budge
from that. Says she don't want to be unneighbourly
to either. But, if you ask me, it's money she smells!

JILL. [*Advancing*] Now, mother!

MRS. H. Well?

JILL. Why did you insult her?

MRS. H. I think I only asked you to take her out.

JILL. Why? Even if she is Old Combustion's
daughter-in-law?

MRS. H. My dear Jill, allow me to judge the sort
of acquaintances I wish to make. [*She looks at* DAWKER.

JILL. She's all right. Lots of women powder and
touch up their lips nowadays. I think she's rather a
good sort; she was awfully upset.

Mrs. H. Too upset.

JILL. Oh! don't be so mysterious, mother. If you know something, do spit it out!

Mrs. H. Do you wish me to—er—"spit it out," Jack?

HILLCRIST. Dawker, if you don't mind——

> DAWKER, *with a nod, passes away out of the French window.*

Jill, be respectful, and don't talk like a bargee.

JILL. It's no good, Dodo. It made me ashamed. It's just as—as caddish to insult people who haven't said a word, in your own house, as it is to be—old Hornblower.

Mrs. H. You don't know what you're talking about.

HILLCRIST. What's the matter with young Mrs. Hornblower?

Mrs. H. Excuse me, I shall keep my thoughts to myself at present.

> *She looks coldly at* JILL, *and goes out through the French window.*

HILLCRIST. You've thoroughly upset your mother, Jill.

JILL. It's something Dawker's told her; I saw them. I don't like Dawker, father, he's so common.

HILLCRIST. My dear, we can't all be uncommon. He's got lots of go. You must apologise to your mother.

JILL. [*Shaking her clubbed hair*] They'll make you do things you don't approve of, Dodo, if you don't look out. Mother's fearfully bitter when she gets her knife in. If old Hornblower's disgusting, it's no reason we should be.

HILLCRIST. So you think I'm capable—that's nice, Jill!

JILL. No, no, darling! I only want to warn you solemnly that mother'll tell you you're fighting fair, no matter what she and Dawker do.

HILLCRIST. [*Smiling*] Jill, I don't think I ever saw you so serious.

JILL. No. Because—[*She swallows a lump in her throat*] Well—I was just beginning to enjoy myself; and now—everything's going to be bitter and beastly, with mother in that mood. That horrible old man! Oh, Dodo! Don't let them make *you* horrid! You're such a darling. How's your gout, ducky?

HILLCRIST. Better; lot better.

JILL. There, you see! That shows! It's going to be half interesting for you, but not for—us.

HILLCRIST. Look here, Jill—is there anything between you and young what's-his-name—Rolf?

JILL. [*Biting her lip*] No. But—now it's *all* spoiled.

HILLCRIST. You can't expect me to regret that.

JILL. I don't mean any tosh about love's young dream; but I do like being friends. I want to *enjoy* things, Dodo, and you can't do that when everybody's on the hate. You're going to wallow in it, and so shall I—oh! I know I shall!—we shall all wallow, and think of nothing but "one for his nob."

HILLCRIST. Aren't you fond of your home?

JILL. Of course. I love it.

HILLCRIST. Well, you won't be able to live in it unless we stop that ruffian. Chimneys and smoke, the trees cut down, piles of pots. Every kind of abomination. There! [*He points*] Imagine! [*He points through the French window, as if he could see those chimneys rising and marring the beauty of the fields*] I was born here, and my father, and his, and his, and his. They loved those fields, and those old trees. And this barbarian, with his "improvement" schemes, forsooth! I learned to ride in the Centry meadows—prettiest spring meadows in the world; I've climbed every tree there. Why my father ever sold——! But who could have imagined this? And come at a bad moment, when money's scarce.

JILL. [*Cuddling his arm*] Dodo!

HILLCRIST. Yes. But you don't love the place as I do, Jill. You youngsters don't love anything, I sometimes think.

JILL. I do, Dodo, I do!

HILLCRIST. You've got it all before you. But you may live your life and never find anything so good and so beautiful as this old home. I'm not going to have it spoiled without a fight.

> *Conscious of having betrayed sentiment, he walks out at the French window, passing away to the Right. JILL, following to the window, looks. Then throwing back her head, she clasps her hands behind it.*

JILL. Oh—oh—oh!

> *A voice behind her says, "JILL!" She turns and starts back, leaning against the right lin-*

> *tel of the window.* ROLF *appears outside
> the window from Left.*

Who goes there?

ROLF. [*Buttressed against the Left lintel*] Enemy—
after Chloe's bag.

JILL. Pass, enemy! And all's ill!

> ROLF *passes through the window, and retrieves
> the vanity bag from the floor where* CHLOE
> *dropped it, then again takes his stand against
> the Left lintel of the French window.*

ROLF. It's not going to make any difference, is it?

JILL. You know it is.

ROLF. Sins of the fathers.

JILL. Unto the third and fourth generations. What
sin has *my* father committed?

ROLF. None, in a way; only, I've often told you I
don't see why you should treat us as outsiders. We
don't like it.

JILL. Well, you shouldn't be, then; I mean, *he*
shouldn't be.

ROLF. Father's just as human as your father; he's
wrapped up in us, and all his "getting on" is for us.
Would you like to be treated as your mother treated
Chloe? Your mother's set the stroke for the other
big-wigs about here; nobody calls on Chloe. And why
not? Why not? I think it's contemptible to bar
people just because they're *new*, as you call it, and have
to make their position instead of having it left them.

JILL. It's *not* because they're new, it's because—if
your father behaved like a gentleman, he'd be treated
like one.

ROLF. Would he? I don't believe it. My father's a very able man; he thinks he's entitled to have influence here. Well, everybody tries to keep him down. Oh! yes, they do. That makes him mad and more determined than ever to get his way. You ought to be just, Jill.

JILL. I *am* just.

ROLF. No, you're not. Besides, what's it got to do with Charlie and Chloe? Chloe's particularly harmless. It's pretty sickening for her. Father didn't expect people to call until Charlie married, but since——

JILL. I think it's all very petty.

ROLF. It *is*—a dog-in-the-manger business; I did think *you* were above it.

JILL. How would you like to have your home spoiled?

ROLF. I'm not going to argue. Only things don't stand still. Homes aren't any more proof against change than anything else.

JILL. All right! You come and try and take ours.

ROLF. We don't want to take your home.

JILL. Like the Jackmans'?

ROLF. All right. I see you're hopelessly prejudiced.

                    [*He turns to go.*

JILL. [*Just as he is vanishing—softly*] Enemy?

ROLF. [*Turning*] Yes, enemy.

JILL. Before the battle—let's shake hands.

       They move from the lintels and grasp each other's hands in the centre of the French window.

CURTAIN

ACT II

ACT II. SCENE I.

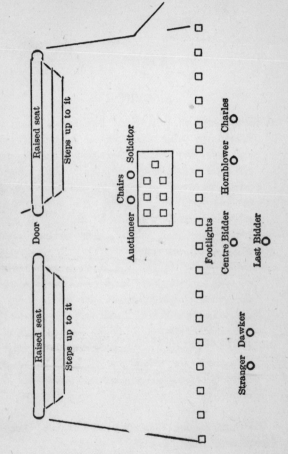

ACT II

SCENE I

*A billiard room in a provincial hotel, where things are
bought and sold. The scene is set well forward,
and is not very broad; it represents the auctioneer's
end of the room, having, rather to stage Left, a narrow
table with two chairs facing the audience, where the
auctioneer will sit and stand. The table, which is
set forward to the footlights, is littered with green-
covered particulars of sale. The audience are in
effect public and bidders. There is a door on the
Left, level with the table. Along the back wall, behind
the table, are two raised benches with two steps up to
them, such as billiard rooms often have, divided by
a door in the middle of a wall, which is panelled in
oak. Late September sunlight is coming from a
skylight (not visible) on to these seats. The stage is
empty when the curtain goes up, but* DAWKER *and*
MRS. HILLCRIST *are just entering through the door
at the back.*

DAWKER. Be out of their way here, ma'am. See old
Hornblower with Chearlie?

[*He points down to the audience.*

39

Mrs. H. It begins at three, doesn't it?

Dawker. They won't be over-punctual; there's only the Centry selling. There's young Mrs. Hornblower with the other boy—[*Pointing*] over at the entrance. I've got that chap I told you of down from town.

Mrs. H. Ah! make sure quite of her, Dawker. Any mistake would be fatal.

Dawker. [*Nodding*] That's right, ma'am. Lot of people—always spare time to watch an auction—ever remark that? The Duke's agent's here; shouldn't be surprised if he chipped in.

Mrs. H. Where did you leave my husband?

Dawker. With Miss Jill, in the courtyard. He's coming to you. In case I miss him, tell him when I reach his limit to blow his nose if he wants me to go on; when he blows it a second time, I'll stop for good. Hope we shan't get to that. Old Hornblower doesn't throw his money away.

Mrs. H. What limit did you settle?

Dawker. Six thousand!

Mrs. H. That's a fearful price. Well, good luck to you, Dawker!

Dawker. Good luck, ma'am. I'll go and see to that little matter of Mrs. Chloe. Never fear, we'll do them in somehow.

> *He winks, lays his finger on the side of his nose, and goes out at the door.*

> Mrs. Hillcrist *mounts the two steps, sits down Right of the door, and puts up a pair of long-handled glasses. Through the door be-*

hind her come CHLOE *and* ROLF. *She makes*
a sign for him to go, and shuts the door.

CHLOE. [*At the foot of the steps—in the gangway—in
a slightly common accent*] Mrs. Hillcrist!

MRS. H. [*Not quite starting*] I beg your pardon?

CHLOE. [*Again*] Mrs. Hillcrist——

MRS. H. Well?

CHLOE. I never did you any harm.

MRS. H. Did I ever say you did?

CHLOE. No; but you act as if I had.

MRS. H. I'm not aware that I've acted at all—as
yet. You are nothing to me, except as one of your
family.

CHOLE. 'Tisn't I that wants to spoil your home.

MRS. H. Stop them then. I see your husband down
there with his father.

CHLOE. I—I have tried.

MRS. H. [*Looking at her*] Oh! I suppose such men
don't pay attention to what women ask them.

CHLOE. [*With a flash of spirit*] I'm fond of my husband. I——

MRS. H. [*Looking at her steadily*] I don't quite know
why you spoke to me.

CHLOE. [*With a sort of pathetic sullenness*] I only
thought perhaps you'd like to treat me as a human
being.

MRS. H. Really, if you don't mind, I should like to
be left alone just now.

CHLOE. [*Unhappily acquiescent*] Certainly! I'll go to
the other end.

*She moves to the Left, mounts the steps and sits
down.*

ROLF, *looking in through the door, and seeing
where she is, joins her.   MRS. HILLCRIST re-
settles herself a little further in on the Right.*

ROLF. [*Bending over to* CHLOE, *after a glance at* MRS.
HILLCRIST] Are you all right?

CHLOE. It's awfully hot.

She fans herself with the particulars of sale.

ROLF. There's Dawker.   I hate that chap!

CHLOE. Where?

ROLF. Down there; see?

He points down to stage Right of the room.

CHLOE. [*Drawing back in her seat with a little gasp*]
Oh!

ROLF. [*Not noticing*] Who's that next him, looking
up here?

CHLOE. I don't know.

*She has raised her auction programme suddenly,
and sits fanning herself, carefully screening
her face.*

ROLF. [*Looking at her*] Don't you feel well?   Shall
I get you some water?   [*He gets up at her nod.*

As he reaches the door, HILLCRIST *and* JILL
come in.   HILLCRIST *passes him abstractedly
with a nod, and sits down beside his wife.*

JILL. [*To* ROLF] Come to see us turned out?

ROLF. [*Emphatically*] No.   I'm looking after Chloe;
she's not well.

JILL. [*Glancing at her*] Sorry.   She needn't have
come, I suppose?   [ROLF *deigns no answer, and goes out.*

JILL glances at CHLOE, *then at her parents talking in low voices, and sits down next her father, who makes room for her.*

MRS. H. Can Dawker see you there, Jack?

[HILLCRIST *nods.*

What's the time?

HILLCRIST. Three minutes to three.

JILL. Don't you feel beastly all down the backs of your legs, Dodo?

HILLCRIST. Yes.

JILL. Do you, mother?

MRS. H. No.

JILL. A wagon of old Hornblower's pots passed while we were in the yard. It's an omen.

MRS. H. Don't be foolish, Jill.

JILL. Look at the old brute! Dodo, hold my hand.

MRS. H. Make sure you've got a handkerchief, Jack.

HILLCRIST. I can't go beyond the six thousand; I shall have to raise every penny on mortgage as it is. The estate simply won't stand more, Amy.

He feels in his breast pocket, and pulls up the edge of his handkerchief.

JILL. Oh! Look! There's Miss Mullins, at the back; just come in. Isn't she a spidery old chip?

MRS. H. Come to gloat. Really, I think her not accepting your offer is disgusting. Her impartiality is all humbug.

HILLCRIST. Can't blame her for getting what she can—it's human nature. Phew! I used to feel like this before a *viva voce*. Who's that next to Dawker?

JILL. What a fish!

MRS. H. [*To herself*] Ah! yes.

> *Her eyes slide round at* CHLOE, *sitting motion-*
> *less and rather sunk in her seat, slowly fan-*
> *ning herself with the particulars of the sale.*

Jack, go and offer her my smelling salts.

HILLCRIST. [*Taking the salts*] Thank God for a
human touch!

MRS. H. [*Taken aback*] Oh! I——

JILL. [*With a quick look at her mother, snatching the*
salts] I will. [*She goes over to* CHLOE *with the salts*] Have
a sniff; you look awfully white.

CHLOE. [*Looking up, startled*] Oh! no thanks. I'm
all right.

JILL. No, do! You must.   [CHLOE *takes them.*

JILL. D'you mind letting me see that a minute?

> *She takes the particulars of the sale and studies*
> *it, but* CHLOE *has buried the lower part of*
> *her face in her hand and the smelling salts*
> *bottle.*

Beastly hot, isn't it? You'd better keep that.

CHLOE. [*Her dark eyes wandering and uneasy*] Rolf's
getting me some water.

JILL. Why do you stay? You didn't want to come,
did you?   [CHLOE *shakes her head.*

All right! Here's your water.

> *She hands back the particulars and slides over*
> *to her seat, passing* ROLF *in the gangway,*
> *with her chin well up.*
>
> MRS. HILLCRIST, *who has watched* CHLOE *and*
> JILL *and* DAWKER *and his friend, makes an*

*enquiring movement with her hand, but gets
a disappointing answer.*

JILL. What's the time, Dodo?

HILLCRIST. [*Looking at his watch*] Three minutes past.

JILL. [*Sighing*] Oh, hell!

HILLCRIST. Jill!

JILL. Sorry, Dodo. I was only thinking. Look!
Here he is! Phew!—isn't he——?

MRS. H. 'Sh!

The AUCTIONEER *comes in Left and goes to the
table. He is a square, short, brown-faced,
common-looking man, with clipped grey hair
fitting him like a cap, and a clipped grey
moustache. His lids come down over his
quick eyes, till he can see you very sharply,
and you can hardly see that he can see you.
He can break into a smile at any moment,
which has no connection with him, as it were.
By a certain hurt look, however, when bidding
is slow, he discloses that he is not merely an
auctioneer, but has in him elements of the
human being. He can wink with anyone,
and is dressed in a snuff-brown suit, with a
perfectly unbuttoned waistcoat, a low, turned-
down collar, and small black and white sailor-
knot tie. While he is settling his papers, the
HILLCRISTS settle themselves tensely. CHLOE
has drunk her water and leaned back again,
with the smelling salts to her nose. ROLF
leans forward in the seat beside her, looking*

sideways at JILL.   *A* SOLICITOR, *with a grey
beard, has joined the* AUCTIONEER *at his table.*

AUCTIONEER. [*Tapping the table*] Sorry to disappoint
you, gentlemen, but I've only one property to offer you
to-day, No. 1, The Centry, Deepwater. The second
on the particulars has been withdrawn. The third—
that's Bidcot, desirable freehold mansion and farmlands
in the Parish of Kenway—we shall have to deal with
next week. I shall be happy to sell it you then without reservation. [*He looks again through the particulars
in his hand, giving the audience time to readjust themselves to his statements*] Now, gen'lemen, as I say, I've
only the one property to sell. Freehold No. 1—all
that very desirable corn and stock-rearing and parklike
residential land known as the Centry, Deepwater,
unique property—an A.1. chance to an A.1. audience.
[*With his smile*] Ought to make the price of the three
we thought we had. Now you won't mind listening to
the conditions of sale; Mr. Blinkard'll read 'em, and
they won't wirry you, they're very short.

> *He sits down and gives two little taps on the
> table.*

> *The* SOLICITOR *rises and reads the conditions
> of sale in a voice which no one practically
> can hear. Just as he begins to read these
> conditions of sale,* CHARLES HORNBLOWER
> *enters at back. He stands a moment, glanc-
> ing round at the* HILLCRISTS *and twirling his
> moustache, then moves along to his wife and
> touches her.*

CHARLES. Chloe, aren't you well?

> *In the start which she gives, her face is fully*
> *revealed to the audience.*

CHARLES. Come along, out of the way of these
people.

> *He jerks his head towards the* HILLCRISTS.
> CHLOE *gives a swift look down to the stage*
> *Right of the audience.*

CHLOE. No; I'm all right; it's hotter there.

CHARLES. [*To* ROLF] Well, look after her—I must
go back.

> ROLF *nods.* CHARLES *slides back to the door,*
> *with a glance at the* HILLCRISTS, *of whom*
> MRS. HILLCRIST *has been watching like a*
> *lynx. He goes out, just as the* SOLICITOR,
> *finishing, sits down.*

AUCTIONEER. [*Rising and tapping*] Now, gen'lemen,
it's not often a piece of land like this comes into the
market. What's that? [*To a friend in front of him*]
No better land in Deepwater—that's right, Mr. Spicer.
I know the village well, and a charming place it is;
perfect locality, to be sure. Now I don't want to
wirry you by singing the praises of this property; there
it is—well-watered, nicely timbered—no reservation of
the timber, gen'lemen—no tenancy to hold you up;
free to do what you like with it to-morrow. You've
got a jewel of a site there, too; perfect position for a
house. It lies between the Duke's and Squire Hillcrist's—an emerald isle. [*With his smile*] No allusion
to Ireland, gen'lemen—perfect peace in the Centry.
Nothing like it in the county—a gen'leman's site, and
you don't get that offered you every day. [*He looks*

down towards HORNBLOWER, *stage Left*] Carries the
mineral rights, and as you know, perhaps, there's the
very valuable Deepwater clay there. What am I to
start it at? Can I say three thousand? Well, anything you like to give me. I'm not particular. Come
now, you've got more time than me, I expect. Two
hundred acres of first-rate grazin' and cornland, with
a site for a residence unequalled in the county; and all
the possibilities! Well, what shall I say?

                                       [*Bid from* SPICER.
Two thousand? [*With his smile*] That won't hurt you,
Mr. Spicer. Why, it's worth that to overlook the
Duke. For two thousand?

                             [*Bid from* HORNBLOWER, *stage Left*.
And five. Thank you, sir. Two thousand five hun-
dred bid.   [*To a friend just below him*.
Come, Mr. Sandy, don't scratch your head over it.

                             [*Bid from* DAWKER, *stage Right*.
And five. Three thousand bid for this desirable property. Why, you'd think it wasn't desirable. Come
along, gen'lemen. A little spirit.   [*A slight pause*.

  JILL. Why can't I *see* the bids, Dodo?

  HILLCRIST. The last was Dawker's.

  AUCTIONEER. For three thousand. [HORNBLOWER]
Three thousand five hundred? May I say four? [*A
bid from the centre*] No, I'm not particular; I'll take
hundreds. Three thousand six hundred bid. [HORN-
BLOWER] And seven. Three thousand seven hundred,
and——   [*He pauses, quartering the audience*.

  JILL. Who was that, Dodo?

HILLCRIST. Hornblower. It's the Duke in the centre.

AUCTIONEER. Come, gen'lemen, don't keep me all day. Four thousand may I say? [DAWKER] Thank you. We're beginning. And one? [*A bid from the centre*] Four thousand one hundred. [HORNBLOWER] Four thousand two hundred. May I have yours, sir? [*To* DAWKER] And three. Four thousand three hundred bid. No such site in the county, gen'lemen. I'm going to sell this land for what it's worth. You can't bid too much for me. [*He smiles*] [HORNBLOWER] Four thousand five hundred bid. [*Bid from the centre*] And six. [DAWKER] And seven. [HORNBLOWER] And eight. Nine, may I say? [*But the centre has dried up*] [DAWKER] And nine. [HORNBLOWER] Five thousand. Five thousand bid. That's better; there's some spirit in it. For five thousand.

[*He pauses while he speaks to the* SOLICITOR.

HILLCRIST. It's a ducl now.

AUCTIONEER. Now, gen'lemen, I'm not going to give this property away. Five thousand bid. [DAWKER] And one. [HORNBLOWER] And two. [DAWKER] And three. Five thousand three hundred bid. And five, did you say, sir? [HORNBLOWER] Five thousand five hundred bid. [*He looks at his particulars.*

JILL. [*Rather agonised*] Enemy, Dodo.

AUCTIONEER. This chance may never come again.

"How you'll regret it
    If you don't get it,"

as the poet says. May I say five thousand six hun-

dred, sir? [DAWKER] Five thousand six hundred bid.
HORNBLOWER] And seven. [DAWKER] And eight. For
five thousand eight hundred pounds. We're gettin' on,
but we haven't got the value yet.

> *A slight pause, while he wipes his brow at the*
> *success of his own efforts.*

JILL. Us, Dodo?

> HILLCRIST *nods.* JILL *looks over at* ROLF, *whose*
> *face is grimly set.* CHLOE *has never moved.*
> MRS. HILLCRIST *whispers to her husband.*

AUCTIONEER. Five thousand eight hundred bid.
For five thousand eight hundred. Come along,
gen'lemen, come along. We're not beaten. Thank
you, sir. [HORNBLOWER] Five thousand nine hundred.
And—? [DAWKER] Six thousand. Six thousand bid.
Six thousand bid. For six thousand! The Centry—
most desirable spot in the county—going for the low
price of six thousand.

HILLCRIST. [*Muttering*] Low! Heavens!

AUCTIONEER. Any advance on six thousand? Come,
gen'lemen, we haven't dried up? A little spirit. Six
thousand? For six thousand? For six thousand
pounds? Very well, I'm selling. For six thousand
once—[*He taps*] For six thousand twice—[*He taps*].

JILL. [*Low*] Oh! we've got it!

AUCTIONEER. And one, sir? [HORNBLOWER] Six thousand one hundred bid.

> *The* SOLICITOR *touches his arm and says some-*
> *thing, to which the* AUCTIONEER *responds*
> *with a nod.*

MRS. H. Blow your nose, Jack.

> [HILLCRIST *blows his nose.*

AUCTIONEER. For six thousand one hundred. [DAW-KER] And two. Thank you. [HORNBLOWER] And three. For six thousand three hundred. [DAWKER] And four. For six thousand four hundred pounds. This coveted property. For six thousand four hundred pounds. Why, it's giving it away, gen'lemen.   [*A pause.*

MRS. H. Giving!

AUCTIONEER. Six thousand four hundred bid. [HORN-BLOWER] And five. [DAWKER] And six. [HORNBLOWER] And seven. [DAWKER] And eight.

> *A pause, during which, through the door Left,*
> *someone beckons to the* SOLICITOR, *who rises*
> *and confers.*

HILLCRIST. [*Muttering*] I've done if that doesn't get it.

AUCTIONEER. For six thousand eight hundred. For six thousand eight hundred—once—[*He taps*] twice—[*He taps*] For the last time. This dominating site. [HORNBLOWER] And nine. Thank you. For six thousand nine hundred.

> [HILLCRIST *has taken out his handkerchief.*

JILL. Oh! Dodo!

MRS. H. [*Quivering*] Don't give in!

AUCTIONEER. Seven thousand may I say? [DAWKER] Seven thousand.

MRS. H. [*Whispers*] Keep it down; don't show him.

AUCTIONEER. For seven thousand—going for seven

thousand—once—[*Taps*] twice—[*Taps*] [HORNBLOWER]
And one. Thank you, sir.

> HILLCRIST *blows his nose.* JILL, *with a choke,*
> *leans back in her seat and folds her arms*
> *tightly on her chest.* MRS. HILLCRIST *passes*
> *her handkerchief over her lips, sitting perfectly*
> *still.* HILLCRIST, *too, is motionless.*
>
> *The* AUCTIONEER *has paused, and is talking to*
> *the* SOLICITOR, *who has returned to his seat.*

MRS. H. Oh! Jack.

JILL. Stick it, Dodo; stick it!

AUCTIONEER. Now, gen'lemen, I have a bid of seven
thousand one hundred for the Centry. And I'm instructed to sell if I can't get more. It's a fair price,
but not a big price. [*To his friend* MR. SPICER] A
thumpin' price? [*With his smile*] Well, you're a judge
of thumpin', I admit. Now, who'll give me seven
thousand two hundred? What, no one? Well, I
can't make you, gen'lemen. For seven thousand one
hundred. Once—[*Taps*] Twice—[*Taps*].

> [JILL *utters a little groan.*

HILLCRIST. [*Suddenly, in a queer voice*] Two.

AUCTIONEER. [*Turning with surprise and looking up*
to receive HILLCRIST'S *nod*] Thank *you*, sir. And two.
Seven thousand two hundred. [*He screws himself round*
so as to command both HILLCRIST *and* HORNBLOWER]
May I have yours, sir? [HORNBLOWER] And three.
[HILLCRIST] And four. Seven thousand four hundred.
For seven thousand four hundred. [HORNBLOWER] Five.
[HILLCRIST] Six. For seven thousand six hundred. [*A*

pause] Well, gen'lemen, this is better, but a record property shid fetch a record price. The possibilities are enormous. [HORNBLOWER] Eight thousand did you say, sir? Eight thousand. Going for eight thousand pounds. [HILLCRIST] And one. [HORNBLOWER] And two. [HILLCRIST] And three. [HORNBLOWER] And four. [HILLCRIST] And five. For eight thousand five hundred. A wonderful property for eight thousand five hundred.

[*He wipes his brow.*

JILL. [*Whispering*] Oh, Dodo!

MRS. H. That's enough, Jack, we must stop some time.

AUCTIONEER. For eight thousand five hundred. Once—[*Taps*] Twice—[*Taps*] [HORNBLOWER] Six hundred. [HILLCRIST] Seven. May I have yours, sir? [HORNBLOWER] Eight.

HILLCRIST. Nine thousand.

MRS. HILLCRIST *looks at him, biting her lips, but he is quite absorbed.*

AUCTIONEER. Nine thousand for this astounding property. Why, the Duke would pay that if he realised he'd be overlooked. Now, sir? [*To* HORNBLOWER. *No response*]. Just a little raise on that. [*No response.*] For nine thousand. The Centry, Deepwater, for nine thousand. Once—[*Taps*] Twice—[*Taps*].

JILL. [*Under her breath*] Ours!

A VOICE. [*From far back in the centre*] And five hundred.

AUCTIONEER. [*Surprised and throwing out his arms towards the voice*] And five hundred. For nine thou-

sand five hundred.   May I have yours, sir?   [*He looks
at* HORNBLOWER.   *No response.*]

> > [*The* SOLICITOR *speaks to him.*

MRS. H. [*Whispering*] It must be the Duke again.

HILLCRIST. [*Passing his hand over his brow*] That's
stopped him, anyway.

AUCTIONEER. [*Looking at* HILLCRIST] For nine thousand five hundred?   [HILLCRIST *shakes his head.*]
Once more.   The Centry, Deepwater, for nine thousand five hundred.   Once—[*Taps*]   Twice—[*Taps*] [*He
pauses and looks again at* HORNBLOWER *and* HILLCRIST]
For the last time—at nine thousand five hundred.
[*Taps*] [*With a look towards the bidder*] Mr. Smalley.
Well! [*With great satisfaction*] That's that!   No more
to-day, gen'lemen.

> > *The* AUCTIONEER *and* SOLICITOR *busy them-
> > selves.   The room begins to empty.*

MRS. H. Smalley?   Smalley?   *Is* that the Duke's
agent?   Jack!

HILLCRIST. [*Coming out of a sort of coma, after the
excitement he has been going through*] What!   What!

JILL. Oh, Dodo!   How splendidly you stuck it!

HILLCRIST. Phew!   What a squeak!   I was clean
out of my depth.   A mercy the Duke chipped in again.

MRS. H. [*Looking at* ROLF *and* CHLOE, *who are
standing up as if about to go*] Take care; they can hear
you.   Find Dawker, Jack.

> > *Below, the* AUCTIONEER *and* SOLICITOR *take up
> > their papers, and move out Left.*

> > HILLCRIST *stretches himself, standing up, as*

*if to throw off the strain. The door behind
is opened, and* HORNBLOWER *appears.*

HORNBLOWER. Ye ran me up a pretty price. Ye
bid very pluckily, Hillcrist. But ye didn't quite get
my measure.

HILLCRIST. Oh! It was *my* nine thousand the Duke
capped. Thank God, the Centry's gone to a gentleman!

HORNBLOWER. The Duke? [*He laughs*] No, the Centry's not gone to a gentleman, nor to a fool. It's gone
to me.

HILLCRIST. What!

HORNBLOWER. I'm sorry for ye; ye're not fit to
manage these things. Well, it's a monstrous price,
and I've had to pay it because of your obstinacy. I
shan't forget that when I come to build.

HILLCRIST. D'you mean to say that bid was for
you?

HORNBLOWER. Of course I do. I told ye I was a
bad man to be up against. Perhaps ye'll believe me
now.

HILLCRIST. A dastardly trick!

HORNBLOWER. [*With venom*] What did ye call it—a
skin game? Remember we're playin' a skin game,
Hillcrist.

HILLCRIST. [*Clenching his fists*] If we were younger
men——

HORNBLOWER. Ay! 'Twouldn't look pretty for us
to be at fisticuffs. We'll leave the fightin' to the young
ones. [*He glances at* ROLF *and* JILL; *suddenly throwing*

out his finger at ROLF] No makin' up to that young woman! I've watched ye. And as for you, missy, you leave my boy alone.

JILL. [*With suppressed passion*] Dodo, may I spit in his eye or something?

HILLCRIST. Sit down.

> JILL *sits down. He stands between her and*
> HORNBLOWER.

You've won this round, sir, by a foul blow. We shall see whether you can take any advantage of it. I believe the law can stop you ruining my property.

HORNBLOWER. Make your mind easy; it can't. I've got ye in a noose, and I'm goin' to hang ye.

MRS. H. [*Suddenly*] Mr. Hornblower, as you fight foul—so shall we.

HILLCRIST. Amy!

MRS. H. [*Paying no attention*] And it will not be foul play towards you and yours. You are outside the pale.

HORNBLOWER. That's just where I am, outside *your* pale all round ye. Ye're not long for Deepwater, ma'am. Make your dispositions to go; ye'll be out in six months, I prophesy. And good riddance to the neighbourhood.   [*They are all down on the level now.*

CHLOE. [*Suddenly coming closer to* MRS. HILLCRIST] Here are your salts, thank you. Father, can't you—?

HORNBLOWER. [*Surprised*] Can't I what?

CHLOE. Can't you come to an arrangement?

MRS. H. Just so, Mr. Hornblower. Can't you?

HORNBLOWER. [*Looking from one to the other*] As

we're speakin' out, ma'am, it's your behaviour to my daughter-in-law—who's as good as you—and better, to my thinking—that's more than half the reason why I've bought this property. Ye've fair got my dander up. Now it's no use to bandy words. It's very forgivin' of ye, Chloe, but come along!

MRS. H. Quite seriously, Mr. Hornblower, you had better come to an arrangement.

HORNBLOWER. Mrs. Hillcrist, ladies should keep to their own business.

MRS. H. I will.

HILLCRIST. Amy, do leave it to us men. You young man [*He speaks to* ROLF] do you support your father's trick this afternoon?

> JILL *looks round at* ROLF, *who tries to speak, when* HORNBLOWER *breaks in.*

HORNBLOWER. *My* trick? And what d'ye call it, to try and put me own son against me?

JILL. [*To* ROLF] Well?

ROLF. I don't, but——

HORNBLOWER. Trick? Ye young cub, be quiet. Mr. Hillcrist had an agent bid for him—I had an agent bid for me. Only his agent bid at the beginnin', an' mine bid at the end. What's the trick in that?

> [*He laughs.*

HILLCRIST. Hopeless; we're in different worlds.

HORNBLOWER. I wish to God we were! Come you, Chloe. And you, Rolf, you follow. In six months I'll have those chimneys up, and me lorries runnin' round ye.

MRS. H. Mr. Hornblower, if you build——

HORNBLOWER. [*Looking at* MRS. HILLCRIST] Ye know—it's laughable. Ye make me pay nine thousand five hundred for a bit o' land not worth four, and ye think I'm not to get back on ye. I'm goin' on with as little consideration as if ye were a family of black-beetles. Good afternoon!

ROLF. Father!

JILL. Oh, Dodo! He's obscene.

HILLCRIST. Mr. Hornblower, my compliments.

> HORNBLOWER, *with a stare at* HILLCRIST'S *half-smiling face, takes* CHLOE'S *arm, and half drags her towards the door on the Left. But there, in the opened doorway, are standing* DAWKER *and a* STRANGER. *They move just out of the way of the exit, looking at* CHLOE, *who sways and very nearly falls.*

HORNBLOWER. Why! Chloe! What's the matter?

CHLOE. I don't know; I'm not well to-day.

> [*She pulls herself together with a great effort.*

MRS. H. [*Who has exchanged a nod with* DAWKER *and the* STRANGER] Mr. Hornblower, you build at your peril. I warn you.

HORNBLOWER. [*Turning round to speak*] Ye think yourself very cool and very smart. But I doubt this is the first time ye've been up against realities. Now, I've been up against them all my life. Don't talk to me, ma'am, about peril and that sort of nonsense; it makes no impression. Your husband called me pachydermatous. I don't know Greek, and Latin, and all that, but I've looked it out in the dictionary, and I find it means thick-skinned. And I'm none the worse for that when I have to deal with folk like you. Good afternoon.

> *He draws* CHLOE *forward, and they pass through the door, followed quickly by* ROLF.

MRS. H. Thank you, Dawker.

> *She moves up to* DAWKER *and the* STRANGER, *Left, and they talk.*

JILL. Dodo! It's awful!

HILLCRIST. Well, there's nothing for it now but to smile and pay up. Poor old home! It shall be his wash-pot. Over the Centry will he cast his shoe. By Gad, Jill, I could cry!

JILL. [*Pointing*] Look! Chloe's sitting down. She nearly fainted just now. It's something to do with Dawker, Dodo, and that man with him. Look at mother! Ask them!

HILLCRIST. Dawker!

> DAWKER *comes to him, followed by* MRS. HILL-CRIST.

What's the mystery about young Mrs. Hornblower?

DAWKER. No mystery.

HILLCRIST. Well, what is it?

MRS. H. You'd better not ask.

HILLCRIST. I wish to know.

MRS. H. Jill, go out and wait for us.

JILL. Nonsense, mother!

MRS. H. It's not for a girl to hear.

JILL. Bosh! I read the papers every day.

DAWKER. It's nothin' worse than you get there, anyway.

MRS. H. Do you wish your daughter——

JILL. It's ridiculous, Dodo; you'd think I was mother
at my age.

MRS. H. I was not so proud of my knowledge.

JILL. No, but you had it, dear.

HILLCRIST. What is it—what is it? Come over
here, Dawker.

> DAWKER *goes to him, Right, and speaks in a
> low voice.*

What!   [*Again* DAWKER *speaks in a low voice.*
Good God!

MRS. H. Exactly!

JILL. Poor thing—whatever it is!

MRS. H. Poor thing?

JILL. What went before, mother?

MRS. H. It's what's coming after that matters,
luckily.

HILLCRIST. How do you know this?

DAWKER. My friend here [*He points to the* STRANGER]
was one of the agents.

HILLCRIST. It's shocking. I'm sorry I heard it.

MRS. H. I told you not to.

HILLCRIST. Ask your friend to come here.

> DAWKER *beckons, and the* STRANGER *joins the
> group.*

Are you sure of what you've said, sir?

STRANGER. Perfectly. I remember her quite well;
her name then was——

HILLCRIST. I don't want to know, thank you. I'm

truly sorry. I wouldn't wish the knowledge of that about his womenfolk to my worst enemy. This mustn't be spoken of.   [JILL *hugs his arm.*

MRS. H. It will not be if Mr. Hornblower is wise. If he is not wise, it must be spoken of.

HILLCRIST. I say no, Amy. I won't have it. It's a dirty weapon. Who touches pitch shall be defiled.

MRS. H. Well, what weapons does he use against us? Don't be quixotic. For all we can tell, they know it quite well already, and if they don't they ought to. Anyway, to know this is our salvation, and we must use it.

JILL. [*Sotto voce*] Pitch! Dodo! Pitch!

DAWKER. The threat's enough! J.P.—Chapel—Future member for the constituency——

HILLCRIST. [*A little more doubtfully*] To use a piece of knowledge about a woman—it's repugnant. I—I won't do it.

MRS. H. If you had a son tricked into marrying such a woman, would you wish to remain ignorant of it?

HILLCRIST. [*Struck*] I don't know—I don't know.

MRS. H. At least you'd like to be in a position to help him, if you thought it necessary?

HILLCRIST. Well—that—perhaps.

MRS. H. Then you agree that Mr. Hornblower at least should be told. What he does with the knowledge is not our affair.

HILLCRIST. [*Half to the* STRANGER *and half to* DAWKER] Do you realise that an imputation of that kind may be ground for a criminal libel action?

STRANGER. Quite.   But there's no shadow of doubt;
not the faintest.   You saw her just now?

HILLCRIST. I did. [*Revolting again*] No; I don't like
it.

> DAWKER *has drawn the* STRANGER *a step or
> two away, and they talk together.*

MRS. H. [*In a low voice*] And the ruin of our home?
You're betraying your fathers, Jack.

HILLCRIST. I can't bear bringing a woman into it.

MRS. H. We don't.   If anyone brings her in, it will
be Hornblower himself.

HILLCRIST. We use her secret as a lever.

MRS. H. I tell you quite plainly: I will only consent to holding my tongue about her, if you agree to
Hornblower being told.   It's a scandal to have a
woman like that in the neighbourhood.

JILL. Mother means that, father.

HILLCRIST. Jill, keep quiet.   This is a very bitter
position.   I can't tell what to do.

MRS. H. You must use this knowledge.   You owe
it to me—to us all.   You'll see that when you've
thought it over.

JILL. [*Softly*] Pitch, Dodo, pitch!

MRS. H. [*Furiously*] Jill, be quiet!

HILLCRIST. I was brought up never to hurt a woman.
I can't do it, Amy—I can't do it.   I should never feel
like a gentleman again.

MRS. H. [*Coldly*] Oh! Very well.

HILLCRIST. What d'you mean by that?

MRS. H. I shall use the knowledge in my own way.

HILLCRIST. [*Staring at her*] You would—against my wishes?

MRS. H. I consider it my duty.

HILLCRIST. If I agree to Hornblower being told——

MRS. H. That's all I want.

HILLCRIST. It's the utmost I'll consent to, Amy; and don't let's have any humbug about its being morally necessary. We do it to save our skins.

MRS. H. I don't know what you mean by humbug?

JILL. He means humbug, mother.

HILLCRIST. It must stop at old Hornblower. Do you quite understand?

MRS. H. Quite.

JILL. Will it stop?

MRS. H. Jill, if you can't keep your impertinence to yourself——

HILLCRIST. Jill, come with me.

> [*He turns towards door, Back.*

JILL. I'm sorry, mother. Only it *is* a skin game, isn't it?

MRS. H. You pride youself on plain speech, Jill. I pride myself on plain thought. You will thank me afterwards that I can see realities. I know we are better people than these Hornblowers. Here we are going to stay, and they—are not.

JILL. [*Looking at her with a sort of unwilling admiration*] Mother, you're wonderful!

HILLCRIST. Jill!

JILL. Coming, Dodo.

> *She turns and runs to the door.   They go out.*

MRS. HILLCRIST, *with a long sigh, draws herself up, fine and proud.*

MRS. H. Dawker!   [*He comes to her.*
I shall send him a note to-night, and word it so that he will be bound to come and see us to-morrow morning. Will you be in the study just before eleven o'clock, with this gentleman?

DAWKER. [*Nodding*] We're going to wire for his partner. I'll bring him too. Can't make too sure.

                   [*She goes firmly up the steps and out.*

DAWKER. [*To the* STRANGER, *with a wink*] The Squire's squeamish—too much of a gentleman. But he don't count. The grey mare's all right. You wire to Henry. I'm off to our solicitors. We'll make that old rhinoceros sell us back the Centry at a decent price. These Hornblowers—[*Laying his finger on his nose*] We've got 'em!

CURTAIN

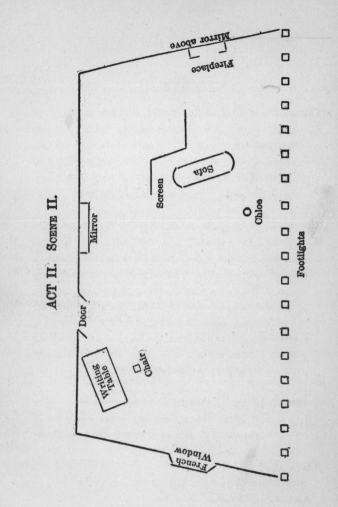

ACT II. SCENE II.

Mirror above

Fireplace

Screen

Sofa

Mirror

Chloe

Footlights

Door

Writing Table

Chair

French Window

SCENE II

CHLOE's *boudoir at half-past seven the same evening. A pretty room. No pictures on the walls, but two mirrors. A screen and a luxurious couch on the fireplace side, stage Left. A door rather Right of Centre Back, opening inwards. A French window, Right forward. A writing table, Right Back. Electric light burning.*

CHLOE, *in a tea-gown, is standing by the forward end of the sofa, very still, and very pale. Her lips are parted, and her large eyes stare straight before them as if seeing ghosts. The door is opened noiselessly and a* WOMAN's *face is seen. It peers at* CHLOE, *vanishes, and the door is closed.* CHLOE *raises her hands, covers her eyes with them, drops them with a quick gesture, and looks round her. A knock. With a swift movement she slides on to the sofa, and lies prostrate, with eyes closed.*

CHLOE. [*Feebly*] Come in!

> *Her* MAID *enters; a trim, contained figure of uncertain years, in a black dress, with the face which was peering in.*

Yes, Anna?

ANNA. Aren't you going in to dinner, ma'am?

CHLOE. [*With closed eyes*] No.

67

ANNA. Will you take anything here, ma'am?

CHLOE. I'd like a biscuit and a glass of champagne.

> *The* MAID, *who is standing between sofa and door, smiles.* CHLOE, *with a swift look, catches the smile.*

Why do you smile?

ANNA. Was I, ma'am?

CHLOE. You know you were. [*Fiercely*] Are you paid to smile at me?

ANNA. [*Immovable*] No, ma'am. Would you like some eau de Cologne on your forehead?

CHLOE. Yes.—No.—What's the good? [*Clasping her forehead*] My headache won't go.

ANNA. To keep lying down's the best thing for it.

CHLOE. I have been—hours.

ANNA. [*With the smile*] Yes, ma'am.

CHLOE. [*Gathering herself up on the sofa*] Anna! Why do you do it?

ANNA. Do what, ma'am?

CHLOE. Spy on me.

ANNA. I—never! I——!

CHLOE. To spy! You're a fool, too. What is there to spy on?

ANNA. Nothing, ma'am. Of course, if you're not satisfied with me, I must give notice. Only—if I were spying, I should expect to have notice given me. I've been accustomed to ladies who wouldn't stand such a thing for a minute.

CHLOE. [*Intently*] Well, you'll take a month's wages and go to-morrow. And that's all, now.

> [ANNA *inclines her head and goes out.*

CHLOE, *with a sort of moan, turns over and
buries her face in the cushion.*

CHLOE. [*Sitting up*] If I could see that man—if only
—or Dawker——

*She springs up and goes to the door, but hesi-
tates, and comes back to the head of the sofa,
as* ROLF *comes in. During this scene the
door is again opened stealthily, an inch or
two.*

ROLF. How's the head?

CHLOE. Beastly, thanks.   I'm not going in to dinner.

ROLF. Is there anything I can do for you?

CHLOE. No, dear boy. [*Suddenly looking at him*]
You don't want this quarrel with the Hillcrists to go
on, do you, Rolf?

ROLF. No; I hate it.

CHLOE. Well, I think I *might* be able to stop it.   Will
you slip round to Dawker's—it's not five minutes—
and ask him to come and see me.

ROLF. Father and Charlie wouldn't——

CHLOE. I know.   But if he comes to the window
here while you're at dinner, I'll let him in, and out,
and nobody'd know.

ROLF. [*Astonished*] Yes, but what—I mean how——

CHLOE. Don't ask me.   It's worth the shot—that's
all. [*Looking at her wrist-watch*] To this window at
eight o'clock exactly.   First long window on the terrace, tell him.

ROLF. It's nothing Charlie would mind?

CHLOE. No; only I can't tell him—he and father are
so mad about it all.

ROLF. If there's a real chance——

CHLOE. [*Going to the window and opening it*] This way, Rolf. If you don't come back I shall know he's coming. Put your watch by mine. [*Looking at his watch*] It's a minute fast, see!

ROLF. Look here, Chloe——

CHLOE. Don't wait; go on.

> *She almost pushes him out through the window, closes it after him, draws the curtains again, stands a minute, thinking hard ; goes to the bell and rings it ; then, crossing to the writing table, Right Back, she takes out a chemist's prescription.*

[ANNA *comes in.*

CHLOE. I don't want that champagne. Take this to the chemist and get him to make up some of these cachets quick, and bring them back yourself.

ANNA. Yes, ma'am; but you have some.

CHLOE. They're too old; I've taken two—the strength's out of them. Quick, please; I can't stand this head.

ANNA. [*Taking the prescription—with her smile*] Yes, ma'am. It'll take some time—you don't want me?

CHLOE. No; I want the cachets. [ANNA *goes out.*

> CHLOE *looks at her wrist-watch, goes to the writing-table, which is old-fashioned, with a secret drawer, looks round her, dives at the secret drawer, takes out a roll of notes and a tissue paper parcel. She counts the notes: " Three hundred." Slips them into her breast*

and unwraps the little parcel. It contains pearls. She slips them, too, into her dress, looks round startled, replaces the drawer, and regains her place on the sofa, lying prostrate as the door opens, and HORNBLOWER *comes in. She does not open her eyes, and he stands looking at her a moment before speaking.*

HORNBLOWER. [*Almost softly*] How are ye feelin', Chloe?

CHLOE. Awful head!

HORNBLOWER. Can ye attend a moment? I've had a note from that woman.   [CHLOE *sits up.*

HORNBLOWER. [*Reading*] "I have something of the utmost importance to tell you in regard to your daughter-in-law. I shall be waiting to see you at eleven o'clock to-morrow morning. The matter is so utterly vital to the happiness of all your family, that I cannot imagine you will fail to come." Now, what's the meaning of it? Is it sheer impudence, or lunacy, or what?

CHLOE. I don't know.

HORNBLOWER. [*Not unkindly*] Chloe, if there's anything—ye'd better tell me. Forewarned's forearmed.

CHLOE. There's nothing; unless it's—[*With a quick look at him*]—Unless it's that my father was a—a bankrupt.

HORNBLOWER. Hech! Many a man's been that. Ye've never told us much about your family.

CHLOE. I wasn't very proud of him.

HORNBLOWER. Well, ye're not responsible for your father. If that's all, it's a relief. The bitter snobs! I'll remember it in the account I've got with them.

CHLOE. Father, don't say anything to Charlie; it'll only worry him for nothing.

HORNBLOWER. Na, no, I'll not. If *I* went bankrupt, it'd upset Chearlie, I've not a doubt. [*He laughs. Looking at her shrewdly*] There's nothing else, before I answer her? [CHLOE *shakes her head.* Ye're sure?

CHLOE. [*With an effort*] She may invent things, of course.

HORNBLOWER. [*Lost in his feud feeling*] Ah! but there's such a thing as the laws o' slander. If they play pranks, I'll have them up for it.

CHLOE. [*Timidly*] Couldn't you stop this quarrel, father? You said it was on my account. But *I* don't want to know them. And they do love their old home. I like the girl. You don't really need to build just there, do you? Couldn't you stop it? Do!

HORNBLOWER. Stop it? Now I've bought? Na, no! The snobs defied me, and I'm going to show them. I hate the lot of them, and I hate that little Dawker worst of all.

CHLOE. He's only their agent.

HORNBLOWER. He's a part of the whole dog-in-the-manger system that stands in my way. Ye're a woman, and ye don't understand these things. Ye wouldn't believe the struggle I've had to make my money and get my position. These county folk talk soft sawder, but to get anything from them's like gettin' butter out of a dog's mouth. If they could drive me out of here by fair means or foul, would they hesitate a moment? Not they! See what they've made me pay; and look at this letter. Selfish, mean lot o' hypocrites!

CHLOE. But they didn't begin the quarrel.

HORNBLOWER. Not openly; but underneath they did —that's their way. They began it by thwartin' me here and there and everywhere, just because I've come into me own a bit later than they did. I gave 'em their chance, and they wouldn't take it. Well, I'll show 'em what a man like me can do when he sets his mind to it. I'll not leave much skin on them.

> *In the intensity of his feeling he has lost sight of her face, alive with a sort of agony of doubt, whether to plead with him further, or what to do. Then, with a swift glance at her wrist-watch, she falls back on the sofa and closes her eyes.*

It'll give me a power of enjoyment seein' me chimneys go up in front of their windies. That was a bonnie thought—that last bid o' mine. He'd got that roused up, I believe he never would a' stopped. [*Looking at her*] I forgot your head. Well, well, ye'll be best [yin' quiet.   [*The gong sounds.* Shall we send ye something in from dinner?

CHLOE. No; I'll try to sleep. Please tell them I don't want to be disturbed.

HORNBLOWER. All right. I'll just answer this note.
                              [*He sits down at her writing-table.*

CHLOE *starts up from the sofa feverishly, look-*
ing at her watch, at the window, at her watch ;
then softly crosses to the window and opens it.

HORNBLOWER. [*Finishing*] Listen ! [*He turns round
towards the sofa*] Hallo !   Where are ye?

CHLOE. [*At the window*] It's so hot.

HORNBLOWER. Here's what I've said:

"MADAM,—You can tell me nothing of my daughter-in-law which can affect the happiness of
my family.   I regard your note as an impertinence, and I shall not be with you at eleven
o'clock to-morrow morning.
                              "Yours truly——"

CHLOE. [*With a suffering movement of her head*] Oh !
—Well !——   [*The gong is touched a second time.*

HORNBLOWER. [*Crossing to the door*] Lie ye down,
and get a sleep.   I'll tell them not to disturb ye; and
I hope ye'll be all right to-morrow.   Good-night, Chloe.

CHLOE. Good-night.   [*He goes out.*

After a feverish turn or two, CHLOE *returns to
the open window and waits there, half screened
by the curtains.   The door is opened inch
by inch, and* ANNA'S *head peers round.   Seeing where* CHLOE *is, she slips in and passes
behind the screen, Left.   Suddenly* CHLOE
backs in from the window.

CHLOE. [*In a low voice*] Come in.

        [*She darts to the door and locks it.*

DAWKER has come in through the window and stands regarding her with a half smile.

DAWKER. Well, young woman, what do you want of me?

In the presence of this man of her own class, there comes a distinct change in CHLOE'S voice and manner; a sort of frank commonness, adapted to the man she is dealing with, but she keeps her voice low.

CHLOE. You're making a mistake, you know.

DAWKER. [*With a broad grin*] No. I've got a memory for faces.

CHLOE. I say you are.

DAWKER. [*Turning to go*] If that's all, you needn't 'ave troubled me to come.

CHLOE. No. Don't go! [*With a faint smile*] You *are* playing a game with me. Aren't you ashamed? What harm have I done you? Do you call this cricket?

DAWKER. No, my girl—business.

CHLOE. [*Bitterly*] What have I to do with this quarrel? I couldn't help their falling out.

DAWKER. That's your misfortune.

CHLOE. [*Clasping her hands*] You're a cruel fellow if you can spoil a woman's life who never did you an ounce of harm.

DAWKER. So they *don't* know about you. That's all right. Now, look here, I serve my employer. But I'm flesh and blood, too, and I always give as good as I get. I hate this family of yours. There's no name too bad for 'em to call me this last month, and no

looks too black to give me. I tell you frankly, I hate
'em.

CHLOE. There's good in them same as in you.

DAWKER. [*With a grin*] There's no good Hornblower
but a dead Hornblower.

CHLOE. But—but I'm *not* one.

DAWKER. You'll be the mother of some, I shouldn't
wonder.

CHLOE. [*Stretching out her hand—pathetically*] Oh!
leave me alone, do! I'm happy here. Be a sport!
Be a sport!

DAWKER. [*Disconcerted for a second*] You can't get
at me, so don't try it on.

CHLOE. I had such a bad time in old days.

> DAWKER *shakes his head ; his grin has dis-
> appeared and his face is like wood.*

CHLOE. [*Panting*] Ah! do! You might! You've
been fond of some woman, I suppose. Think of her!

DAWKER. [*Decisively*] It won't do, Mrs. Chloe.
You're a pawn in the game, and I'm going to use you.

CHLOE. [*Despairingly*] What is it to you? [*With a
sudden touch of the tigress*] Look here! Don't you
make an enemy of me. I haven't dragged through
hell for nothing. Women like me can bite, I tell
you.

DAWKER. That's better. I'd rather have a woman
threaten than whine, any day. Threaten away!
You'll let 'em know that you met me in the Prom-
enade one night. Of course you'll let 'em know that,
won't you?—or that——

CHLOE. Be quiet! Oh! Be quiet! [*Taking from her bosom the notes and the pearls*] Look! There's my savings—there's all I've got! The pearls'll fetch nearly a thousand. [*Holding it out to him*] Take it, and drop me out—won't you? Won't you?

DAWKER. [*Passing his tongue over his lips—with a hard little laugh*] You mistake your man, missis. I'm a plain dog, if you like, but I'm faithful, and I hold fast. Don't try those games on me.

CHLOE. [*Losing control*] You're a beast!—a beast! a cruel, cowardly beast! And how dare you bribe that woman here to spy on me? Oh! yes, you do; you know you do. If you drove me mad, you wouldn't care. You beast!

DAWKER. Now, don't carry on! That won't help you.

CHLOE. What d'you call it—to dog a woman down like this, just because you happen to have a quarrel with a man?

DAWKER. Who made the quarrel? Not me, missis. *You* ought to know that in a row it's the weak and helpless—we won't say the innocent—that get it in the neck. That can't be helped.

CHLOE. [*Regarding him intently*] I hope your mother or your sister, if you've got any, may go through what I'm going through ever since you got on my track. I hope they'll know what fear means. I hope they'll love and find out that it's hanging on a thread, and—and—— Oh! you coward, you persecuting coward! Call yourself a man!

DAWKER. [*With his grin*] Ah! You look quite pretty like that. By George! you're a handsome woman when you're roused.

> CHLOE'S *passion fades out as quickly as it blazed up. She sinks down on the sofa, shudders, looks here and there, and then for a moment up at him.*

CHLOE. Is there *anything* you'll take, not to spoil my life? [*Clasping her hands on her breast ; under her breath*] Me?

DAWKER. [*Wiping his brow*] By God! That's an offer. [*He recoils towards the window*] You—you touched me there. Look here! I've got to use you and I'm going to use you, but I'll do my best to let you down as easy as I can. No, I don't want anything you can give me—that is—[*He wipes his brow again*] I'd like it —but I won't take it.

> [CHLOE *buries her face in her hands.*

There! Keep your pecker up; don't cry. Good-night!
> [*He goes through the window.*

CHLOE. [*Springing up*] Ugh! Rat in a trap! Rat——!
> *She stands listening ; flies to the door, unlocks it, and, going back to the sofa, lies down and closes her eyes.* CHARLES *comes in very quietly and stands over her, looking to see if she is asleep. She opens her eyes.*

CHARLES. Well, Clo! Had a sleep, old girl?

CHLOE. Ye—es.

CHARLES. [*Sitting on the arm of the sofa and caressing her*] Feel better, dear?

CHLOE. Yes, better, Charlie.

CHARLES. That's right.   Would you like some soup?

CHLOE. [*With a shudder*] No.

CHARLES. I say—what gives you these heads? You've been very on and off all this last month.

CHLOE. I don't know.   Except that—except that I *am* going to have a child, Charlie.

CHARLES. After all! By Jove! Sure?

CHLOE. [*Nodding*] Are you glad?

CHARLES. Well—I suppose I am. The guv'nor will be mighty pleased, anyway.

CHLOE. Don't tell him—yet.

CHARLES. All right! [*Bending over and drawing her to him*] My poor girl, I'm so sorry you're seedy. Give us a kiss.

> CHLOE *puts up her face and kisses him passionately.*

I say, you're like fire.   You're not feverish?

CHLOE. [*With a laugh*] It's a wonder if I'm not. Charlie, are you happy with me?

CHARLES. What do you think?

CHLOE. [*Leaning against him*] You wouldn't easily believe things against me, would you?

CHARLES. What! Thinking of those Hillcrists? What the hell that woman means by her attitude towards you—— When I saw her there to-day, I had all my work cut out not to go up and give her a bit of my mind.

CHLOE. [*Watching him stealthily*] It's not good for me, now I'm like this. It's upsetting me, Charlie.

CHARLES. Yes; and we won't forget. We'll make 'em pay for it.

CHLOE. It's wretched in a little place like this. I say, must you go on spoiling their home?

CHARLES. The woman cuts you and insults you. That's enough for me.

CHLOE. [*Timidly*] Let her. *I* don't care; I can't bear feeling enemies about, Charlie, I—get nervous—I——

CHARLES. My dear girl! What is it?

[*He looks at her intently.*

CHLOE. I suppose it's—being like this. [*Suddenly*] But, Charlie, do stop it for my sake. Do, do!

CHARLES. [*Patting her arm*] Come, come; I say, Chloe! You're making mountains. See things in proportion. Father's paid nine thousand five hundred to get the better of those people, and you want him to chuck it away to save a woman who's insulted you. That's not sense, and it's not business. Have some pride.

CHLOE. [*Breathless*] I've got no pride, Charlie. I want to be quiet—that's all.

CHARLES. Well, if the row gets on your nerves, I can take you to the sea. But you ought to enjoy a fight with people like that.

CHLOE. [*With calculated bitterness*] No, it's nothing, of course—what *I* want.

CHARLES. Hallɔ! Hallo! You *are* on the jump!

CHLOE. If you want me to be a good wife to you, make father stop it.

CHARLES. [*Standing up*] Now, look here, Chloe, what's behind this?

CHLOE. [*Faintly*] Behind?

CHARLES. You're carrying on as if—as if you were really scared! We've *got* these people. We'll have them out of Deepwater in six months. It's absolute ruination to their beastly old house; we'll put the chimneys on the very edge, not three hundred yards off, and our smoke'll be drifting over them half the time. You won't have this confounded stuck-up woman here much longer. And then we can really go ahead and take our proper place. So long as she's here, we shall never do that. We've only to drive on now as fast as we can.

CHLOE. [*With a gesture*] I see.

CHARLES. [*Again looking at her*] If you go on like this, you know, I shall begin to think there's something you——

CHLOE [*softly*] Charlie!   [*He comes to her.*]
Love me!

CHARLES. [*Embracing her*] There, old girl! I know women are funny at these times. You want a good night, that's all.

CHLOE. You haven't finished dinner, have you? Go back, and I'll go to bed quite soon. Charlie, don't stop loving me.

CHARLES. Stop? Not much.

> *While he is again embracing her,* ANNA *steals from behind the screen to the door, opens it noiselessly, and passes through, but it clicks as she shuts it.*

CHLOE. [*Starting violently*] Oh—h!

CHARLES. What is it? What is it? You are nervy, my dear.

CHLOE. [*Looking round with a little laugh*] I don't know. Go on, Charlie. I'll be all right when this head's gone.

CHARLES. [*Stroking her forehead and looking at her doubtfully*] You go to bed; I won't be late coming up.

He turns and goes, blowing a kiss from the doorway. When he is gone, CHLOE gets up and stands in precisely the attitude in which she stood at the beginning of the Act, thinking, and thinking. And the door is opened, and the face of the MAID peers round at her.

CURTAIN

ACT III

ACT III

SCENE I

MORNING

HILLCRIST'S *study next morning.*

> JILL, *coming from Left, looks in at the open French window.*

JILL. [*Speaking to* ROLF, *invisible*] Come in here. There's no one.

> *She goes in.* ROLF *joins her, coming from the garden.*

ROLF. Jill, I just wanted to say—Need we?

> [JILL *nods.*

Seeing you yesterday—it did seem rotten.

JILL. *We* didn't begin it.

ROLF. No; but you don't understand. If you'd made yourself, as father has——

JILL. I hope I should be sorry.

ROLF. [*Reproachfully*] That isn't like you. Really he can't help thinking he's a public benefactor.

JILL. And we can't help thinking he's a pig. Sorry!

ROLF. If the survival of the fittest is right——

JILL. He may be fitter, but he's not going to survive.

ROLF. [*Distracted*] It looks like it, though.

JILL. Is that all you came to say?

Rolf. No. Suppose we joined, couldn't we stop it?

Jill. I don't feel like joining.

Rolf. We *did* shake hands.

Jill. One can't fight and not grow bitter.

Rolf. *I* don't feel bitter.

Jill. Wait; you'll feel it soon enough.

Rolf. Why? [*Attentively*] About Chloe? I do think your mother's manner to her is——

Jill. Well?

Rolf. Snobbish.   [Jill *laughs*.
She may not be your class; and that's just why it's snobbish.

Jill. I think you'd better shut up.

Rolf. What my father said was true; your mother's rudeness to her that day she came here, has made both him and Charlie ever so much more bitter.

[Jill *whistles the Habanera from* "*Carmen*."
[*Staring at her, rather angrily*] Is it a whistling matter?

Jill. No.

Rolf. I suppose you want me to go?

Jill. Yes.

Rolf. All right. Aren't we ever going to be friends again?

Jill. [*Looking steadily at him*] I don't expect so.

Rolf. That's very—horrible.

Jill. Lots of horrible things in the world.

Rolf. It's our business to make them fewer, Jill.

Jill. [*Fiercely*] Don't be moral.

Rolf. [*Hurt*] That's the last thing I want to be. I only want to be friendly.

JILL. Better be real first.

ROLF. From the big point of view——

JILL. There isn't any. We're all out for our own. And why not?

ROLF. By jove, you have got——

JILL. Cynical? Your father's motto—"Every man for himself." That's the winner—hands down. Goodbye!

ROLF. Jill! Jill!

JILL. [*Putting her hands behind her back, hums*]—
"If auld acquaintance be forgot
And days of auld lang syne"——

ROLF. Don't!

*With a pained gesture he goes out towards Left,
through the French window.*

JILL, *who has broken off the song, stands with
her hands clenched and her lips quivering.*

[FELLOWS *enters Left.*

FELLOWS. Mr. Dawker, Miss, and two gentlemen.

JILL. Let the three gentlemen in, and me out.

[*She passes him and goes out Left.*

And immediately DAWKER *and the* TWO
STRANGERS *come in.*

FELLOWS. I'll inform Mrs. Hillcrist, sir. The Squire is on his rounds. [*He goes out Left.*

The THREE MEN *gather in a discreet knot at
the big bureau, having glanced at the two
doors and the open French window.*

DAWKER. Now this may come into Court, you know. If there's a screw loose anywhere, better men-

tion it. [*To* SECOND STRANGER] You knew her personally?

SECOND S. What do you think? I don't take girls
on trust for that sort of job. She came to us highly
recommended, too; and did her work very well. It
was a double stunt—to make sure—wasn't it, George?

FIRST S. Yes; we paid her for the two visits.

SECOND S. I should know her in a minute; striking
looking girl; had something in her face. Daresay she'd
seen hard times.

FIRST S. We don't want publicity.

DAWKER. Not likely. The threat'll do it; but the
stakes are heavy—and the man's a slogger; we must
be able to push it home. If you can both swear to
her, it'll do the trick.

SECOND S. And about—I mean, we're losing time,
you know, coming down here.

DAWKER. [*With a nod at* FIRST STRANGER] George
here knows me. That'll be all right. I'll guarantee it
well worth your while.

SECOND S. I don't want to do the girl harm, if she's
married.

DAWKER. No, no; nobody wants to hurt *her*. We
just want a cinch on this fellow till he squeals.

> They separate a little as MRS. HILLCRIST *enters
> from Right*.

DAWKER. Good morning, ma'am. My friend's partner. Hornblower coming?

MRS. H. At eleven. I had to send up a second
note, Dawker.

DAWKER. Squire not in?

MRS. H. I haven't told him.

DAWKER. [*Nodding*] Our friends might go in here [*Pointing Right*] and we can use 'em as we want 'em.

MRS. H. [*To the* STRANGERS] Will you make yourselves comfortable?

> *She holds the door open, and they pass her into the room, Right.*

DAWKER. [*Showing document*] I've had this drawn and engrossed. Pretty sharp work. Conveys the Centry, *and* Longmeadow, to the Squire at four thousand five hundred. Now, ma'am, suppose Hornblower puts his hand to that, he'll have been done in the eye, and six thousand all told out o' pocket. You'll have a very nasty neighbour here.

MRS. H. But we shall still have the power to disclose that secret at any time.

DAWKER. Yeh! But things might happen here you could never bring home to him. You can't trust a man like that. He isn't goin' to forgive *me*, I know.

MRS. H. [*Regarding him keenly*] But if he signs, we couldn't honourably——

DAWKER. No, ma'am, *you* couldn't; and I'm sure *I* don't want to do that girl a hurt. I just mention it because, of course, you can't guarantee that it doesn't get out.

MRS. H. Not absolutely, I suppose.

> *A look passes between them, which neither of them has quite sanctioned.*

There's his car. It always seems to make more noise than any other.

DAWKER. He'll kick and flounder—but you leave

him to ask what you want, ma'am; don't mention this [*He puts the deed back into his pocket*]. The Centry's no mortal good to him if he's not going to put up works; I should say he'd be glad to save what he can.

Mrs. Hillcrist *inclines her head.* Fellows *enters Left.*

Fellows. [*Apologetically*] Mr. Hornblower, ma'am; by appointment, he says.

Mrs. H. Quite right, Fellows.

Hornblower *comes in, and* Fellows *goes out.*

Hornblower. [*Without salutation*] I've come to ask ye point blank what ye mean by writing me these letters. [*He takes out two letters*] And we'll discuss it in the presence of nobody, if ye please.

Mrs. H. Mr. Dawker knows all that I know, and more.

Hornblower. Does he? Very well! Your second note says that my daughter-in-law has lied to me. Well, I've brought her, and what ye've got to say—if it's not just a trick to see me again—ye'll say to her face.   [*He takes a step towards the window.*

Mrs. H. Mr. Hornblower, you had better decide that after hearing what it is—we shall be quite ready to repeat it in her presence; but we want to do as little harm as possible.

Hornblower. [*Stopping*] Oh! ye do! Well, what lies have ye been hearin'? Or what have ye made up? You and Mr. Dawker? Of course ye know there's a law of libel and slander. I'm not the man to stop at that.

MRS. H. [*Calmly*] Are you familiar with the law of divorce, Mr. Hornblower?

HORNBLOWER. [*Taken aback*] No, I'm not. That is——

MRS. H. Well, you know that misconduct is required. And I suppose you've heard that cases are arranged.

HORNBLOWER. I know it's all very shocking—what about it?

MRS. H. When cases are arranged, Mr. Hornblower, the man who is to be divorced often visits an hotel with a strange woman. I am extremely sorry to say that your daughter-in-law, before her marriage, was in the habit of being employed as such a woman.

HORNBLOWER. Ye dreadful creature!

DAWKER. [*Quickly*] All proved, up to the hilt!

HORNBLOWER. I don't believe a word of it. Ye're lyin' to save your skins. How dare ye tell me such monstrosities? Dawker, I'll have ye in a criminal court.

DAWKER. Rats! You saw a gent with me yesterday? Well, *he's* employed her.

HORNBLOWER. A put-up job! Conspiracy!

MRS. H. Go and get your daughter-in-law.

HORNBLOWER. [*With the first sensation of being in a net*] It's a foul shame—a lying slander!

MRS. H. If so, it's easily disproved. Go and fetch her.

HORNBLOWER. [*Seeing them unmoved*] I will. I don't believe a word of it.

MRS. H. I hope you are right.

> HORNBLOWER *goes out by the French window,*
> DAWKER *slips to the door Right, opens it,*
> *and speaks to those within.* MRS. HILLCRIST
> *stands moistening her lips, and passing her*
> *handkerchief over them.* HORNBLOWER *re-*
> *turns, preceding* CHLOE, *strung up to hard-*
> *ness and defiance.*

HORNBLOWER. Now then, let's have this impudent story torn to rags.

CHLOE. What story?

HORNBLOWER. That you, my dear, were a woman— it's too shockin'—I don't know how to tell ye——

CHLOE. Go on!

HORNBLOWER. Were a woman that went with men, to get them their divorce.

CHLOE. Who says that?

HORNBLOWER. That lady [*Sneering*] there, and her bull-terrier here.

CHLOE. [*Facing* MRS. HILLCRIST] That's a charitable thing to say, isn't it?

MRS. H. Is it true?

CHLOE. No.

HORNBLOWER. [*Furiously*] There! I'll have ye both on your knees to her!

DAWKER. [*Opening the door, Right*] Come in.

> *The* FIRST STRANGER *comes in.* CHLOE, *with*
> *a visible effort, turns to face him.*

FIRST S. How do you do, Mrs. Vane?

CHLOE. I don't know you.

FIRST S. Your memory is bad, ma'am. You knew me yesterday well enough. One day is not a long time, nor are three years.

CHLOE. Who *are* you?

FIRST S. Come, ma'am, come! The Custer case.

CHLOE. I don't know you, I say. [*To* MRS. HILL-CRIST] How can you be so vile?

FIRST S. Let me refresh your memory, ma'am. [*Producing a notebook*] Just on three years ago: "Oct. 3. To fee and expenses Mrs. Vane with Mr. C——, Hotel Beaulieu, Twenty pounds. Oct. 10, Do., Twenty pounds." [*To* HORNBLOWER] Would you like to glance at this book, sir? You'll see they're genuine entries.

> HORNBLOWER *makes a motion to do so, but checks himself and looks at* CHLOE.

CHLOE. [*Hysterically*] It's all lies—lies!

FIRST S. Come, ma'am, we wish you no harm.

CHLOE. Take me away. I won't be treated like this.

MRS. H. [*In a low voice*] Confess.

CHLOE. Lies!

HORNBLOWER. Were ye ever called Vane?

CHLOE. No, never.

> *She makes a movement towards the window, but* DAWKER *is in the way, and she halts.*

FIRST S. [*Opening the door, Right*] Henry.

> *The* SECOND STRANGER *comes in quickly. At sight of him* CHLOE *throws up her hands, gasps, breaks down, stage Left, and stands covering her face with her hands. It is so*

complete a confession that HORNBLOWER
*stands staggered; and, taking out a coloured
handkerchief, wipes his brow.*

DAWKER. Are you convinced?

HORNBLOWER. Take those men away.

DAWKER. If you're not satisfied, we can get other
evidence; plenty.

HORNBLOWER. [*Looking at* CHLOE] That's enough.
Take them out. Leave me alone with her.

[DAWKER *takes them out Right.*
MRS. HILLCRIST *passes* HORNBLOWER *and goes
out at the window.* HORNBLOWER *moves
down a step or two towards* CHLOE.

HORNBLOWER. My God!

CHLOE. [*With an outburst*] Don't tell Charlie! Don't
tell Charlie!

HORNBLOWER. Chearlie! So that was your manner
of life. [CHLOE *utters a moaning sound.*
So that's what ye got out of by marryin' into my
family! Shame on ye, ye Godless thing!

CHLOE. Don't tell Charlie!

HORNBLOWER. And that's all ye can say for the
wreck ye've wrought. My family, my works, my
future! How dared ye!

CHLOE. If you'd been me!——

HORNBLOWER. An' these Hillcrists. The skin game
of it!

CHLOE. [*Breathless*] Father!

HORNBLOWER. Don't call me that, woman!

CHLOE. [*Desperate*] I'm going to have a child.

HORNBLOWER. God! Ye are!

CHLOE. Your grandchild. For the sake of it, do what these people want; and don't tell anyone—*Don't tell Charlie!*

HORNBLOWER. [*Again wiping his forehead*] A secret between us. I don't know that I can keep it. It's horrible. Poor Chearlie!

CHLOE. [*Suddenly fierce*] You must keep it, you shall! I won't have him told. Don't make me desperate! I can be—I didn't live that life for nothing.

HORNBLOWER. [*Staring at her revealed in a new light*] Ay; ye look a strange, wild woman, as I see ye. And we thought the world of ye!

CHLOE. I love Charlie; I'm faithful to him. I can't live without him. You'll never forgive me, I know; but Charlie——! [*Stretching out her hands.*

HORNBLOWER *makes a bewildered gesture with his large hands.*

HORNBLOWER. I'm all at sea here. Go out to the car and wait for me.

[CHLOE *passes him and goes out, Left.*

[*Muttering to himself*] So I'm down! Me enemies put their heels upon me head! Ah! but we'll see yet!

He goes up to the window and beckons towards the Right.

[MRS. HILLCRIST *comes in.*

What d'ye want for this secret?

MRS. H. Nothing.

HORNBLOWER. Indeed! Wonderful!—the trouble ye've taken for—nothing.

MRS. H. If you harm us we shall harm you. Any use whatever of the Centry——

HORNBLOWER. For which ye made me pay nine thousand five hundred pounds.

MRS. H. We will buy it from you.

HORNBLOWER. At what price?

MRS. H. The Centry at the price Miss Mullins would have taken at first, and Longmeadow at the price you gave us—four thousand five hundred altogether.

HORNBLOWER. A fine price, and me six thousand out of pocket. Na, no! I'll keep it and hold it over ye. Ye daren't tell this secret so long as I've got it.

MRS. H. No, Mr. Hornblower. On second thoughts, you *must* sell. You broke your word over the Jackmans. We can't trust you. We would rather have our place here ruined at once, than leave you the power to ruin it as and when you like. You will sell us the Centry and Longmeadow now, or you know what will happen.

HORNBLOWER. [*Writhing*] I'll not. It's blackmail.

MRS. H. Very well then! Go your own way and we'll go ours. There is no witness to this conversation.

HORNBLOWER. [*Venomously*] By heaven, ye're a clever woman. Will ye swear by Almighty God that you and your family, and that agent of yours, won't breathe a word of this shockin' thing to mortal soul.

MRS. H. Yes, if you sell.

HORNBLOWER. Where's Dawker?

MRS. H. [*Going to the door, Right*] Mr. Dawker!

[DAWKER *comes in.*

HORNBLOWER. I suppose ye've got your iniquity ready.   [DAWKER *grins and produces the document.* It's mighty near conspiracy, this. Have ye got a Testament?

MRS. H. My word will be enough, Mr. Hornblower.

HORNBLOWER. Ye'll pardon me—I can't make it solemn enough for you.

MRS. H. Very well; here is a Bible.

[*She takes a small Bible from the bookshelf.*

DAWKER. [*Spreading document on bureau*] This is a short conveyance of the Centry and Longmeadow— recites sale to you by Miss Mullins of the first, John Hillcrist of the second, and whereas you have agreed for the sale to said John Hillcrist, for the sum of four thousand five hundred pounds, in consideration of the said sum, receipt whereof, you hereby acknowledge you do convey all that, etc.   Sign here.   I'll witness.

HORNBLOWER. [*To* MRS. HILLCRIST] Take that Book in your hand, and swear first.   I swear by Almighty God never to breathe a word of what I know concerning Chloe Hornblower to any living soul.

MRS. H. No, Mr. Hornblower; you will please sign first.   *We* are not in the habit of breaking our words.

HORNBLOWER, *after a furious look at them,*
          seizes a pen, runs his eye again over the deed,
          and signs, DAWKER *witnessing.*

To that oath, Mr. Hornblower, we shall add the words, "So long as the Hornblower family do us no harm."

HORNBLOWER. [*With a snarl*] Take it in your hands, both of ye, and together swear.

MRS. H. [*Taking the Book*] I swear that I will

breathe no word of what I know concerning Chloe
Hornblower to any living soul, so long as the Hornblower family do us no harm.

DAWKER. I swear that too.

MRS. H. I engage for my husband.

HORNBLOWER. Where are those two fellows?

DAWKER. Gone. It's no business of theirs.

HORNBLOWER. It's no business of any of ye what
has happened to a woman in the past. Ye know that.
Good-day!

> *He gives them a deadly look, and goes out, Left,
> followed by* DAWKER.

MRS. H. [*With her hand on the Deed*] Safe!

> HILLCRIST *enters at the French window, fol-
> lowed by* JILL.

[*Holding up the Deed*] Look! He's just gone! I told
you it was only necessary to use the threat. He caved
in and signed this; we are sworn to say nothing. We've
beaten him.   [HILLCRIST *studies the Deed.*

JILL. [*Awed*] We saw Chloe in the car. How did
she take it, mother?

MRS. H. Denied, then broke down when she saw
our witnesses. I'm glad you were not here, Jack.

JILL. [*Suddenly*] I shall go and see her.

MRS. H. Jill, you will *not ;* you don't know what
she's done.

JILL. I shall. She must be in an awful state.

HILLCRIST. My dear, you can do her no good.

JILL. I think I can, Dodo.

MRS. H. You don't understand human nature.

We're enemies for life with those people. You're a little donkey if you think anything else.

JILL. I'm going, all the same.

MRS. H. Jack, forbid her.

HILLCRIST. [*Lifting an eyebrow*] Jill, be reasonable.

JILL. Suppose I'd taken a knock like that, Dodo, I'd be glad of friendliness from someone.

MRS. H. You never *could* take a knock like *that*.

JILL. You don't know what you can do till you try, mother.

HILLCRIST. Let her go, Amy. I'm sorry for that young woman.

MRS. H. You'd be sorry for a man who picked your pocket, I believe.

HILLCRIST. I certainly should! Deuced little he'd get out of it, when I've paid for the Centry.

MRS. H. [*Bitterly*] Much gratitude I get for saving you both our home!

JILL. [*Disarmed*] Oh! Mother, we *are* grateful. Dodo, show your gratitude.

HILLCRIST. Well, my dear, it's an intense relief. I'm not good at showing my feelings, as you know. What d'you want me to do? Stand on one leg and crow?

JILL. *Yes*, Dodo, yes! Mother, hold him while I— [*Suddenly she stops, and all the fun goes out of her*] No! I can't—I can't help thinking of *her*.

CURTAIN *falls for a Minute.*

SCENE II

EVENING

When it rises again, the room is empty and dark, save for moonlight coming in through the French window, which is open.

The figure of CHLOE, *in a black cloak, appears outside in the moonlight ; she peers in, moves past, comes back, hesitatingly enters. The cloak, fallen back, reveals a white evening dress ; and that magpie figure stands poised watchfully in the dim light, then flaps unhappily Left and Right, as if she could not keep still. Suddenly she stands listening.*

ROLF'S VOICE. [*Outside*] Chloe! Chloe!

[*He appears.*

CHLOE. [*Going to the window*] What are you doing here?

ROLF. What are *you?* I only followed you.

CHLOE. Go away!

ROLF. What's the matter? Tell me!

CHLOE. Go away, and don't say anything. Oh! The roses! [*She has put her nose into some roses in a bowl on a big stand close to the window*] Don't they smell lovely?

ROLF. What did Jill want this afternoon?

100

CHLOE. I'll tell you nothing.   Go away!

ROLF. I don't like leaving you here in this state.

CHLOE. What state?   I'm all right.   Wait for me down in the drive, if you want to.

> [ROLF *starts to go, stops, looks at her, and does go.*
> CHLOE, *with a little moaning sound, flutters again, magpie-like, up and down, then stands by the window listening.   Voices are heard, Left.   She darts out of the window and away to the Right, as* HILLCRIST *and* JILL *come in.   They have turned up the electric light, and come down in front of the fireplace, where* HILLCRIST *sits in an armchair, and* JILL *on the arm of it.   They are in undress evening attire.*

HILLCRIST. Now, tell me.

JILL. There isn't much, Dodo.   I was in an awful funk for fear I should meet any of the others, and of course I did meet Rolf, but I told him some lie, and he took me to her room—boudoir, they call it—isn't boudoir a "dug-out" word?

HILLCRIST. [*Meditatively*] The sulking room.   Well?

JILL. She was sitting like this. [*She buries her chin in her hands, with her elbows on her knees*] And she said in a sort of fierce way: "What do you want?"   And I said: "I'm awfully sorry, but I thought you might like it."

HILLCRIST. Well?

JILL. She looked at me hard, and said: "I suppose you know all about it."   And I said: "Only vaguely," because of course I don't. And she said: "Well, it was decent of you to come." Dodo, she looks like a lost soul. What has she done?

HILLCRIST. She committed her real crime when she married young Hornblower without telling him. She came out of a certain world to do it.

JILL. Oh! [*Staring in front of her*] Is it very awful in that world, Dodo?

HILLCRIST. [*Uneasy*] I don't know, Jill. Some can stand it, I suppose; some can't. I don't know which sort she is.

JILL. One thing I'm sure of: she's awfully fond of Chearlie.

HILLCRIST. That's bad; that's very bad.

JILL. And she's frightened, horribly. I think she's desperate.

HILLCRIST. Women like that are pretty tough, Jill; don't judge her too much by your own feelings.

JILL. No; only— Oh! it was beastly; and of course I dried up.

HILLCRIST. [*Feelingly*] H'm! One always does. But perhaps it was as well; you'd have been blundering in a dark passage.

JILL. I just said: "Father and I feel awfully sorry; if there's anything we can do——"

HILLCRIST. That was risky, Jill.

JILL. [*Disconsolately*] I had to say something. I'm glad I went, anyway. I feel more human.

HILLCRIST. We *had* to fight for our home. I should have felt like a traitor if I hadn't.

JILL. I'm not *enjoying* home to-night, Dodo.

HILLCRIST. I never could hate properly; it's a confounded nuisance.

JILL. Mother's fearfully bucked, and Dawker's simply oozing triumph. I *don't* trust him, Dodo; he's too —not pugilistic—the other one with a pug—naceous.

HILLCRIST. He is rather.

JILL. I'm sure he wouldn't care tuppence if Chloe committed suicide.

HILLCRIST. [*Rising uneasily*] Nonsense! Nonsense!

JILL. I wonder if mother would.

HILLCRIST. [*Turning his face towards the window*] What's that? I thought I heard—[*Louder*] Is there anybody out there?

> *No answer.* JILL *springs up and runs to the window.*

JILL. You! [*She dives through to the Right, and returns, holding* CHLOE's *hand and drawing her forward*] Come in! It's only us! [*To* HILLCRIST] Dodo!

HILLCRIST. [*Flustered, but making a show of courtesy*] Good evening! Won't you sit down?

JILL. Sit down; you're all shaky.

> *She makes* CHLOE *sit down in the armchair, out of which they have risen, then locks the door, and closing the windows, draws the curtains hastily over them.*

HILLCRIST. [*Awkward and expectant*] Can I do anything for you?

CHLOE. I couldn't bear it—he's coming to ask you——

HILLCRIST. Who?

CHLOE. My husband. [*She draws in her breath with a long shudder, then seems to seize her courage in her hands*] I've got to be quick. He keeps on asking— he knows there's something.

HILLCRIST. Make your mind easy. We shan't tell him.

CHLOE. [*Appealing*] Oh! that's not enough. Can't you tell him something to put him back to thinking it's all right? I've done him such a wrong. I didn't realise till after—I thought meeting him was just a piece of wonderful good luck, after what I'd been through. I'm not such a bad lot—not really.

> *She stops from the over-quivering of her lips.*
> JILL, *standing beside the chair, strokes her shoulder.* HILLCRIST *stands very still, painfully biting at a finger.*

You see, my father went bankrupt, and I was in a shop till——

HILLCRIST. [*Soothingly, and to prevent disclosures*] Yes, yes; yes, yes!

CHLOE. I never gave a man away or did anything I was ashamed of—at least—I mean, I had to make my living in all sorts of ways, and then I met Charlie.

> *Again she stopped from the quivering of her lips.*

JILL. It's all right.

CHLOE. He thought I was respectable, and that **was** such a relief, you can't think, so—so I let him.

JILL. Dodo! It's awful!

HILLCRIST. It is!

CHLOE. And after I married him, you see, I fell in love. If I had before, perhaps I wouldn't have dared— only, I don't know—you never know, do you? When there's a straw going, you catch at it.

JILL. Of course you do.

CHLOE. And now, you see, I'm going to have a child.

JILL. [*Ayhast*] Oh! *Are* you?

HILLCRIST. Good God!

CHLOE. [*Dully*] I've been on hot bricks all this month, ever since—that day here. I knew it was in the wind. What gets in the wind never gets out. [*She rises and throws out her arms*] Never! It just blows here and there [*Desolately*] and then blows home. [*Her voice changes to resentment*] But I've paid for being a fool—'tisn't fun, that sort of life, I can tell you. I'm not ashamed and repentant, and all that. If it wasn't for him! I'm afraid he'll never forgive me; it's such a disgrace for him—and then, to have his child! Being fond of him, I feel it much worse than anything I ever felt, and that's saying a good bit. It is.

JILL. [*Energetically*] Look here! He simply mustn't find out.

CHLOE. That's it; but it's started, and he's bound to keep on because he knows there's something. A man isn't going to be satisfied when there's something he suspects about his wife. Charlie wouldn't—never. He's clever, and he's jealous; and he's coming here.

[*She stops, and looks round wildly, listening.*

JILL. Dodo, what can we say to put him clean off the scent?

HILLCRIST. Anything in reason.

CHLOE. [*Catching at this straw*] You will! You see,
I don't know what I'll do. I've got soft, being looked
after—he does love me. And if he throws me off, I'll
go under—that's all.

HILLCRIST. Have you any suggestion?

CHLOE. [*Eagerly*] The only thing is to tell him something positive, something he'll believe, that's not *too*
bad—like my having been a lady clerk with those people who came here, and having been dismissed on sus-
picion of taking money. I could get him to believe
that wasn't true.

JILL. Yes; and it isn't—that's splendid! You'd be
able to put such conviction into it. Don't you think
so, Dodo?

HILLCRIST. Anything I can. I'm deeply sorry.

CHLOE. Thank you. And don't say I've been here,
will you? He's very suspicious. You see, he knows
that his father has re-sold that land to you; that's what
he can't make out—that, and my coming here this
morning; he knows something's being kept from him;
and he noticed that man with Dawker yesterday.
And my maid's been spying on me. It's in the air.
He puts two and two together. But I've told him
there's nothing he need worry about; nothing that's
true.

HILLCRIST. What a coil!

CHLOE. I'm very honest and careful about money.
So he won't believe that about me, and the old man
wants to keep it from Charlie, I know.

HILLCRIST. That does seem the best way out.

CHLOE. [*With a touch of defiance*] I'm a true wife to him.

JILL. Of course we know that.

HILLCRIST. It's all unspeakably sad. Deception's horribly against the grain—but——

CHLOE. [*Eagerly*] When I deceived him, I'd have deceived God Himself—I was so desperate. You've never been right down in the mud. You can't understand what I've been through.

HILLCRIST. Yes, yes. I daresay I'd have done the same. I should be the last to judge——

> [CHLOE *covers her eyes with her hands.*

There, there! Cheer up!

> [*He puts his hand on her arm.*

JILL. [*To herself*] Darling Dodo!

CHLOE. [*Starting*] There's somebody at the door. I must go; I must go.

> She runs to the window and slips through the
> curtains.

> [*The handle of the door is again turned.*

JILL. [*Dismayed*] Oh! It's locked—I forgot.

> She springs to the door, unlocks and opens it,
> while HILLCRIST goes to the bureau and sits
> down.

It's all right, Fellows; I was only saying something rather important.

FELLOWS. [*Coming in a step or two and closing the door behind him*] Certainly, Miss. Mr. Charles 'Ornblower is in the hall. Wants to see you, sir, or Mrs. Hillcrist.

JILL. What a bore! Can you see him, Dodo?

HILLCRIST. Er—yes. I suppose so. Show him in here, Fellows.

> As FELLOWS *goes out,* JILL *runs to the window, but has no time to do more than adjust the curtains and spring over to stand by her father, before* CHARLES *comes in. Though in evening clothes, he is white and dishevelled for so spruce a young man.*

CHARLES. Is my wife here?

HILLCRIST. No, sir.

CHARLES. Has she been?

HILLCRIST. This morning, I believe, Jill?

JILL. Yes, she came this morning.

CHARLES. [*Staring at her*] I know that—*now*, I mean?

JILL. No.   [HILLCRIST *shakes his head.*

CHARLES. Tell me what was said this morning.

HILLCRIST. I was not here this morning.

CHARLES. Don't try to put me off. I know too much. [*To* JILL] You.

JILL. Shall I, Dodo?

HILLCRIST. No; I will. Won't you sit down?

CHARLES. No. Go on.

HILLCRIST. [*Moistening his lips*] It appears, Mr. Hornblower, that my agent, Mr. Dawker——

> CHARLES, *who is breathing hard, utters a sound of anger.*

—that my agent happens to know a firm, who in old days employed your wife. I should greatly prefer not to say any more, especially as we don't believe the story.

JILL. No; we don't.

CHARLES. Go on!

HILLCRIST. [*Getting up*] Come! If I were you, I should refuse to listen to anything against my wife.

CHARLES. Go on, I tell you.

HILLCRIST. You insist? Well, they say there was some question about the accounts, and your wife left them under a cloud. As I told you, we don't believe it.

CHARLES. [*Passionately*] Liars!

                         [*He makes a rush for the door.*

HILLCRIST. [*Starting*] What did you say?

JILL. [*Catching his arm*] Dodo! [*Sotto voce*] We are, you know.

CHARLES. [*Turning back to them*] Why do you tell me that lie? When I've just had the truth out of that little scoundrel! My wife's been here; she put you up to it.

> *The face of* CHLOE *is seen transfixed between the curtains, parted by her hands.*

She—she put you up to it. Liar that she is—a living lie. For three years a living lie!

> HILLCRIST, *whose face alone is turned towards the curtains, sees that listening face. His hand goes up from uncontrollable emotion.*

And hasn't now the pluck to tell me. I've done with her. I won't own a child by such a woman.

> *With a little sighing sound* CHLOE *drops the curtain and vanishes.*

HILLCRIST. For God's sake, man, think of what you're saying. She's in great distress.

CHARLES. And what am I?

JILL. She loves you, you know.

CHARLES. Pretty love! That scoundrel Dawker told me—told me— Horrible! Horrible!

HILLCRIST. I deeply regret that our quarrel should have brought this about.

CHARLES. [*With intense bitterness*] Yes, you've smashed my life.

> *Unseen by them,* MRS. HILLCRIST *has entered and stands by the door, Left.*

MRS. H. Would you have wished to live on in ignorance?   [*They all turn to look at her.*

CHARLES. [*With a writhing movement*] I don't know. But—*you—you* did it.

MRS. H. You shouldn't have attacked us.

CHARLES. What did we do to you—compared with this?

MRS. H. All you could.

HILLCRIST. Enough, enough! What can we do to help you?

CHARLES. Tell me where my wife is.

> JILL *draws the curtains apart—the window is open—*JILL *looks out. They wait in silence.*

JILL. We don't know.

CHARLES. Then she *was* here?

HILLCRIST. Yes, sir; and she heard you.

CHARLES. All the better if she did. She knows how I feel.

HILLCRIST. Brace up; be gentle with her.

CHARLES. Gentle? A woman who—who——

HILLCRIST. A most unhappy creature. Come!

CHARLES. Damn your sympathy!

> *He goes out into the moonlight, passing away, Left.*

JILL. Dodo, we ought to look for her; I'm awfully afraid.

HILLCRIST. I saw her there—listening. With child! Who knows where things end when they once begin? To the gravel pit, Jill; I'll go to the pond. No, we'll go together.   [*They go out.*

> Mrs. HILLCRIST *comes down to the fireplace, rings the bell and stands there, thinking. * FELLOWS *enters.*

MRS. H. I want someone to go down to Mr. Dawker's.

FELLOWS. Mr. Dawker is here, ma'am, waitin' to see you.

MRS. H. Ask him to come in. Oh! and Fellows, you can tell the Jackmans that they can go back to their cottage.

FELLOWS. Very good, ma'am.   [*He goes out.*

> Mrs. HILLCRIST *searches at the bureau, finds and takes out the deed.* DAWKER *comes in ; he has the appearance of a man whose temper has been badly ruffled.*

MRS. H. Charles Hornblower—how did it happen?

DAWKER. He came to me. I said I knew nothing. He wouldn't take it; went for me, abused me up hill

and down dale; said he knew everything, and then he
began to threaten me. Well, I lost my temper, and
I told him.

MRS. H. That's very serious, Dawker, after our
promise. My husband is most upset.

DAWKER. [*Sullenly*] It's not my fault, ma'am; he
shouldn't have threatened and goaded me on. Besides,
it's got out that there's a scandal; common talk in the
village—not the facts, but quite enough to cook their
goose here. They'll have to go. Better have done
with it, anyway, than have enemies at your door.

MRS. H. Perhaps; but— Oh! Dawker, take
charge of this. [*She hands him the deed*] These people
are desperate—and—I'm not sure of my husband when
his feelings are worked on.

[*The sound of a car stopping.*

DAWKER. [*At the window, looking to the Left*] Hornblower's, I think. Yes, he's getting out.

MRS. H. [*Bracing herself*] You'd better wait, then.

DAWKER. He mustn't give me any of his sauce; I've
had enough.

The door is opened and HORNBLOWER *enters,
pressing so on the heels of* FELLOWS *that the
announcement of his name is lost.*

HORNBLOWER. Give me that deed! Ye got it out
of me by false pretences and treachery. Ye swore
that nothing should be heard of this. Why! me own
servants know!

MRS. H. That has nothing to do with us. Your
son came and wrenched the knowledge out of Mr.
Dawker by abuse and threats; that is all. You will

kindly behave yourself here, or I shall ask that you be shown out.

HORNBLOWER. Give me that deed, I say! [*He suddenly turns on* DAWKER] Ye little ruffian, I see it in your pocket.

> *The end indeed is projecting from* DAWKER'S *breast pocket.*

DAWKER. [*Seeing red*] Now, look 'ere, 'Ornblower, I stood a deal from your son, and I'll stand no more.

HORNBLOWER. [*To* MRS. HILLCRIST] I'll ruin your place yet! [*To* DAWKER] Ye give me that deed, or I'll throttle ye.

> *He closes on* DAWKER, *and makes a snatch at the deed.* DAWKER *springs at him, and the two stand swaying, trying for a grip at each other's throats.* MRS. HILLCRIST *tries to cross and reach the bell, but is shut off by their swaying struggle.*
>
> *Suddenly* ROLF *appears in the window, looks wildly at the struggle, and seizes* DAWKER'S *hands, which have reached* HORNBLOWER'S *throat.* JILL, *who is following, rushes up to him and clutches his arm.*

JILL. Rolf! All of you! Stop! Look!

> DAWKER'S *hand relaxes, and he is swung round.* HORNBLOWER *staggers and recovers himself, gasping for breath. All turn to the window, outside which in the moonlight* HILLCRIST *and* CHARLES HORNBLOWER *have* CHLOE'S *motionless body in their arms.*

In the gravel pit. She's just breathing; that's all.

MRS. H. Bring her in. The brandy, Jill!

HORNBLOWER. No. Take her to the car. Stand back, young woman! I want no help from any of ye. Rolf—Chearlie—take her up.

> *They lift and bear her away, Left.* JILL *follows.*

Hillcrist, ye've got me beaten and disgraced hereabouts, ye've destroyed my son's married life, and ye've killed my grandchild. I'm not staying in this cursed spot, but if ever I can do you or yours a hurt, I will.

DAWKER. [*Muttering*] That's right. Squeal and threaten. You began it.

HILLCRIST. Dawker, have the goodness! Hornblower, in the presence of what may be death, with all my heart I'm sorry.

HORNBLOWER. Ye hypocrite!

> *He passes them with a certain dignity, and goes out at the window, following to his car.*
>
> HILLCRIST, *who has stood for a moment stockstill, goes slowly forward and sits in his swivel chair.*

MRS. H. Dawker, please tell Fellows to telephone to Dr. Robinson to go round to the Hornblowers *at once.*

> DAWKER, *fingering the deed, and with a noise that sounds like "The cur!" goes out, Left.*

[*At the fireplace*] Jack! Do you blame me?

HILLCRIST. [*Motionless*] No.

MRS. H. Or Dawker? He's done his best.

HILLCRIST. No.

MRS. H. [*Approaching*] What is it?

HILLCRIST. Hypocrite!

[JILL *comes running in at the window.*

JILL. Dodo, she's moved; she's spoken. It may not be so bad.

HILLCRIST. Thank God for that!

[FELLOWS *enters, Left.*

FELLOWS. The Jackmans, ma'am.

HILLCRIST. Who? What's this?

The JACKMANS *have entered, standing close to the door.*

MRS. J. We're so glad we can go back, sir—ma'am, we just wanted to thank you.

There is a silence. They see that they are not welcome.

Thank you kindly, sir. Good-night, ma'am.

[*They shuffle out.*

HILLCRIST. I'd forgotten their existence. [*He gets up*] What is it that gets loose when you begin a fight, and makes you what you think you're not? What blinding evil! Begin as you may, it ends in this—skin game! Skin game!

JILL. [*Rushing to him*] It's not you, Dodo; it's not you, beloved Dodo.

HILLCRIST. It is me. For I am, or should be, master in this house!

MRS. H. I don't understand.

HILLCRIST. When we began this fight, we had clean hands—are they clean now? What's gentility worth if it can't stand fire?

CURTAIN

The
Great Theatres
of London

The
Great Theatres
of London

New Edition

RONALD BERGAN

and Jane Burnard
Edited by Robyn Karney

ANDRE
DEUTSCH

First published in 1990 by
Prion, an imprint of Multimedia Books Ltd.

This revised edition published in 2004 by
André Deutsch
an imprint of the
Carlton Publishing Group
20 Mortimer Street
London
W1T 3JW

A catalogue record for this book is available
from the British Library

ISBN 0-233-00066-6

Printed and bound in China

Contents

Foreword

Architecture and drama are brother arts, but like many siblings they don't always get along. The perfect performance, if there is such a thing, is the communion of actors, audience and the building itself. The acoustics, the sightlines, the comfort of the seats, the atmosphere of the auditorium, the service at the bars and the size of the dressing rooms all contribute to the success or failure of a production. Sometimes there is too great a contrast between the glamour and the luxury of the front of house and the cramped squalor of backstage. But, for an actor, there is nothing equal to playing before a laughing, weeping, snoring, coughing, shocked or enraptured audience in a space created for the purpose.

After years in the USA, I returned to find the architectural face of London changing rapidly, in some cases for the better. However, it is pleasing to see that the great London theatres, part of the glory of the city, remain virtually untouched by 'progress'. Fortunately, most of them are protected from the clutches of property developers. One doesn't have to believe in ghosts to feel a frisson when one enters these ornate and showy playhouses of yesteryear, the architectural equivalents of how we imagine the flamboyant actor-managers like Tree and Irving to have been.

I have been lucky enough to have played at the Royal Court, which has a tradition going back to the era of Pinero and Shaw, combined with the reputation for radical contemporary drama; and for some years with Sir Laurence Olivier's National Theatre Company at the Old Vic, a theatre with one

As Lambert Le Roux in *Pravda* (1985)

foreword

With Judi Dench in *Antony and Cleopatra* (1987)

of the richest of histories. And I've played at the National Theatre on the South Bank, the concrete proof that modern theatres can have an ambience, excitement and personality of their own. That wonderful Olivier stage on which one can mount a vast battle or play the most intimate of scenes!

Yet we actors 'are the abstracts and brief chronicles of the time', and although Keen and Garrick and other great names that fill the pages of this book have come to dust, most of the theatres they played in still remain. The history of the theatre is also the history of the theatres, a fact that this beautifully illustrated, entertaining and informative book celebrates.

Introduction

Amodern-day Wordsworth, standing upon Westminster bridge, would still be able to contemplate 'ships, towers, domes, theatres and temples', although there are far more theatres than the poet dreamed of in 1807. In fact, London has more mainstream theatres than any other city in the world, most of them dating from the Victorian era, and clustered mainly in the West End, the area bounded by Oxford Street to the north, the Strand to the south, Regent Street to the west and Kingsway to the east, with Shaftesbury Avenue running like an arrow through this heart of the capital's playground.

Apart from the 40 or so theatres in the West End there are the two great government-subsidised companies – the National on the South Bank and the Royal Shakespeare Company at the Barbican in the City – as well as the two famous opera houses, and important theatres at Blackfriars, Hammersmith, Sloane Square, Victoria, Hampstead and in the East End, plus the many fringe theatres that have mushroomed in and around London since the 1970s.

These many hives of theatrical activity are sustained by a standard of acting that has gained a justifiably high international reputation. In other words, theatre is alive and well and living in London, despite bitter economic realities and competition from cinema, TV and video. Continuing queues at the box-office testify to the fact that there is no substitute for live entertainment.

The first playhouse, erected in London in April 1576, was aptly named The Theatre. When it was pulled down in 1597, its timber was used to build the Globe, Shakespeare's famous wooden O. The company there was led by Richard Burbage who was the first Hamlet, Lear and Othello, and one of the first in a long line of actor-managers who ran, and often owned, the theatres in which they performed. Laurence Olivier, in his tenure at the National Theatre at the Old Vic (which he quit in 1974), was probably the last of a species.

It took over a century for the playhouse to emerge from the unroofed, circular Globe into the familiar horseshoe-shaped auditorium with its tiered boxes. It was only in the 18th century that the theatre took on the trappings of pomp hitherto reserved for palaces and churches. In the 19th century, with the rise of the civic-proud middle classes, theatres were erected with porticos and columns echoing Imperial Rome, and decor of florid baroque motifs, a mode that continued until the end of World War I. There was a reaction in the '20s and '30s, when theatres went in for simpler lines and Art Deco interiors, while others were influenced by cinema architecture. The following generation broke away from the tyranny of the proscenium arch, moving towards the open stage and theatre in the round, as well as the more democratic seating of the raked auditorium. From the Theatre Royal, Drury Lane to the Barbican, London encompasses the visible history of theatre architecture.

In the process of reseaching this book, I would often have to visit theatres in the cold light of morning. Without the lights, the curtains or eager audiences, they resembled glamorous but ageing women caught before they were able to dress and make up. Thus it was possible to view the theatres as buildings of instrinsic interest, detached from their function, as one visits a cathedral when no service is in progress. However, an audience is an essential ingredient in making these architectural glories or extravagant follies come alive 'The play's the thing', of course, but spectators are aware of the spacial relationship between the stage and the auditorium, the shape of the theatre and the decor, and the history, which makes theatregoing far more than what is happening over the footlights at a given moment.

I hope that my text, enriched immeasurably by the splendid photography taken for the book by Kirsty McLaren, will increase your pleasure in visiting the great theatres of London.

Ronald Bergan

The Adelphi

The king of musical comedy, George Edwardes, always maintained there was box-office magic in the word 'girl' and he was right – at least as far as the last 80 or so years of the Adelphi's history is concerned. Edwardes himself produced *The Quaker Girl* (1908), which ran here for 536 performances, followed by *The Girl In The Taxi* (1912) and *The Girl From Utah* (1913). The theatre's longest-running success was *Charlie Girl* starring Anna Neagle, which ran from December 1965 to early 1971, despite a lambasting from the critics. The 'Lambeth Walk Musical', *Me And My Girl* (1985), continued in the happy line of 'girl' hits, and ran for an amazing nine years.

The first theatre on the site in the Strand was built for a girl. John Scott, who made a fortune from the invention of a washing blue, built the Sans Pareil in 1806 for his stage-struck daughter. It opened with *Miss Scott's Entertainments* in which the talented Jane Scott sang songs, recited poems, spoke monologues written by herself, and danced. A series of melodramas followed, with Miss Scott usually in the leading role. In 1819, John Scott sold the theatre to two gentlemen called Jones and Rodwell, who gave it a facelift and renamed it the Adelphi. As the Lord Chamberlain's licence given to the theatre did not cover 'straight dramas', they were obliged to put on what were called burlettas, being plays containing no less than five pieces of vocal music in each act. This meant that even *Othello* had to be interrupted every few minutes by a song. This unhappy situation lasted until the monopoly of the Patent Theatres was broken in 1843. Despite this restriction, the Adelphi was one of the most popular theatres in London in the 1820s. William Moncrieff's *Tom And Jerry; Or, Life In London* (1821) ran a record 100 consecutive performances, but was surpassed a few years later by *The Pilot* (1825), adapted from

'His murder marked the passing of the kind of melodrama so long associated with the theatre where he died.'

— Lynton Hudson on William Terriss, *The English Stage*

James Fenimore Cooper's sea novel under the new management of Frederick Yates and Daniel Terry.

Adaptations from novels seemed to be the thing in the 1830s, with Charles Dickens's serials being the favourites. Moncrieff rapidly dramatised *The Pickwick Papers*, calling it *Sam Weller; Or, The Pickwickians* (1837), *Nicholas Nickleby* (1838) and *Oliver Twist* (1839). Dickens called Moncrieff 'the literary gentleman... who had dramatised 247 novels as fast as they had come out – some of them faster than they had come out'. In 1844, the famous French dancer Madame Céline Céleste and the actor-manager Benjamin Webster took over what a contemporary described as 'by far the most fashionably attended theatre in London', where they staged what came to be known as 'Adelphi Dramas', mostly written by John Buckstone. Shaw wrote that 'a really good Adelphi melodrama is of first-rate literary importance because it only needs elaboration to become a masterpiece'.

After Webster became sole manager, he decided to demolish the theatre which had fallen into 'incurable disrepair' and built a larger one in its place in 1858. The New Adelphi was among the first London theatres to evoke the epithet 'luxurious' from the press. During the building's 42 years of existence it saw the successes of Dion Boucicault's *The Colleen Bawn* (1860) and *The Octoroon* (1861), the latter being the first play to treat the Afro-American seriously. From 1879, the handsome and debonair William Terriss, father of the future actress Ellaline Terriss, appeared in a celebrated series of melodramas. On 16 December 1897, life imitated art when he was stabbed to death by a vengeful actor as he was entering the stage door to appear in *Secret Service*.

the adelphi

In 1901 the theatre was extensively altered and the name changed to the Century, but public pressure caused the old name to be restored. Under Otho Stuart, whose 'management was distinguished for its judgement, enterprise and liberality', the Adelphi became the home of Shakespeare and modern poetic dramas from 1904 to 1908. Then musical comedy established itself here, first under George Edwardes and later Alfred Butt. As described above, 'girl' titles were popular, but *The Boy*, a musical version of Pinero's *The Magistrate* (1917), ran 810 performances. Another 'boy' was Peter Pan in the shape of Gladys Cooper at Christmas 1923. After two hit revues starring the husband-and-wife team Jack Hulbert and Cicely Courtneidge, and the musical *Mr Cinders* (1929), the theatre was once again pulled down.

What arose in 1930 was a plain linear terracotta structure designed by Ernest Schaufelberg, with its handsome lettering across the top. (In 1993, when Andrew Lloyd Webber and James Nederlander became the new owners, the Adelphi was lavishly restored, and many of the Art Deco fittings and features were reinstated.)

The 1930s decor was a perfect setting for its opening productions, many of them modern musical comedies and revues produced by Charles B. Cochran, including *Evergreen* (1930) starring Jessie Matthews; Noël Coward's *Words And Music* (1932) with Ivy St Helier, Doris Hare and the 23-year-old John Mills; *Follow The Sun* (1936) with Claire Luce; and *Home And Beauty* (1937) in which Binnie Hale sang the praises of 'A Nice Cup Of Tea'.

During the 1940s there was not much at the Adelphi worthy of the theatrical history books other than Marie Tempest's London farewell in a revival of Dodie Smith's popular family comedy-drama *Dear Octopus* (1940);

A typical Adelphi extravaganza *circa* 1840

13

Robert Lindsay and Emma Thompson in the smash-hit revival of Noel Gay's musical, *Me And My Girl* (1983)

Ivor Novello's *The Dancing Years* (1942), which ran for most of the war; and Vivian Ellis's *Bless The Bride* (1947). For most of the 1950s producer Jack Hylton presented a series of variety shows featuring popular radio and television personalities such as Jimmy Edwards, Vera Lynn, Tony Hancock, Arthur Askey,

the adelphi

Shirley Bassey, and the Tiller Girls, the English equivalent of the Radio City Rockettes.

Before musicals completely dominated the fare at the Adelphi, Beatrice Lillie in *Auntie Mame* (1958) held the stage here for two years. Van Johnson in *The Music Man* (1961) gave way to three home-grown musicals – *Blitz!* (1962), of which a critic commented that 'one comes out humming the sets by Sean Kenny', and *Maggie May* (1963), both by Lionel Bart, and the aforementioned *Charlie Girl*. Broadway returned with *Show Boat* (1971), *The King And I* (1973) and Stephen Sondheim's *A Little Night Music* (1975) starring Jean Simmons, Hermione Gingold, Maria Aitken and Liz Robertson. After Miss Robertson became Alan Jay Lerner's seventh wife, she played Eliza in her husband's *My Fair Lady* (1979). In 1982, the D'Oyly Carte Company made its valedictory appearances, sadly not yet back at its spiritual home, the Savoy across the road. The following year, Stephanie Lawrence had a personal triumph in the musical *Marilyn,* but the show died prematurely, to be replaced by the long-running *Me And My Girl*. *Sunset Boulevard* followed, another great success with 1,500 performances, and now the Adelphi is entertaining audiences with the Broadway hit *Chicago* – winner of 1998's Olivier Award for Outstanding Musical Production. *Chicago's* glamorous, stylish design fits very well with the Adelphi's Art Deco auditorium, and the theatre looks set for another great run.

the adelphi theatre
strand = wc2e

15

The Albery

Virtually back to back and boasting similar decorative, late-Victorian facades are the Wyndham's Theatre, facing Charing Cross Road, and the Albery on St Martin's Lane. They have more in common than the same architect, W. G. R. Sprague. On entering the foyer of the Albery, one is faced by a bust of Sir Bronson Albery after whom the theatre was named in 1973. For its previous seventy years of existence, it was known as the New Theatre. The change of name was a fitting tribute to the dedicated theatrical dynasty that has played such a significant role in the history of the West End for more than a century.

The dramatist James Albery married sixteen-year-old Mary Moore in 1878. Seven years later, with three children and a husband whose health and income had been ruined by the demon drink, Mary joined actor-manager Charles Wyndham's company at the Criterion Theatre and soon became his leading lady and business partner. This successful collaboration enabled Wyndham to build the theatre that bears his name in 1899 and, four years later, the New on the vacant lot just behind it. After the deaths of James Albery (from cirrhosis of the liver) and Wyndham's first wife, Charles and Mary married in 1916. When his mother died, Bronson Albery (knighted in 1949) took control of the three theatres. His son Donald (knighted in 1977) followed in his footsteps and then Bronson's grandson Ian became managing director of what is called the Maybox Group, expanded to include the Piccadilly and Whitehall theatres.

Sprague, architect of eight extant London theatres, designed the New with a capacity of 877 seats, far larger than Charles Wyndham's other two theatres. It boasts a spacious entrance and a large and attractive dress-circle bar. Above the proscenium can be seen two golden angels, representing Peace and Music, with Cupids on either side. Much of the Louis XVI flavour of the

'Here was a gathering together of 400 years of tradition, and the New seemed alive with distinguished ghosts.'

— Bryan Forbes on the Old Vic tenancy

white and gold decoration has been maintained, but the building lacks the intimacy, atmosphere and prettiness of its near neighbour. What it certainly does not lack is a rich heritage.

The newly knighted Sir Charles Wyndham appeared opposite Mary Moore in the first production at the New in March 1903, a revival of a play called *Rosemary*. They were followed by such luminaries as Forbes Robertson, Mrs Patrick Campbell and Cyril Maude before Fred Terry (Ellen's younger brother) and his wife Julia Neilson took over for six months annually from 1905 to 1913. Among their successes were *The Scarlet Pimpernel*, *Dorothy O' The Hall* and *Henry of Navarre*, in the latter of which Fred's daughter, Phyllis Neilson-Terry, made her first appearance. Phyllis, a member of another legendary theatrical dynasty, was cousin to John Gielgud, who was to figure so prominently at the same theatre.

In 1915 Dion Boucicault, son of the playwright of the same name, became manager. His first presentation was a revival of *Peter Pan*, which flew high for a further four Christmas seasons, the Peter of 1917 being Fay Compton. Boucicault, known as 'Dot', also distinguished himself by producing a series of plays by leading playwrights such as Somerset Maugham (*Caroline,* 1916; *The Land Of Promise*, 1917), A. A. Milne (*Belinda*, 1918; *Mr Pim Passes By*, 1920), Sir Arthur Wing Pinero (*The Freaks*, 1918) and J. M. Barrie (*The Old Lady Shows Her Medals*, 1917). The distinguished American actress Katharine Cornell made her only London appearance as Jo in *Little Women* (1919) and, in 1920, 21-year-old Noël Coward had a play of his produced in the West End for the first time. Despite a successful first night and good

The great Sybil (later Dame Sybil) Thorndike gave well over 200 performances of her legendary *St Joan* at this theatre in 1924

notices, *I'll Leave It To You*, with Coward himself in the lead, flickered out after five weeks. The failure was blamed on the economy-conscious Lady Wyndham (Mary Moore) who removed half the stage lighting. But she was also responsible for inviting Sybil Thorndike and her husband Lewis Casson to appear in Shelley's *The Cenci* (1922) and *Cymbeline* (1923) among other plays. Then came Sybil's great triumph – her creation of the title role in Shaw's *St Joan* in March 1924, which ran for 244 performances.

Enter 21-year-old John Gielgud as Lewis Dodd (succeeding Noël Coward in the role) in Margaret Kennedy's *The Constant Nymph* (1925). His association with the theatre was resumed in the famous 'black and white' production of *Twelfth Night* (1932), followed by his first popular success in the title role in *Richard Of*

19

Bordeaux (1933) by Gordon Daviot (a pseudonym of Josephine Tay). The actor with the most mellifluous of voices then established himself as a star in *Hamlet* (1934), one of the longest runs ever of the play at 155 performances. After taking the title role in André Obey's *Noah* (1935), Gielgud invited Laurence Olivier to alternate with him as Romeo and Mercutio to Peggy Ashcroft's Juliet, with Edith Evans as the Nurse, and it was during the run that he found his real-life Juliet in Vivien Leigh.

When the Old Vic Theatre and Sadler's Wells were bombed out in 1941, the two companies sought refuge at the New Theatre, which became the site of many glittering evenings. For nine years, youthful queues gathering in the morning at the side of the theatre were a common sight. They were rewarded with such memorable performances as Ralph Richardson in *Peer Gynt* (1944), Olivier and Richardson in *Uncle Vanya* (1946) and Edith Evans in *The Cherry Orchard* (1948). After the Old Vic returned to its renovated home, the high standard at the New was maintained. Female stars such as Katharine Hepburn in Shaw's

Fagin (Ron Moody) surrounded by his young apprentice pickpockets in *Oliver!* Lionel Bart's musical ran for a record-breaking seven years

the albery

The Millionairess (1952), Dorothy Tutin in *I Am A Camera* (1954) and Leslie Caron in *Gigi* (1956) sparkled brightly, before all gave way to the boy *Oliver!*, Lionel Bart's musical version of *Oliver Twist*, which ran from 1960 to 1967, breaking all records for this theatre.

In 1971, Olivier returned as head of the as yet homeless National Theatre company for a season which included his James Tyrone in Eugene O'Neill's *Long Day's Journey Into Night*. The next year, the RSC's production of Boucicault's *London Assurance*, with Donald Sinden and Judi Dench, transferred from the Aldwych and enjoyed a successful run, as did Somerset Maugham's *The Constant Wife* (1974), starring Ingrid Bergman, and *A Month in the Country* with Helen Mirren and John Hurt. The theatre's change of name to the Albery did not alter its policy of presenting quality productions with top-ranking actors. In the 1980s, for example, were three sensitive American plays on serious issues: *Children Of A Lesser God* (1981); *Torch Song Trilogy* (1985); and *The Normal Heart* (1986).

These days, the Albery is gaining a reputation as a venue that presents West End showcases of work by leading producing theatres – such as the National Theatre's acclaimed production of *Baby Doll*; the Donmar Warehouse's *Company* (1996); the RSC's *The Cherry Orchard* with Judi Dench (1995); *An Ideal Husband* by the Peter Hall Company; an extraordinary season in 1998 by the Almeida Theatre Company – opening with Racine's *Phèdre* and *Britannicus* (with Diana Rigg), followed by Sheila Hancock in *Vassa* and Cate Blanchett in David Hare's *Plenty*.

Home to Noël Coward's very first produced play in 1920, the Albery has now brought him into the twenty-first century with the sell-out, award-winning production of *Private Lives*, starring Lindsay Duncan and Alan Rickman.

the albery theatre
st martin's lane = wc2n

The Aldwych

There are few theatres in London that have had three such distinct and diverse reputations as the Aldwych. For the pre-war generation it was the home of the 'Aldwych Farces'; from 1960 the Aldwych is remembered as having been the London base of the Royal Shakespeare Company for 22 glorious years; and since then it has been the home of quality drama with productions such as *The Cherry Orchard* with Judi Dench, Sam Mendes's production of *The Rise and Fall of Little Voice* and *Who's Afraid of Virginia Woolf?* with Diana Rigg and David Suchet.

The Aldwych is the twin of the Strand Theatre on the opposite corner of the same block, not far from Drury Lane and the Royal Opera House. They were opened within seven months of each other in 1905 and designed by W. G. R. Sprague with identical facades and almost the same seating capacity of over 1000. The interior decoration of the Aldwych is a mixture of Georgian and French baroque, the dominant colour being a greyish blue with gilt ornamentation. A dual stairway ascends past three huge mirrors and meets in the handsome plush Circle Bar under chandeliers from where one can look down into the vestibule from a circular ramp. *The Era* magazine in 1905 wrote that 'one of the innovations that will be greatly appreciated by the male members of the audience is a commodious smokers' gallery above the entrance hall'.

The Aldwych was built for actor-manager-dramatist Seymour Hicks in association with the famed American impresario Charles Frohman. Hicks and his wife, the beautiful Ellaline Terriss (born in the Falkland Islands in 1871), starred in the opening productions, often musical comedies such as *Blue Bell* (1905) and *The Gay Gordons* (1907). In 1909 Chekhov's *The Cherry Orchard* was given its first performance in England. Nigel Playfair, who

22

'It was the happiest of choices for the RSC. A real theatre, not a culture bunker.'
— Janet Suzman

was in the cast, related how the actors had little understanding of their roles, most of the audience walked out, and the critics complained that the play was gloomy and formless. It was to return to the Aldwych triumphantly in Michel Saint Denis's celebrated production for the RSC in 1961.

During the Great War the theatre put on a few popular revivals but was also used for a time as a club for Australian servicemen. In 1920, Sacha Guitry and Yvonne Printemps, the second of his four wives, came from Paris to appear in several of the Frenchman's pieces, including *Nono* (written when Guitry was 16). However, with the transfer of *Tons Of Money* from the old Shaftesbury Theatre (destroyed by bombs in 1941), the Aldwych began its renowned reign as the home of English farce, a title it held until the Whitehall achieved a similar reputation in the '50s. In the main its shows were written by Ben Travers, and relied on mistaken identities, comical coincidences and ludicrous characters played by accomplished comedians such as Tom Walls, Ralph Lynn, Robertson Hare, Mary Brough and Winifred Shotter. *A Cuckoo In The Nest* (1925), *Rookery Nook* (1926), *Thark* (1927), *Plunder* (1928), *A Cup Of Kindness* (1929) and others made the Aldwych one of the most popular places of entertainment in London until 1933.

There followed a lean period, despite the introduction of the Privilege Ticket – two seats for the price of one – until the wartime successes: Lillian Hellman's effective anti-Nazi play *Watch On The Rhine* (1942) starring Diana Wynyard and Anton Walbrook; and Lynn Fontanne and Alfred Lunt in Robert Sherwood's *There Shall Be No Night* (1943), written in response to the German invasion of Finland. This was followed by two fine actors in Shakespeare: Robert Donat in *Much Ado About Nothing*

Janet Suzman as Helen of Troy in John Barton's epic cycle of Greek dramas

(1946); and Michael Redgrave as Macbeth (1947). America was represented strongly in the next few years. Gian Carlo Menotti introduced his opera double bill, *The Medium* and *The Telephone,* in 1948, and there was the first English production of Tennessee Williams's steamy drama *A Streetcar Named Desire* (1949), in which Vivien Leigh, in one of the few great female roles in English-speaking contemporary theatre, proved her powers as never before. The year 1955 saw another American hit, *The Bad Seed* by Maxwell Anderson, but, in the same year, Christopher Fry's long-awaited *The Dark Is Light Enough*, despite Edith Evans's superb performance, was not a success.

Farce returned to the Aldwych in more ways than one in 1958 when Peter Sellers, appearing in the legitimate theatre (for the first and last time) in *Brouhaha*, stumbled onto the stage one night in a state of inebriation and announced, 'I'm sloshed. Do you want my understudy to go on?' A vociferous 'No!' allowed him to give an outrageously funny performance, sometimes from the stalls.

For some years, the Shakespeare Memorial Theatre Company at Stratford-on-Avon had been looking for a second home in London. In 1960, when Peter Hall became artistic director, they acquired the Aldwych. Before moving in on 15 December, 1960 with Peggy Ashcroft in the title role in *The Duchess Of Malfi*, an apron stage (as at Stratford) was created by bringing the forestage forward to the line of the stage boxes and eliminating the curtain. The interior was re-painted a dark olive, with the gilt left intact.

Roger Rees (foreground right) was Dickens' hero Nicholas Nickleby in the RSC's magnificent dramatisation of the novel

the aldwych

During their long tenancy, the Royal Shakespeare Company (so named in 1961) set new standards for Shakespeare production, and for other classical and modern plays, building up a brilliant ensemble company of actors in the hands of inspired directors. Among the multitude of memorable productions were three directed by Peter Brook – a hippy *Midsummer Night's Dream*, a Samuel Beckett-like *King Lear* with Paul Scofield, and the revolutionary *Marat/Sade* which brought Glenda Jackson to the public attention. There was Pinter's *The Homecoming*, Brecht's *The Caucasian Chalk Circle*, the landmark sequence of eight of Shakespeare's history plays, *The Wars Of The Roses*, and their tenure culminated in their greatest hit, *Nicholas Nickleby* in 1979. The Aldwych also played host to Peter Daubeny's World Theatre season every summer from 1964 to 1973.

Since the departure of the RSC for the Barbican in 1982, the theatre has not disappointed. The early '90s saw the magnificent revival of *The Cherry Orchard* with Judi Dench and *The Rise and Fall of Little Voice* with Jane Horrocks, Pete Postlethwaite and Alison Steadman – both productions directed by a very young Sam Mendes, before his stint at the Donmar Warehouse. In 1996 came the Almeida's production of *Who's Afraid of Virginia Woolf?*, starring Diana Rigg and David Suchet; then the acclaimed *Tom & Clem*, with Michael Gambon and Alec McCowen; Simon Gray's *Life Support*, starring Alan Bates; and the Royal National Theatre's *Amy's View* by David Hare, starring Judi Dench. The Andrew Lloyd Webber/Jim Steinman musical, *Whistle Down the Wind*, ran for two and a half years, followed by Mahler's *Conversion* by Ronald Harwood, starring Antony Sher. Next a revival of Caryl Churchill's '80s masterpiece *Top Girls* and a run of the Royal National Theatre's acclaimed adult comedy, *Mother Clap's Molly House* – in fact, it's been winners all the way.

the aldwych theatre
aldwych = wc2b

The Almeida

Islington, North London, is the home of three great theatres, all of which are exceptional in their own right, despite being twenty minutes from the West End – Sadler's Wells, the Kings Head pub/fringe theatre and the Almeida.

The Almeida's astonishing rise to become what *The Times* describes as 'one of the world's greatest theatres' has taken place in just over ten years. Like the Donmar Warehouse under Sam Mendes, the Almeida's reputation has been built on the energies and talent of two men: Jonathan Kent and Ian McDiarmid. But they needed the right space to realise their visions, and the Almeida is perfect. It is a unique arena for public performance, with its curved back wall, which enfolds performers and audiences in an embrace, resulting in an acting area as large as the auditorium is small. The fact that the Almeida is not a purpose-built theatre but a 'found' space has given a particular quality to performances there; something of the building's various pasts lingers.

The Almeida Theatre is on Almeida Street, just off Islington's Upper Street. It was first built in 1837 as reading rooms and a lecture hall for Islington's newly formed Scientific and Literary Institution. The Institution used the space for 35 years, until the society wound up and the contents were sold. In 1874 the building was bought by the Wellington Club to be used more frivolously as a music hall. In 1904 it fell into more sober hands and was taken over by the Salvation Army, but in 1956 frivolity struck once more and the building became a factory and showroom for Becks Carnival Novelties. By the 1960s it was nearly derelict, and in 1971 the building was put on the market again. Interest was shown by several theatre companies, and in 1972 Pierre Audi and his associates, realising its potential as an extraordinary performance

'My experience at the Almeida, both on stage and off, has to rank as the finest in my memory.'
— Kevin Spacey

venue, bought and renovated the building. It finally opened as the Almeida Theatre, under the directorship of Audi, in 1980, with a Grade II listing. The venue gained a high reputation almost immediately, particularly for Audi's renowned International Festival of Contemporary Music, staged every summer, which won the overall Prudential Award in 1989.

Actors Ian McDiarmid and Jonathan Kent both worked at the Almeida under Pierre Audi. One day, he simply asked them if they'd ever thought of running a theatre. The rest, as they say, is history. In 1990, Audi left the Almeida to head the Netherlands Opera, handing over to McDiarmid and Kent as joint Artistic Directors. Since then, the Almeida has become one of the world's leading independent producing theatres and a world-class institution. To date, the theatre has won 45 theatre awards, including a Laurence Olivier Award and an *Evening Standard* Award, both for Outstanding Achievement, taken 15 productions to the West End and a similar number to New York, and created the internationally acclaimed Almeida Opera. As well as the Almeida at Islington, the theatre has experimented with all kinds of different performance space, to brilliant effect: the Hackney Empire; the Gainsborough Studios in Shoreditch; a converted coach station in King's Cross (home to the theatre in 2002, while the Islington building was being refurbished); a year-long season at the Albery Theatre and a season at the Playhouse, as well as touring nationally and internationally.

Turning what had been a receiving house into a producing house was quite a challenge. McDiarmid and Kent started more or less from scratch, and with very little capital. 'We've run a National Theatre repertoire on a twentieth of their budget,' says Kent of the early days at the Almeida. 'We initially announced a season we didn't have money for. And when we opened with Howard Barker's *Scenes From an Execution*, I could never quite believe that its star, Glenda Jackson, would turn up.'

But turn up she did, and world-class performers have been turning up at the Almeida ever since, despite Equity-minimum pay-rates and working conditions described as 'little better than primitive'. Kevin Spacey, Hollywood star and award-winning as Hickey in Howard Davies's brilliant production of O'Neill's *The Iceman Cometh* (1998), said at the time, 'My experience at the Almeida, both on stage and off, has to rank as the finest in my memory. The world that the Almeida creates is a safe environment where work can be tried and where one feels that the best is being asked for and given.' In fact, the past ten years' history of the Almeida could be told solely in glowing tributes

Kevin Spacey in *The Iceman Cometh*

from actors and reviewers and the long list of prizes and Broadway/West End transfers.

In the same year that McDiarmid and Kent took over the theatre, *The Rehearsal* transferred to the West End. The next year, *All for Love* was the first production to tour internationally, Almeida Opera was launched, Anthony Burgess's new version of Griboyedov's *Chatsky* was the first production to have a UK tour, and Harold Pinter's *Moonlight* had its world premiere. In 1994 Diana Rigg's *Medea* was the theatre's first Broadway transfer, followed the next year by Ralph Fiennes's *Hamlet*. In 1997, in the theatrical equivalent of taking coals to Newcastle, the Almeida took Chekhov's *Ivanov* to Moscow, tailed by a Channel 4 documentary crew. In 1998 Jonathan Kent's production of *Naked* with Juliet Binoche, together with the world premiere of *The Judas Kiss* by David Hare, starring Liam Neeson, transferred to the Playhouse, marking the first time that the Almeida produced its own work in the West End. In the same year, the seminal and multi-award-winning production of *The Iceman Cometh*, with magnificent performances all round, notably from Kevin Spacey and Tim Piggott-Smith, transferred to the Old Vic. *Mr Puntila and His Man Matti* by Brecht, in a new version by Lee Hall, was the first Almeida production to open at the Edinburgh Festival, and *Phèdre* and *Brittanicus*, Jean Racine in new versions by Ted Hughes and Robert David MacDonald respectively, were staged to great acclaim, with Diana Rigg and Toby Stephens leading the casts. Both Racine plays and *The Iceman Cometh* were staged in New York the following year. The year 2000 saw a production, directed by the author, of Harold Pinter's *Celebration* and the world premiere of *The Room*, with Keith Allen and Lindsay Duncan, and the British premiere of Arthur Miller's *Mr Peters' Connections*, directed by Michael Blakemore. In 2002, Jonathan Kent directed Anna Friel in the title role in Nicholas Wright's new adaptation of Wedekind's *Lulu*, and David Hare's new version of Chekhov's *Platanov*. In the same year, Neil LaBute's world premiere of *The Distance From Here* and Jonathan Miller's *Camera Obscura* both toured the UK.

the almeida

It was also the year that McDiarmid and Kent left the Almeida for the Royal National Theatre. They left behind them an incredibly rich, 12-year episode of modern theatrical history. They have been a formidable team, their productions full of adventure, irony and sensitivity. They were able to say, on the announcement of their departure: 'The British theatre's oldest phrase was always, "That's impossible." No one ever dares to say that at the Almeida. People now say, "There must be a way."'

the almeida theatre
almeida street
islington = n1

The Apollo

The smallest of the six theatres that greet one on strolling up Shaftesbury Avenue from Piccadilly Circus is the intimate Apollo with its French Renaissance facade. Four angels perched on two domed towers look down on 'London's Broadway' from the Apollo, which was opened in February 1901, a month after the death of Queen Victoria, thus making it the first playhouse of the new Edwardian age.

Henry Lowenfeld, the owner and manager, originally wished to call it The Mascot because of the badge of a clan of German gypsies – featuring a flying lizard supported by lions on a silver chain and buckle – that was incorporated into the decor to bring good luck. This can still be seen on the right-hand side of the main entrance. The emblem's propitious qualities did not have much effect on the opening offering, *The Belle Of Bohemia*, a musical farce that flopped. Thereafter, the theatre has been lucky enough to have enjoyed a string of successes over the years.

Designed by Lewen Sharp, it is entirely without the pillars of its period that continue to obscure some seats in a number of older West End theatres. Another innovation was the orchestra pit, which Lowenfeld claimed to be 'a free adaptation of Wagner's construction of the orchestra at Bayreuth', to provide a clearer, unmuffled sound from the instruments. It was hoped that, despite its 796-seat capacity which made it more suitable for straight plays, musical comedies would be the theatre's main attraction. George Edwardes, the manager, did more to popularise the genre than anyone else: *Kitty Grey* ran for 220 performances and *The Girl From Kay's* (1902) almost doubled the previous run. Further musical comedies and operettas followed, including André Messager's *Veronique* (1904) and Edward German's *Tom Jones* (1907), a long way from Fielding's novel, in which Cicely Courtneidge made her London debut.

'One night during the run [of Home*] at the Apollo a man in the stalls suffered a heart attack... The dream remained unbroken. They continued with the play.'*
— Garry O'Connor in *Ralph Richardson, An Actor's Life*

From 1908 to 1912, Harry Gabriel Pélissier's *The Follies* was staged here, exceeding 500 performances a season. Pélissier, first husband of Fay Compton, who made her debut in his show, wrote most of the music, lyrics and satirical sketches as well as performing with his company, dressed mainly in Pierrot costumes against black and white curtains. It laid the foundations for intimate revue. After Pélissier died in 1913, aged 39, *The Follies* was disbanded. Mostly straight plays occupied the Apollo during the Great War, the most popular being Harold Brighouse's often-revived and twice-filmed working-class Lancashire comedy, *Hobson's Choice* (1916), with Norman McKinnel as the patriarchal shoe shop owner.

Between the wars many theatrical treasures were dug out of a mixed bag. Ian Hay's thrice-filmed comedy, *Tilly Of Bloomsbury* (1919), continued for 400 performances, Phyllis Neilson-Terry appeared in J. B. Fagan's *The Wheel* in 1922 and in a revival of *Trilby* in the same year, while Frederick Lonsdale's *The Fake* (1924) gave way to two revues in 1925. These were *By The Way,* starring Jack Hulbert and Cicely Courtneidge, and *Tricks* with 21-year-old dancer Marjorie Robertson (later Anna Neagle). The American 'borscht' circuit hit, *Abie's Irish Rose* (1927), Edgar Wallace's thriller *The Squeaker* (1928), Sean O'Casey's stylised World War I play *The Silver Tassie* (1929), Ivor Novello's *A Symphony In Two Flats* (1929) – not a musical – and John Van Druten's *There's Always Juliet* (1930) with Edna Best, Herbert Marshall and Cyril Raymond, provided the varied fare. In 1933, after Diana Wynyard, returning from Broadway, played Charlotte Brönte in Clemence Dane's *Wild Decembers*, Polish-born actress Elisabeth Bergner, forced to flee the Nazis, made her triumphant London debut in Margaret Kennedy's weepie, *Escape Me Never*.

Marion Lorne starred in a number of plays written for her by her husband Walter Hackett between 1934 and 1937, the best of which were *Hyde Park Corner* (1934), *Espionage* (1935) and *London After Dark* (1937). The last laugh at the theatre for some time came with Ian Hay's two-year run of *The Housemaster*. During the Munich crisis, Robert Sherwood's Pulitzer Prize-winner, *Idiot's Delight* (1938), with Raymond Massey, warned audiences of the coming of World War II, before they retreated into Patrick Hamilton's absorbing Victorian thriller *Gaslight* (1939).

The Apollo continued to shine dauntlessly through the dark years with *The Light Of Heart* (1940) by Emlyn Williams, *Old Acquaintance* (1941) by John Van Druten, and 670 performances of Terence Rattigan's *Flare Path* (1942). In 1944 was the first major revival of *Private Lives*, with John Clements and his wife Kay Hammond in the roles Noël Coward had written for himself and Gertrude Lawrence 14 years earlier; that year, too, the profitable theatre was taken over by Prince Littler. For the next 40 years, the theatre gained a reputation for being the home of long-running light comedies, the sort to attract 'the tired businessman'. These included the lovable, eccentric Margaret Rutherford as Miss Whitchurch in John Dighton's school farce, *The Happiest Days Of Your Life* (1948), Marie Löhr, Sybil Thorndike and Lewis Casson in *Treasure Hunt* (1949), and Hugh Hastings's service comedy *Seagulls Over Sorrento* (1950), which ran for over three years. Revue came back smartly with *For Amusement Only* (1956) featuring Ron Moody, and Peter Cook's *Pieces Of Eight* (1959) with Kenneth Williams and

(above) Two great Grand Old Men of the British theatre – Sir Ralph Richardson (left) and Sir John Geilgud – in David Storey's *Home*

(left) Paul Scofield and Howard Rollins triumphed in *I'm Not Rappaport* (1986)

the apollo

Fenella Fielding. The sequence of 'for amusement only' shows was broken briefly by Christopher Fry's two adaptations from Jean Giraudoux, *Tiger At The Gates* (1955) with Michael Redgrave as Hector, and Vivien Leigh and Claire Bloom in *Duel Of Angels* (1958). In February 1962, Marc Camoletti's sex comedy *Boeing-Boeing* took the theatre over for a record-breaking 2035 performances before flying off to the Duchess in St Martin's Lane.

The theatre was redecorated in 1965, but its repertoire was little renovated. Apart from two visits by John Gielgud as the prudish headmaster in Alan Bennett's nostalgic satire *Forty Years On* (1968) and in David Storey's Pinteresque *Home* (1969) with his old friend Ralph Richardson, Eileen Heckart repeating her Broadway triumph in *Butterflies Are Free* (1970) and Albert Finney in *Orphans* (1986), the main fare was bedroom farces with titles such as *The Mating Game* (1972) and *Shut Your Eyes And Think Of England* (1977). Since then, however, there have been some fine productions to redress the balance – the return of John Gielgud in Hugh Whitemore's *The Best of Friends*, Wendy Hiller in *Driving Miss Daisy* (1988), the National Theatre's *Mrs Klein* with Francesca Annis and Zoe Wanamaker (1989), Peter O'Toole, James Bolan and Tom Conti (successively) in *Jeffrey Bernard is Unwell* (1990) and Rattigan's *The Deep Blue Sea*, starring Penelope Wilton, from the Almeida. In 1997 came a two-year run for Ben Elton's *Popcorn*, in 2000 the Pulitzer Prize-nominated *Side Man* featuring Jason Priestley, then fine productions of Noël Coward's *Fallen Angels*, *Gondoliers* and *Star Quality* – a term which could well be used to sum up the Apollo's last fifteen years.

the apollo theatre
shaftesbury avenue = wlv

Apollo Victoria

Of all the theatres considered in these pages, the only one built specifically as a 'Picture Palace' is the Apollo Victoria, which opened as the New Victoria Cinema in 1930. By becoming an active theatre in 1981, it reversed a lengthy trend of theatres being transformed into movie houses – the Carlton, Dominion (since reclaimed), Leicester Square, London Pavilion, Prince Charles and Saville all went that way. But the Apollo eschewed its cinematic past with a vengeance when the auditorium was drastically reorganised to fit Andrew Lloyd Webber's hit musical on wheels, *Starlight Express* (1984). The multi-tiered set, ramps extending around the theatre and rock music are a far cry from the golden age of cinema when the Mighty Wurlitzer rose up, its multicoloured lights flashing, before the 'big picture'.

The great decade of British cinema design was the 1930s, that of the USA the 1920s. It was said that the New Victoria was the most architecturally important cinema building to have been erected in Britain. W. Lewis, the architect, provided a modern marble and concrete exterior and an auditorium, with a single long balcony, to seat 2,500 people. In those days full houses at weekends would usually cover costs for the whole week. The carefully wrought Art Deco designs and technically ambitious lighting effects created the impression of a sub-aquatic wonderland. It was decorated with fish, shell and sea flora motifs, and walls of marine colours. The circle, reached by a salmon pink staircase, had the design of an ocean liner with portholes on the doors. Despite some crass redecoration by the Rank Organization in the 1950s, some of the original decor can be seen today. Above the Gents lavatory is a seductively reclining bronze mermaid in a Cleopatra hairdo, and in the foyer a nude female figure is in the process of throwing reels of film about.

'People do not want this sort of thing: they want architecture with marble columns, gilt and mirrors. This won't pay.'
— Sidney Bernstein to the architect

When *Starlight Express* steamed in, special listed building consent was sought to construct the multi-tiered set which largely obscured the original look of the auditorium. The '80s were the heyday of the modern musical, epitomised by Andrew Lloyd Webber's productions, and *Starlight Express* was a shining example of the genre. It was an extravaganza of a musical, using every new theatrical device at its disposal: 1000 seats were lost in order to accommodate the roller-skating ramps that spilled into the auditorium; races took place along these ramps and over a railway bridge while large video screens allowed the audience to watch their progress; and small model trains moved along tracks around the theatre. New lighting was installed and the overhang of the circle painted black. In 1992, a new production of *Starlight Express* was launched, and the foyer and exterior (especially on the Wilton Road frontage) were handsomely improved.

It could be said that *Starlight Express* put the Apollo Victoria 'on the map'. Before that, the super-cinema, built at a cost of a quarter of a million pounds, opposite Victoria Station, had a less than glorious past. As a cinema, after the honeymoon cruise was over, it struggled for many years, interrupted occasionally by the London Festival Ballet, pop concerts and cabarets. Its location and size found it failing to compete with first television, then the smaller cinemas and the video boom. The New Victoria closed down in 1976, emerging five years later under its new name when bought by Apollo Leisure (UK) Ltd.

It opened with a Shirley Bassey recital, followed by the revival of Rodgers and Hammerstein's *The Sound Of Music* (1981) with Petula Clark as the singing novice. Another failed attempt to resurrect a hit musical was *Camelot* (1982) starring Richard

Sholom Aleichem's immortal Jewish milkman, Tevye, was given life by Topol (foreground in red cap) in the 1983 revival of *Fiddler on the Roof*

Harris. Dancer Wayne Sleep showed his range in *Dash*, and the Israeli star Topol returned to play Tevye for the second time in London in a short but successful season of *Fiddler On The Roof* (both 1983), before the Apollo was filled with – in the words of Lloyd Webber and Richard Stilgoe's song – 'A Lotta Locomotion'. *Starlight Express* ran for an amazing 18 years, finally closing in 2002, the same year that *Cats* had its last performance at the New London (after a run of 21 years). The Apollo Victoria followed *Starlight Express* with another big Andrew Lloyd Webber musical, *Bombay Dreams*, for which the theatre was again refurbished, with an enlarged auditorium to seat 2,000 (it had previously seated 1,600). *Bombay Dreams* is a romantic comedy, set in India and based on the wonderful world of Bollywood. Let's hope it follows in the successful tracks of *Starlight Express* ...

the apollo victoria
wilton road = swlv

The Arts

In the 1940s and 1950s, the Arts Theatre was described as 'a pocket National Theatre', with one daring theatrical first after another – the British premiere of Beckett's *Waiting for Godot*, the world premiere of Eugene O'Neill's *The Iceman Cometh* and of Christopher Fry's *The Lady's Not For Burning*, as well as staging Harold Pinter and Joe Orton's first plays. It's had its ups and downs since then, but now, with a bright new frontage and auditorium, this little theatre is going into the twenty-first century with a brave new programme of cutting-edge productions and an enthusiastic new management.

The Arts Theatre, with its simple, unpretentious entrance and small auditorium seating 360, is in the heart of the West End on Great Newport Street, between Leicester Square and St Martin's Lane. It opened on 20 April 1927 as the Arts Theatre Club, to provide 'the amenities of a London Club and a congenial place for those interested in the theatre on both sides of the curtain', with an intimate revue called *Picnic*. The Arts Theatre Club was an 'other' theatre, one of many that opened around this time outside the mainstream West End, to stage unlicensed and experimental plays under club conditions. In this way these brave little theatres eluded the heavy hand of the Lord Chamberlain, who at that time had the power to ban or censor anything he considered inappropriate. Along with other experimental 'try-out' theatres, such as the Gate, the Players', Q Theatre and Embassy at Swiss Cottage, the Arts Theatre Club was able to play host to producing groups like the Stage Society, the new Three Hundred Club and later the London International Theatre, as well as actor-based organisations such as the Repertory Players and the Play Actors, in order to stage theatre that would be impossible on the conventional West End stage, being too risky commercially or in content. These 'other theatres' became very

'It is good to have the Arts Theatre, where Beckett's tramps first waited for Godot, back in business.'

— The *Guardian* on the re-opening of the theatre in 2000

useful as try-out spaces, and as springboards to West End runs. The Arts and the Players' Theatre were particularly important, as their locations in the West End gave them a bit more of a toe-hold geographically.

The Arts' first important production was staged a year after it opened. *Young Woodley*, by John Van Druten, was a slight but charming study of adolescence, first produced in New York in 1925 but unaccountably banned by the censor in England. Produced privately at the Arts by the Three Hundred Club, the play later had a successful run at the Savoy after the ban was removed. Throughout the '20s and '30s a good deal of new plays shown first at the Arts – including Gordon Daviot's *Richard of Bordeaux* (1932) and Norman Ginsbury's *Viceroy Sarah* (1934) – went on to be West End successes. The Arts also played host to progressive foreign artists and companies – La Compagnie des Quinze appeared in 1931, Yvette Guilbert had a season, and Karsavina danced there.

In 1942 the actor Alec Clunes (father of actor Martin) took over as Artistic Director of the Arts Theatre, and with him came a rich new era in the theatre's history. Beginning with a revival of Odet's *Awake and Sing*, his was a tenure rich in stylish revivals and exciting new writing. Clunes was eager to use the Arts Theatre's 'small' status to stage more from the classical repertoire and give leading performers a far wider range of acting opportunities. In this very creative atmosphere, many new young directors and playwrights premiered significant and ground-breaking productions.

Clunes himself produced and directed numerous plays, many of which he also appeared in – taking the title role in *Macbeth* on its hundredth performance, for instance. Productions included revivals of English classics, such as Farquhar's *The Constant Couple*, and new plays, among them the very first performance of *The Lady's Not For Burning* (1948), the play which first brought author Fry into the limelight, and in which Clunes played the part of Thomas Mendip.

However, of the dozen or so such theatres operating in the late 1940s, by 1955 the only notable survivors of the 'try-out' theatres were the Players' and the Arts, and in the early '50s Alec Clunes left the theatre. In 1954 the new management brought in Peter Hall, then only 25, who quickly established his directorial

Billy McElhaney, Michael Moreland, Michael Nardone and John Stahl from the Traverse Theatre/RNT Production of *Gagarin Way* by Gregory Burke

reputation with a mix of European and American imports. In 1955, Hall directed the seminal English premiere of an unknown playwright's first play – *Waiting For Godot*, by Samuel Beckett – to a bemused audience (some of whom walked out). Important European plays followed: Anouilh's *The Waltz of the Toreadors* (1956); the world premiere, in 1957, of Genet's *The Balcony*; and a staging of Harold Pinter's first success, *The Caretaker* (1960). In 1956 Hall left the Arts and was invited to the Shakespeare Memorial Theatre in Stratford (soon to become the RSC). Like his predecessor Clunes, Hall had, in an incredibly short amount of time, made theatrical history at the Arts. This noble tradition continued under the artistic direction of another young man, Peter Wood, who directed an Ionesco double-bill and produced the brilliant premiere of *The Iceman Cometh* (1958) and the premiere of Pinter's second play, *The Birthday Party*, in the same year.

But by 1960 the Arts Theatre was struggling financially and lacked a resident artistic director. The theatre still managed to create waves, however – in 1961, when Miss Jeanne Moody appeared naked in a bedroom scene of *Lady Chatterley's Lover*, questions were asked in the House, and the run of the play was extended by several months as a result.

Peter Hall returned to the theatre in 1962 with the fledgling RSC for a major experimental season, introducing the company to works ranging from Thomas Middleton's *Women Beware Women*, David Rudkin's *Afore Night Came* – which transferred to the Aldwych as the RSC's first truly modern success – and Maxim Gorky's *The Lower Depths*, which was later to become one of four plays by the Russian writer to be directed for the RSC by David Jones. Two years later came another important premiere for the Arts, when Joe Orton's first play, *Entertaining Mr Sloane*, was performed here.

From 1966 Caryl Jenner's Unicorn Theatre for Children took over the building for over 30 years, showing matinees for children. There were still some significant adult plays in this time: in 1975 Robert Patrick's *Kennedy's Children* came to the Arts

Theatre from the King's Head, Islington, making it the first Fringe theatre production originating in a public house to transfer to the West End. The play was subsequently performed on Broadway and then toured the US. There was also a double bill by Tom Stoppard, *Dirty Linen* and *New Found Land* (1976), which ran for four years. John Godber's *Bouncers* (1986) and *Teechers* (1988) and the musical *A Slice of Saturday Night* (1989) all did well too. For the following ten years, no adult drama was produced at the theatre.

Then, in 2000, the Arts Theatre was taken up by a consortium of UK and New York producers, who brushed it down and polished it up with a £250,000 refurbishment (including the installation of a brand-new basement restaurant), and reopened it in the same year with a successful new production of *Another Country* by Julian Mitchell, 20 years after it first opened in the West End. This was followed by *Entertaining Mr Sloane* (with Alison Steadman), which won the *Evening Standard's* award for Best Play of the Year – back at the Arts, 36 years on. The Pet Shop Boys and Jonathan Harvey's musical collaboration, *Closer to Heaven,* was a more risky venture, but received good reviews. Then came Eve Ensler's highly acclaimed *Vagina Monologues* and in 2002 the award-winning *Gagarin Way*, a stunning first play by Gregory Burke, which arrived at the Arts in 2002 after two sell-out seasons at the National.

The future is looking bright again for the little theatre with the very important history.

the arts theatre
great newport street = wc2

The Barbican

After emerging from the Barbican underground station, follow the yellow brick line, alongside towering apartment buildings, and you will suddenly come across an artificial lake, fountains and the wonder of a modern arts complex complete with concert hall, art galleries, libraries, cinemas, restaurants, conference halls and theatres. This is Britain's first – and still this country's only – fully integrated arts centre. Until the new Barbican Centre's automatic doors slid open to the public in March 1982, the City, the commercial heart of London that throbs with capitalist activity by day, was a cultural desert by night. Adolf Hitler was indirectly responsible for the creation of this artistic oasis.

Before World War II, Cripplegate, situated north of St Paul's Cathedral and the Bank of England, was a busy area of small streets and warehouses – the home of the rag trade – in the centre of which stood St Giles's Church. In December 1940, the district was bombed unmercifully by the Luftwaffe in an attack that flattened most of the buildings but spared St Giles, which still stands demurely behind the modern centre. The surroundings lay as a neglected bomb site for 12 years before various proposals were put forward for development. Office blocks seemed the inevitable fate of the once lively area until in 1959 Duncan Sandys, the Minister for Housing and Local Development, suggested that 'a genuine residential neighbourhood, incorporating schools, shops, open spaces and other amenities' should be created 'even if this means forgoing a more remunerative return on the land'.

In April 1959, the Corporation of the City of London approved a scheme proposed by architects Chamberlin, Powell and Bon for apartment blocks and an arts centre, including a concert hall and theatre, as the new premises for the Guildhall

'The absence of aisles in the stalls will obviate the horror of actors fooling about in them – a dated practice...that should be forbidden.'
— Victor Gladstone

School of Music and Drama. Three years later it was decided that the Guildhall School 'be planned as a self-contained entity which would not share the use of the theatre or concert hall, so that these two elements would be available for full-time occupation by professional companies'. In 1964 the Royal Shakespeare Company and the London Symphony Orchestra, then sharing the Royal Festival Hall with other orchestras, became involved in the planning of the theatre and concert hall. It was a rare opportunity for the future occupants actually to play a part in the design of their new homes.

Of the two large subsidised theatres, the National company was installed at the Old Vic while waiting for its new building; the RSC was doing its best to function in its rather cramped London quarters at the Aldwych. Peter Hall, then the artistic director, and the stage designer John Bury worked in close contact with the architects. Out of their discussions came the basic fan-shape or 'modified horseshoe' and, as theatre architect Victor Gladstone wrote, 'most dramatically, the entirely novel scheme of shallow balconies, each thrusting forward one over the other; a concept quite unique, as far as I know'. However, it would take 18 years after its inception before the RSC could move in.

There were many construction difficulties to surmount along the way to completion of the vast and daring concept that eventually became the Barbican Centre. The name derives from its location, in proximity to where Roman walls once existed on which were built barbicans or watch towers. Foundations had to be sunk up to 80 feet below ground level without disturbing the foundations of the nearby buildings. Literally crowning it all is the widest unsupported flat roof in Europe.

the barbican

The auditorium of the main theatre, with a total seating capacity of 1,166, consists of raked stalls, and three narrow circles of only two rows each jutting forward one above the other towards the stage – the most distant seat being a mere 65 feet away. There is no permanent orchestra pit, but the first three rows of the stalls can be removed to provide one, and there is provision for a proscenium arch. The interior finish was arrived at after consultation with Trevor Nunn, who became artistic director of the RSC in 1968. He asked that the house lighting 'glitter not dazzle', and for the walls to be darker than the pale yew originally chosen. They were replaced by a sensuous Peruvian walnut. There are no aisles in the stalls and each row leads to its own individual door, held open before the performance and during the intervals by electromagnets. When the house lights dim, all the doors close in unison, creating a theatrical atmosphere even before the stage is lit. As in most modern theatres there is no curtain, but at intervals a huge black stainless-steel fire curtain rises from the floor to meet another descending from the ceiling.

David Troughton and William Houston as Henry IV and Prince Hal in Michael Attenborough's *Henry IV Part I*

In fact, the whole building is a show in itself. One is constantly surprised when wandering around its spacious and comfortable halls – there are often art exhibitions to be seen or musicians to be heard in odd corners. Also worth a visit is the magnificent wood-panelled 2,026-seat concert hall. On a summer's day, one can sit on the Lakeside Terrace, wander in the beautiful glass conservatory, or enjoy a meal in the Cut Above restaurant with its panoramic views of St Paul's and St Giles's Church. All of which gives the lie to those oft-heard derogatory cries of 'airport architecture', although it does have the feel of an 'Arts Hilton'.

In 2002, after a 20-year tenure at the Barbican, the RSC (under the directorship of Adrian Noble) announced that it would be leaving the centre in order to perform in a range of different venues. This new creative phase began in spring 2002 at the Roundhouse in Camden, with three of Shakespeare's late plays – *The Winter's Tale*, *The Tempest* and *Pericles*. The RSC will continue to use the Barbican theatre occasionally, but only as one amongst others. Shortly after announcing this new programme, as well as other changes to the structure of the RSC which will take the company back to being more 'production-led', Adrian Noble left the company. His last task will be to direct Ralph Fiennes in Ibsen's *Brand* in March 2003. But the play's the thing! The RSC's time at the Barbican was very rich. From the opening productions of both parts of *Henry IV* in 1982 to Edward Hall's *Julius Caesar* with Tim Piggott-Smith in 2002, the dust was never allowed to settle on Shakespeare's works. Other memorable evenings which thrust the Barbican into instant theatrical fame were an Edwardian *All's Well That Ends Well* (1982) with Peggy Ashcroft as the Countess, a circus *Comedy Of Errors* (1984), the extraordinarily dextrous crutch-wielding Antony Sher as *Richard III* (1984–1985), Jeremy Irons's poignant *Richard II* (1987), Adrian Noble's *The Plantaganets* (1988), adapted from *Henry VI* and *Richard III*, Kenneth Branagh's brilliant *Hamlet* (1992), directed by Adrian Noble, and Toby Stephens in the lead role in *Coriolanus* (1995), a fresh, contemporary, young take on the play directed by David Sacker. Apart from Shakespeare, there was Judi Dench triumphant as Brecht's Mother Courage, and Derek Jacobi shining as Cyrano de Bergerac, both marathon performances in 1984, and Ibsen's *The Master Builder* in 1989. There was also Trevor Nunn and John Caird's English version of the French musical *Les Misérables* by Alain Boublil and Claude-Michel Schonberg, which turned out to be one of the company's greatest successes, transferring for a long run at London's Palace Theatre and on Broadway. Another hit that started small and moved to the West End and Broadway was Christopher Hampton's skilful adaptation of Laclos's *Les Liaisons Dangereuses* (1986). The latter was originally given at The Pit, the RSC's intimate (200 seats) and flexible studio theatre situated under the main auditorium.

The RSC will be sorely missed, but the Barbican has already established an exciting theatrical reputation of its own. Since 1998, for six months each year, the theatre is home to the Bite season (Barbican International Theatre Event) – which offers a unique and very important space on the London stage for international performance, dance and drama. Bite has hosted companies such as the world-famous Comédie Française, the Steppenwolf Theater Company from Chicago and the Maly Drama Theatre of St Petersburg, as well as the Barbican's first performance by the Royal Ballet and the Beckett Festival from Dublin's Gate Theatre. Productions from as far away as Japan, South Africa, India and Israel have been staged, and there have been some important premieres – amongst them Peter Hall's *Tantalus*.

the barbican theatre
barbican = ec2

The Cambridge

On a corner where seven streets meet to form what is known as Seven Dials stands the Cambridge Theatre, which has been at the crossroads many times in its 72-year existence. It was the second of six theatres built in London in 1930, each claiming to be more modern than the last. The others were the Prince Edward, the Phoenix, the Whitehall, the Adelphi and the Leicester Square (now a cinema). The claim to modernity of the Cambridge (designed by the firm of Wimperis, Simpson and Guthrie) was its use of concrete and steel, its clean lines, lively gold and silver decor by Serge Chermayeff (much of which was painted over in red in 1950) and its concealed lighting (replaced by gilt candelabras and chandeliers in 1950). The complete overhaul of the theatre by the Stoll Moss group and designer Carl Toms in 1987 resulted in a larger stage, a reconstitution of much of the earlier ambience and a thorough cleaning, leaving the stone facade and interior gleaming. At the entrance, the 1930 mural of nude chorus girls has been retained.

Anton Dolin and Dora Vadimova were among the clothed dancers in Charlot's *Masquerade*, the opening production, which also featured Beatrice Lillie, Florence Desmond and Henry Kendall. France was well represented in the first years by seasons of Sacha Guitry (1932) and the Comédie Française (1934), but the English contingent failed to make a go of the theatre, and it became a venue for trade film shows in the late 1930s. The war years brought it back into circulation with Edith Evans, Robert Donat and Isabel Jeans in Shaw's *Heartbreak House* (1943) and Johann Strauss's operetta *A Night In Venice* (1944). In 1946, Jan Pomeroy founded the New London Opera Company, which made the Cambridge its home for two years before moving to Sadler's Wells. Opera and ballet seemed particularly suitable for the large house of 1,275 seats. Menotti's opera *The Consul* had its

'The Cambridge Theatre...originally decorated with amusing Jazz Age Motifs by Serge Chermayeff, is now covered in dull ox-blood paint.'
— Simon Tidworth, *Theatres*, 1973

British premiere here with a mainly American cast, and Peter Daubeny presented seasons of foreign dance companies between 1951 and 1952. Previously, there were two popular revues, *Sauce Tartare* (1949) and *Sauce Piquante* (1950), the latter having a 21-year-old unknown named Audrey Hepburn in the chorus.

Straight plays returned to the Cambridge in 1952 with *Affairs Of State,* starring Joyce Redman, Coral Browne, Hugh Williams, Basil Radford and Wilfrid Hyde-White, running for 18 months. An even longer run was clocked up by William Douglas Home's *The Reluctant Debutante* (1955), a typically pre-'kitchen sink' drawing room comedy. In 1960, ripples of the New Wave were felt at the Cambridge with John Mortimer's first full-length play, *The Wrong Side Of The Park*, with Margaret Leighton and Robert Stephens; and in the same year 24-year-old Albert Finney starred in Keith Waterhouse and Willis Hall's *Billy Liar*. Other successes of the period were Margaret Lockwood in *Signpost To Murder* (1962); Tommy Steele as Kipps in the British musical *Half A Sixpence* (1963), which earned considerably more than the title;

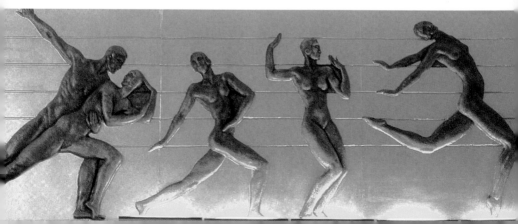

Ingrid Bergman and Michael Redgrave in *A Month In The Country* (1965)

and Bruce Forsyth playing seven roles in the American musical *Little Me* (1964).

In September 1965, Ingrid Bergman, Michael Redgrave and Emlyn Williams triumphed in Turgenev's *A Month In The Country*, the Redgrave production that had opened the new

Maggie Smith starred in *Hedda Gabler* (1970) in a revelatory production by Ingmar Bergman

Yvonne Arnaud Theatre in Guildford a few months earlier. But the prestige this generated did not sustain the theatre for too long, and a number of flops forced it to become a cinema for six months from September 1967. Then, in 1968, tenor John Hanson rode to the rescue as the Red Shadow in *The Desert Song*, and as the romantic young royal in *The Student Prince*, old-fashioned productions of old-time Sigmund Romberg operettas, which found an audience.

A very different audience converged on the Cambridge in 1970 for the National Theatre Company season, the highlights of which were Maggie Smith in Ingmar Bergman's production of *Hedda Gabler* and Laurence Olivier's Shylock in Jonathan Miller's nineteenth-century updating of *The Merchant Of Venice*. Quality was maintained in 1971, which saw contrasting Hamlets from Alan Bates and Ian McKellen, the return of Ingrid Bergman in Shaw's *Captain Brassbound's Conversion* and Ralph

Richardson and Jill Bennett in John Osborne's *West Of Suez*. But a number of duds and transfers had the Cambridge floundering again until two archetypal British farces – *Two And Two Make Sex* (1973) and *A Bit Between The Teeth* (1974) – brought business back. The '80s offered a variety of entertainment, from Joan Collins in *The Last of Mrs Cheyney* to a brilliant Peter O'Toole in Shaw's *Man and Superman* (1983). Since reopening after refurbishment in 1987 with Lulu and George Cole in *Peter Pan – The Musical*, the theatre has chosen musical entertainment as its mainstay. In 1988 the New D'Oyly Carte Company was launched at the Cambridge, with glorious productions of *Iolanthe* and *The Yeoman of the Guard*. Then came Bob Carlton's Olivier Award-winning *Return to the Forbidden Planet*, with its three-year run. This was followed by the first stage production of *Fame – The Musical* (1995); *Grease*, for three years; the world premiere of Ben Elton and Lloyd Webber's *The Beautiful Game* (2000); and in 2001 *Fame – The Musical* once again, returning to the West End theatre where it first opened.

the cambridge theatre
earlham street = wc2h

The Coliseum

One of the most eye-catching landmarks of the West End is the spinning globe of the Coliseum, dominating St Martin's Lane. The colourful sphere tops off an enormous square tower with solid columns, bold carved figures at each end representing Art, Music, Science and Literature, and a pride of sculptured lions. Today the globe, lit from within to give the impression of movement, is the beckoning sign for opera lovers – London's largest theatre (with a current seating capacity of 2,358) has been the home of the prestigious and enterprising English National Opera Company since 1974.

This grandiose Edwardian edifice was the dreamchild of the great theatre manager Oswald Stoll. An Australian of Irish parentage, he found himself, on the death of his stepfather, running the family's music hall in Liverpool at the tender age of 14. Stoll was soon controlling an extensive chain of halls throughout the country. In Victorian times the music hall, whose origin lay in the entertainments at taverns in the eighteenth century, had a bawdy and boisterous reputation. Stoll planned to build a theatre where a man could bring his family without fear of shocking them.

The imposing playhouse with its Italian Renaissance-style facade, designed by the renowned Frank Matcham, leading theatre architect of the day, opened its doors on 24 December, 1904. Crowds flocked out of curiosity to see the palace of pleasures as much as from any desire to attend the four-shows-a-day variety programme. The latter contained such delights as The American Sisters Meredith singing 'Oowana', an Indian love song, Madge Lessing accompanied by a troop of Highland soldiers with pipe band, and a Derby finale in which real horses were ridden on the huge revolving stage, the first such in Great Britain.

*'In between the matinee and evening performance,
the Coliseum stage appeared vaster and more
mysterious, like an empty, echoing
cathedral smelling faintly of dust.'*
— Noël Coward

In the first week, 67,000 people came to marvel at the mosaic and marble walls and ceilings, elaborate Grand Salon and Grand Staircase, and 'the only theatre in Europe which provides lifts to take the audience to the upper parts of the building. . . primarily for elevation to the handsome Terrace Tea Room', as an early programme sheet proclaimed. (The roof garden was pulled down in 1951.) But the novelty of the structure soon wore off, and the shows were not sufficiently good to continue drawing the crowds. By expunging the more ribald elements and substituting decorous spectacles, Stoll lost the working and lower middle-class

Opera-goers fill the beautiful Matcham-designed auditorium

audiences that were the mainstay of music hall. 'Coarseness and vulgarity are not allowed at the Coliseum,' read an unenticing advertisement.

In an attempt to revitalise the box-office, Stoll presented *The Revue* in 1906, 'invented and produced' by Victor de Cottens of the Folies Bergères in Paris. The commère (female compère) was 20-year-old Billie Burke, who was to marry Florenz Ziegfeld, the master of the American revue, seven years later. Despite its success, the 300-cast show cost Stoll a fortune to mount, and he was forced to close the theatre in June of the same year. It remained dark until December 1907, when the globe lit up the London skyline again. Stoll returned, having formed a new syndicate, cut the four shows a day by half and tempted in the great names of the music hall who had previously been put off by the theatre's earlier slogan of *Pro Bono Publico* (For the Public Good). From 1909 to 1931 the 2,358-seat auditorium was packed to the rafters by crowds enjoying such legendary entertainers as Harry Lauder, Little Tich, Harry Tate, Albert Chevalier, Nellie Wallace and male impersonator Vesta Tilley. These acts were interspersed with performing animals, jugglers, acrobats and curiosities like Fräulein Brunnhilde, 'the tallest pianist in the world' at seven feet eleven. Who would have predicted that Wagner's Brunnhilde would appear on the same stage one day?

When Stoll invited Sergei Diaghilev to bring his Russian Ballet to the Coliseum after their sensational visit to Paris in 1909, the famed impresario said, 'The Russian Ballet sandwiched between performing dogs and a fat lady playing a silver-plated trombone! Never! Never!' However, his troupe did leap the boards of the Coliseum in 1917 after their brilliant pre-war period. In fact, it was not unusual for stars of the 'legitimate' theatre to appear between 'performing dogs and a fat lady'. Ellen Terry played Portia in the trial scene from *The Merchant Of Venice* in 1918, Lillie Langtry paid two glowing visits in 1917 and 1918, and Sarah Bernhardt appeared each year between 1910 and 1913. Her last visit in 1916 was after the amputation of her leg forced her to perform sitting down. Opera was first staged here in 1912 when the Beecham Opera Company presented *Hansel And Gretel*, but was not to return for some years.

Despite a range of dazzling artists, including Jack Buchanan, Gertrude Lawrence, Beatrice Lillie, Jack Hulbert, Cicely Courtneidge and Ronald Colman from England and Marie Dressier, Helen Morgan, W. C. Fields and the Marx Brothers from the USA, by 1931 variety was no longer the spice of live theatre. It was time for the Coliseum to change direction. In April, a new policy was instituted with the opening of *White Horse Inn*. The size of the auditorium, never kind to straight theatre, proved ideal for musical comedy, which held centre stage in the theatre's history for the next three decades. *White Horse Inn*, which ran for 651 performances, was followed by *Casanova* in the same lavish vein. Other large-scale productions included a 'real ice' spectacle called *St Moritz* in 1937.

During World War II the theatre remained open, bringing cheer to besieged Londoners. It was twice hit by incendiary bombs, but only minor damage was done. In January 1942, Sir Oswald Stoll (he had been knighted in 1919) died aged 76. The theatre was bought by Prince Littler who revived *White Horse Inn*, *Me And My Girl*, *Maid Of The Mountains*, *The Belle Of New York* and *The Merry Widow*. But on 7 June, 1947 *Annie Get Your Gun* proved that anything the West End could do in musical comedy, Broadway could do better. The energetic, witty and tuneful Irving Berlin show burst onto the London stage, running for three years, the longest in this theatre's history. *Kiss Me Kate* (1951), *Call Me Madam* (1952), *Guys And Dolls* (1953), *Can Can* (1954), *The Pyjama Game* (1955), *Damn Yankees*, *Bells Are Ringing* (both 1957) and *The Most Happy Fella* (1960) proved that the Broadway musical was here to stay. Sadly, because two of the greatest Broadway musicals, *My Fair Lady* and *West Side Story*, with better casts, were occupying Drury Lane and Her Majesty's respectively, the Coliseum found it increasingly difficult to compete. In 1961, MGM, sniffing around for a large theatre in which to instal Cinerama equipment, took a long lease on the

the coliseum

building, turning it into a cinema. As the widest of wide screen processes needed three massive projectors to be placed at the back of the stalls, extensive alterations were made to the auditorium. It remained a none-too-successful enterprise until MGM decided not to renew the lease in 1967.

Meanwhile, Sadler's Wells Opera was beginning to find its theatre in Islington too small and too far from the West End. Stephen Arlen, managing director of the company, entered into negotiations with Prince Littler and took a ten-year lease. A great deal had to be done to repair the damage caused by the Cinerama misadventure in order to achieve the warm, welcoming, comfortable opera house, with superb acoustics, that we know today. In 1992 the building was purchased by the Department of Heritage for the company, renamed the English National Opera in 1974. This vastly successful venture has introduced a whole new generation to opera in less elitist and stuffy confines than the Royal Opera House – and at cheaper prices. In each ten-month season, more than 20 works are given, and often four different operas can be seen in a week. An

ambitious and confident programme of restoration is now being undertaken, over a four-year period, to bring the Coliseum back to its former glory in time for its centenary in 2004. The Arts Team at RHWL (architects of the new Sadler's Wells building, 1998) plan to recreate many of the original features, including the splendid facade and the glass roof which covered the Terrace Bar.

ENO's policy has been, from the opening production of *Don Giovanni* on 21 August, 1968, to perform a wide range of operas,

including new works, all in English. Each year, the Company aims to stage a world premiere or a British stage premiere, and it also nurtures young British talent through the Eno Jerwood Young Singers programme. Apart from their achievements in the classics of the operatic repertoire, such as a complete and impressive Ring cycle, they have tackled many less familiar operas of merit. Prokofiev's *The Gambler* and his spectacular *War And Peace*, Tchaikovsky's *Mazeppa*, Martinu's *Julietta*, Wagner's *Rienzi* and Spontini's *La Vestale* are examples of the latter. Proving that opera is a living art form, contemporary works have included Ligeti's *Le Grand Macabre*, Philip Glass's *Akhnaten* and Mark-Anthony Turnage's award-winning *The Tassie*, one of the most successful new operas of recent times, while a new slant is given to more traditional operas as in Jonathan Miller's brilliant New York Mafia *Rigoletto*, his production of *The Mikado* with an English 1920s setting – first performed in 1986 and revived to brilliant effect in 2001 and his award-winning *Carmen* (1996). All performed in the inspirational setting of the Coliseum, of which Lord Harwood, the ENO's first managing director, said '[it] combines the sometimes opposing attributes of style and unpretentiousness, beauty and the sort of familiarity which quickly makes one feel at home.'

the coliseum
st martin's lane = wc2n

(facing page) The famous opera singer Willard White performing at the Coliseum

The Comedy

'Panton Street in the Haymarket has for very many years past enjoyed a dubious reputation owing to the numerous "night-houses" once existing in this vicinity. Recent improvements in this and the adjacent thoroughfares have now removed altogether the doubtful resorts of the roisterers of other days, and the demolition of a large pile of buildings on the south side has enabled a spacious theatre to be constructed which seems likely to take a prominent place among the West End establishments devoted to public amusement.' So wrote the *Daily Telegraph* on 14 October, 1881 on the opening of the Comedy Theatre.

Today, there are still plenty of 'roisterers' and 'doubtful resorts' in nearby Soho, but the Comedy is coyly tucked away from the hurly-burly in a quiet side street. On visiting it, one enters the past. The pedimented classical facade, with its Greek 'Lady with the Lamp' sculpture above the entrance, is virtually the same as when it was conceived by Thomas Verity over a century ago, but for the addition of a modern wrought-iron canopy. Built in a record time of six months, the building also has one of the few extant pre 1890 auditoria in London, despite some alterations along the way. This has its disadvantages: pillars hold up the Dress Circle, obscuring the view from certain seats, and the stage is the smallest of any theatre of comparable size in London. The dominant colour of the French Renaissance decor – from the exquisite ceiling to the wallpaper – is gold. Many of its productions, too, have been pure gold, with a fair portion of dross in between.

The Comedy's first manager, Alexander Henderson, intended the venue to be a house of comic opera to rival Gilbert and Sullivan's Savoy Theatre, which had opened only five days earlier. The premiere production was an English version of Edmond

'The architect Sir John Summerson wrote that the Comedy Theatre was the best and most originally preserved of London theatres, and I must say that I agree with him.'
— Sir Ralph Richardson

Audran's French operetta, *The Mascotte*. Similar works followed, some of them featuring Violet Melnotte (born Rosenberg in Birmingham), who took over the Comedy for a while before moving into the Trafalgar Square Theatre (later the Duke Of York's) in 1892. In 1887, Herbert Beerbohm Tree had his first big success as actor-manager with *The Red Lamp*, which he later transferred to the Haymarket when he took over the management there. Another legend of the age, Sarah Bernhardt, appeared in Sardou's *Tosca* and *Fédora*, roles written with her in mind.

In the last decade of the century, managers and plays came and went until Lewis Wailer, one of the outstanding romantic actors of the day, rescued the theatre from the doldrums by presenting Booth Tarkington's *Monsieur Beaucaire* (1902), with himself in the title role, for 430 performances. The equally romantic 23-year-old John Barrymore made his first London appearance in *The Dictator* (1905), while the following year E. W. Hornung's *Raffles*, coincidentally played by Barrymore in a 1917 silent film, started the Edwardian craze for 'crook' plays. The glamorous Gerald du Maurier (father of novelist Daphne) portrayed the dapper gentleman burglar, altering tradition by turning the villain into the hero. Somerset Maugham, the darling of the West End, had three plays performed at the Comedy between 1908 and 1911. They starred Marie Tempest (who made her debut here in *Boccaccio* [1895]) in *Mrs Dot* and *Penelope*, and Marie Löhr in *Smith*.

During World War I, Laurette Taylor recreated her New York triumph here in her husband John Hartley Manners's play *Peg O'*

The finely detailed auditorium ceiling

My Heart (1914) for 710 performances. Six revues then occupied the stage until the end of the war, produced by the kings of revue, Albert de Courville, Charles B. Cochran and André Charlot. It was in Charlot's *Tails Up* (1918), starring Jack Buchanan, that Noël Coward's name first appeared in the West End as a lyric writer. Revues continued to be a significant part of the Comedy's programmes for the next few decades. Douglas Byng was in *How D'You Do?* (1933) and *Hi Diddle-Diddle* (1934), the two Hermiones (Gingold and Baddeley) in *Rise Above It* (1941) and Gingold in *Slings And Arrows* (1948); there was the Flanders and Swann *Fresh Airs* (1956), 23-year-old Maggie Smith's West End debut in *Share My Lettuce* (1957) and *The Premise* (1962), an American revue which relied on improvisation.

The Comedy certainly lived up to its name, and dramas were not the theatre's strong point. Then, in 1956, the theatre played a vital part in helping to undermine the archaic censorship laws of Britain. Until 1968, the unlamented Lord Chamberlain had the right to ban plays if the subject or language was deemed unsuitable. Since it was forbidden to portray homosexuality (or even the suggestion of it), a group of West End managers got together to form the New Watergate Club at the Comedy where they could present banned plays under club conditions. By paying a five-shilling subscription, audiences were able to see three American plays refused a licence: Arthur Miller's *A View From The Bridge* (1956); Robert Anderson's *Tea And Sympathy* (1957); and Tennessee Williams's *Cat On A Hot Tin Roof* (1958). Some time later the Lord Chamberlain's office admitted that homosexuality 'is now so widely debated, written about and talked over that its complete exclusion from the stage can no longer be regarded as justifiable'. The club, therefore, became unnecessary.

The newly gained concession allowed Peter Shaffer's first play, *Five Finger Exercise*, with its subtle homosexual thread, to enjoy a two-year commercial run from 1958. The passing of both time and the Lord Chamberlain brought male and female nudity to the same theatre in the prison drama *Fortune And Men's Eyes* and in Nell Dunn's long-running *Steaming* (1980), set in a women's Turkish bath. Other controversial productions included Peter Nichols's *A Day In The Death Of Joe Egg* (1967) – which enjoyed a hugely successful revival in 2002, with Eddie Izzard and Prunella Scales – Christopher Hampton's *Savages* (1973), starring Paul Scofield, and David Hare's *Knuckle* (1974) with Edward Fox.

The Comedy has been an important venue for Harold Pinter's works – *The Caretaker, No Man's Land, Moonlight, The Hothouse* and *The Homecoming* have all been presented in recent years. In the 1990s Alan Bennett appeared with Patricia Routledge in his

the comedy

Anthony Andrews and Francesca Annis in Ibsen's *Ghosts* (2001)

Talking Heads, and later so did Maggie Smith. There followed a series of star performances: the Donmar Warehouse's *The Glass Menagerie* with Zoe Wanamaker; Edward Fox and Claire Higgins in *A Letter of Resignation*; Ewan McGregor in *Little Malcolm and His Struggle Against the Eunuchs*; Peter Nichol's *Passion Play*; Simon Callow in *The Mystery of Charles Dickens*; Francesca Annis in Ibsen's *Ghosts*; and the brilliant production of Pinter's *The Caretaker* (2000) directed by Patrick Marber and starring Michael Gambon. The Comedy's brave and continuing tradition of staging daring, quality drama has ensured that this theatre enters its third century in great style.

the comedy theatre
panton street = wly

The Criterion

Opposite the statue of Eros at Piccadilly Circus stands a Second Empire-style facade, in which a tiny entrance leads into one of London's most entrancing and historically important theatres. Apart from the vestibule (where hangs a full-length portrait of actress-manager Mary Moore), the entire theatre, as conceived by Thomas Verity, is underground. To reach the almost perfectly preserved mid-Victorian auditorium, one descends a flight of stairs between striking tiled walls painted with classical figures, muses and the names of famous composers. The mini-maze of corridors, large mirrors and ceilings adorned with cherubs on clouds gives audiences a feeling of space to counteract any claustrophobia. Indeed, for ten years after the opening in 1874 – until the building was enlarged and properly ventilated – it was necessary to pump air into the theatre to prevent the public from suffocating.

It is easy to imagine, when seated and waiting for the curtain to rise, lovely bejewelled ladies and their Victorian toff escorts surrounded by the pink and aubergine decor of the stalls or leaning forward on the curved-front boxes. In the Royal Box, still used for royalty and VIPs, one might have spotted the Prince of Wales applauding his mistress, Lillie Langtry, appearing opposite Charles Wyndham in *The Fringe Of Society* (1892). If they could be brought back to life, they would still recognise the house, but might be a trifle disturbed by the plays. After all, there were gasps of horror when Kate Rorke, playing a rebellious girl in *Fourteen Days*, lit up a cigarette.

What audiences would have seen and enjoyed in 1877 was a French farce, adapted by James Albery, called *Pink Dominoes*. In the cast was Charles Wyndham, who took over the theatre in 1879 and whose initials are seen in decorative monograms on the walls. Enter Albery's wife, Mary Moore (billed as Miss M.

'The Criterion Theatre, transformed from a stuffy band-box to a convenient, handsome and well-ventilated house...'

- Dramatic Notes, 1884

Mortimer), making her first appearance here in *The Candidate* (1884). A woman of great beauty and intelligence, she soon became Wyndham's leading lady (they married in 1916) with such roles as Lady Amaranthe in John O'Keefe's *Wild Oats* and Ada Ingot in Tom Robertson's *David Garrick* (both 1886). A year later the future King Edward VII invited them to give a command performance of the latter play at Sandringham.

Although the theatre gained a reputation for light comedy, it was Arthur Henry Jones's dramas of social criticism that attracted attention in the last years of the century, notably *The Bauble Shop* (1893), *The Case Of Rebellious Susan* (1894) and *The Liars* (1897). In 1899, Wyndham left to go to the theatre that bears his name. He returned eight years later with a production of Hubert Henry Davies's *The Mollusc*, in which Mary Moore's performance was a tour de force, although she barely stirred from a settee throughout. From 1915 to 1919 ran a farce entitled *A Little Bit Of Fluff*, of which Lynton Hudson in *The English Stage, 1850–1950* commented that although 'its illusory suggestion of naughtiness – and one solitary and by modern standards entirely decorous glimpse of a silk-clad shapely leg – dominated the wartime theatre, it would be unfair to blame the innocents who enjoyed this light-hearted fare for a deterioration in public taste'. It ran for an amazing 1,241 performances – a figure which, though impressive, pales into insignificance when compared to the theatre's six-year run of *Run for Your Wife* (1983–89) and the over 2,500 performances of the Reduced Shakespeare Company's *The Complete Works of Shakespeare (abridged)*.

Cyril Maude in *Lord Richard In The Pantry* (1919), Charles Hawtrey in *Ambrose Applejohn's Adventure* (1921), Sybil

Thorndike in *Advertising April* (1923) and Marie Tempest in five plays between 1926 to 1929 enlivened the rather scanty comedies, and brought in the public. At the death of Mary Moore in 1931, her son Bronson Albery took over the running of the theatre. He presented John Gielgud in *Musical Chairs* (1932), by the young and talented Ronald MacKenzie who was killed in a car crash after the play had been running a year. In 1936, 24-year-old Terence Rattigan's *French Without Tears* started its three-year run, making its author rich and famous. Lesley Storm's comedy *Tony Draws A Horse* was the last pre-war success.

During World War II, the Criterion proved to be a perfect underground shelter for a BBC studio to beam light entertainment to the nation. It was from here that the wartime radio hit *ITMA* (*It's That Man Again*) was broadcast. As soon as peace was declared, the theatre opened its doors for business again with Edith Evans a delightful Mrs Malaprop in *The Rivals* (1945). For the next ten years the Criterion offered a number of profitable comedies including *The Guinea* Pig (1946), in which the expression 'kick up the arse' caused audiences to fall about; Gladys Cooper varying her lines from night to night in Peter Ustinov's *The Indifferent Shepherd* (1948) and Rattigan's *Who Is Sylvia?* (1950). A very different kind of play, Samuel Beckett's modern classic, *Waiting For Godot* (1955), surprised everybody by running a year. At one particular performance, when an old bearded gentleman made his way belatedly to his seat, a cry from the gallery went up that Godot had arrived at last. Jean Anouilh's *The Waltz Of The Toreadors* (1956) followed for a long run. Both these plays were directed by 25-year-old Peter Hall, who had transferred them from the Arts Theatre Club. Other 'avant garde' productions included *Three* (1961), a triple bill of plays by Harold Pinter, John Mortimer and N. F. Simpson, and James Saunders's *Next Time I'll Sing To You* (1962) with an unknown Michael Caine in the cast. More conventional hits were the marital comedies, *The Irregular Verb To Love* (1961) with Joan Greenwood, *A Severed Head* (1963), adapted by J. B. Priestley and Iris Murdoch from the latter's novel, and Alan Ayckbourn's *Absurd Person Singular* (1973). In between, Simon Gray's acerbic *Butley* (1971), starring Alan Bates, kept the theatre full. Among the few flops was a revue called *Hulla Baloo* (1972), set in a 'loo', with contributions from two young men named Andrew Lloyd Webber and Tim Rice – perhaps not something they would now wish to remember!

In the few years before the farce *Run For Your Wife!* began its incredible run, quality productions included Ibsen's *A Doll's House* (1973), with Claire Bloom repeating her Broadway triumph, *Bent* (1978) and Dario Fo's *Can't Pay, Won't Pay* (1981). Through the early 1990s productions ranged from *The Flying Karamazov Brothers* to *Misery*, and since 1996 the wacky and improvisational Reduced Shakespeare Company have made the Criterion their London home, providing delighted audiences with all of Shakespeare's 37 plays in 97 minutes.

the criterion

The Reduced Shakespeare Company's comic abridged version of the complete works of Shakespeare has been nominated for the Laurence Olivier Audience Award for the Most Popular Show

The Criterion has weathered many storms in recent times. Its subterranean location makes it susceptible to damp – £45,000 was spent on improvements in 1972. Then in 1985 the theatre suffered extensive flood damage which ruined some of its unique tiles. In the '70s and early '80s the Criterion was under very real threat of closure when the site on which it stands was proposed for redevelopment. Happily, high-profile demonstrations, with campaigners such as John Gielgud, Edward Woodward and Diana Rigg, assured its future. After three years' careful renovation work, the block that stands today was rebuilt around the theatre, preserving it perfectly. And so the Criterion survives and flourishes, continuing to give pleasure to playgoers.

the criterion theatre
piccadilly circus = wlv

The Dominion

'In the opinion of the Board, the most popular form of entertainment today consists of musical productions, which must be staged on so lavish a scale and be of such magnificence that a theatre with a very large seating capacity is required to render the production commercially successful, and there is undoubtedly a large public demand for big spectacular musical productions at popular prices with high class artistes.' This extract from a report on the building of 'A New Super-Theatre in the Centre of London' was issued in February 1928, just before construction began on the 2,800-seat Dominion Theatre, which stands on the busy intersection of Tottenham Court Road and Oxford Street. Despite alterations to the auditorium, the Dominion is still one of the largest theatres in the West End, with a seating capacity of 2,182.

For many years, the Dominion was used as a cinema, or temporary home for short seasons of opera, dance and rock until it re-entered the mainstream of West End theatres with its production of Dave Clark's space-age musical *Time* (1986). But it opened first as a theatre in October 1929 with an American musical comedy on golf by De Sylva, Brown and Henderson called *Follow Through* (*Follow Thru* on Broadway) starring Elsie Randolph, Ivy Tresmand and Leslie Henson. Neither this, nor a follow-up musical, *Silver Wings*, made much impression. So, in 1930, it provided a venue for Lon Chaney's *The Phantom Of The Opera* with dialogue and some new footage added to the 1925 silent movie. The next year, Charlie Chaplin appeared on stage to make a 'thank you' speech after the first showing of his *City Lights*, in the presence of George V. The screen was folded up in 1932 to allow Richard Tauber to move his ample form, from which emanated his dulcet tenor tones, in a revival of Franz Lehar's *The Land Of Smiles*. A number of film stars, including Maurice

'At first sight the interior of the house gives one the impression it was really meant for a super cinema.'
— The Stage, 1929

Chevalier, Jeanette MacDonald, Sophie Tucker and Judy Garland, made appearances in variety seasons.

In 1958, Todd-AO equipment was installed for the showing of the movie musical *South Pacific* which ran four years, a record surpassed by *The Sound Of Music*, which resounded through the Dominion from 1965 to 1973. For over a decade thereafter, blockbuster films shared the auditorium with the Welsh National Opera, the Georgian dancers from the USSR, Chinese acrobats and pop groups. In a way, this was reminiscent of the days when there was a fun fair and a huge tent, where variety shows were given, on the empty site on which the Dominion was built. Long before, as far back as the twelfth century, the St Giles Leper Hospital had stood on the spot. Some six centuries later, a brewery was built here containing a 22-foot vat of porter ale. In October 1814, the vat burst, pouring its contents into the streets and literally drowning eight people in alcohol.

The site was chosen for the theatre 'owing to its central position, [and] its proximity to the reconstructed Tube station'. Designed by W. and T. R. Milburn, its broad Portland stone facade is now obscured by a giant sign announcing the entertainment within. The interior with its large mirrored lobby, twin stairways and wide corridors is very much on the lines of 'the modern picture palaces' built in the 1930s. In order to accommodate *Time*, one of the most expensive stage musicals of its day, a few alterations had to be made to the theatre's interior.

Since then, the Dominion has been home to several major musicals – *Grease* (1993), *Scrooge* (1996), Disney's *Beauty and the Beast* (1997) and *Notre-Dame de Paris* (2000). The production of *Beauty and the Beast*, as well as being a huge hit, was particularly

A scene from the 'space-age' musical, *Time*

notable as it marked Disney's first venture into the West End. And in between these big productions, the Dominion continued its tradition of offering all-round entertainment, with one-off pop shows, operas and other entertainments, ranging from a performance of *Swan Lake* by the celebrated dance company Adventures in Motion Pictures to Michael Ball in concert. And the Dominion still occasionally acts as a cinema – *Return of the Jedi* opened here in 1983, as well as London Film Festival Shows. It's also a regular home to the Royal Variety Performance. And so 1929's 'New Super-Theatre' still entertains and impresses audiences.

the dominion theatre
tottenham court road = wlp

The Donmar
Warehouse

What the *New York Times* has described as 'the current epicenter of theatre glamour in London' is deceptively small and simple. Off a narrow, cobbled street in the middle of London's former fruit and vegetable market, Covent Garden, the Donmar Warehouse comprises a two-level square room with seating around three sides of the acting area for an audience of 250 people. Yet this little theatre is a dazzling hotbed of dynamic creativity, attracting the world's finest theatrical and performing talent. The theatre's reputation has been made in an amazingly short amount of time, and centres on the figure of Artistic Director Sam Mendes.

Back in Victorian times, the building which now houses the Donmar was a vat room and hop warehouse for the local brewery. In the 1920s the space was used as a film studio, then, appropriately for its location, as a banana-ripening warehouse. In 1961, theatre impresario Donald Albery (son of theatre manager Sir Bronson Albery) bought the warehouse and converted it into a private rehearsal studio for the London Festival Ballet, a company he formed with his friend, prima ballerina Margot Fonteyn. The amalgamation of their Christian names, and the previous function of the building, gave the space its current title – the Donmar Warehouse.

From 1977 to 1981, the Royal Shakespeare Company made the Donmar its London home to complement the Stratford venue and to present the company's studio work. Among their noted productions here were the stark Ian McKellen/Judi Dench *Macbeth*, *Piaf* and the first performance of Willy Russell's

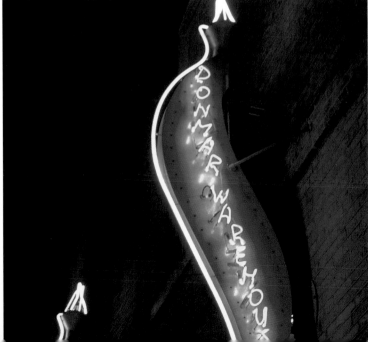

'Powerhouses do not come much smaller, nor much more powerful, than the Donmar Warehouse.'

— *Sunday Times*

Educating Rita with Mark Kingston and Julie Walters, which was followed by a long West End run and a subsequent film adaptation.

When the RSC left to go to its new home at the Barbican, Ian Albery (Donald's son) and Nica Burns formed a non-profit making company called Omega to take the Donmar Warehouse over. At that point, it was the only theatre of its size which was able to rely wholly on the box-office for its revenue. It survived through the brilliant administrative skills of Nica Burns, and through its fast-growing reputation as a home for Britain's most innovative touring companies, with residences from Cheek by Jowl and Hull Truck, amongst others. The Donmar presented a wide spectrum of entertainment, including *Blues in the Night*, Fascinating Aida and the Annual Perrier Comedy Awards, further establishing the theatre as a showcase for cabaret and comedy.

In 1989 the Ambassador Theatre Group acquired the Donmar, with the intention of redeveloping the theatre, and in 1990, 24-year-old Sam Mendes was invited to take up residency as Artistic Director, with the challenge of presenting an annual eight-month season of home-produced work. Like the young Peter Hall at the Arts Theatre back in the '50s, he rose to the challenge with incredible confidence and panache. Mendes was already a well-established West End director, having produced *The Rise and Fall of Little Voice* at the Aldwych, and Chekhov's *The Sea* and *The Cherry Orchard* with Judi Dench. He asked Caro Newling – Senior Press Representative at the Royal Shakespeare Company – to join him as Administrative Director. For the next two years, and on a shoestring budget, Mendes and Newling oversaw the redesign of the theatre, retaining the distinctive characteristics of the former warehouse and the unique thrust

the donmar warehouse

Nicole Kidman in Sam Mendes' production of *The Blue Room* (1998)

stage and adding two bars and significant improvements backstage. In 1992 the theatre reopened as an independent producing house with the triumphant British premiere of Stephen Sondheim's *Assassins*. Its feet have hardly touched the ground since. In 2002 the Donmar celebrated ten years as a producing house under Mendes's artistic direction with, to date, fifteen Laurence Olivier Awards, seven Tony Awards from their Broadway transfers, four *Evening Standard* Awards, six Critics' Circle Awards, and *The Times* Critics' Award for 'epitomising all that is best and boldest about British cultural life'.

The Donmar Warehouse has attracted exceptional directors to its stage. As well as Sam Mendes's own productions (*The Glass Menagerie*, *The Blue Room* and *Cabaret* to name but three), Associate Director Michael Grandage has directed the triple Olivier Award-winning Stephen Sondheim musical *Merrily We Roll Along* (2000), swiftly followed by a brilliant revival of *Passion Play* by Peter Nichols, *Good*, with Charles Dance, and the wartime musical comedy *Privates on Parade* (2002). John Crowley, also an Associate Director, had enormous success with *Juno and the Paycock* (1999) starring Colm Meaney, which transferred to New York, and 2001's *Tales From Hollywood*, a revival of Christopher Hampton's play. In 2001 Nicholas Hytner directed Tennessee Williams's rarely seen *Orpheus Descending*, starring Helen Mirren. Phyllida Lloyd directed *The Threepenny Opera* in 1994, and then the premiere of David Mamet's *Boston Marriage*, starring Zoe Wanamaker (2001), which transferred to the West End. The Donmar has also seen the work of directors such as Robin Lefevre, with *Three Days of Rain* (1999), David Leveaux (*Electra*, 1997), Sean Matthias, Matthew Warchus, Katie Mitchell and James Kerr.

As well as revivals, the Donmar is active in commissioning new work for its intimate auditorium. This has involved collaborations with celebrated playwrights such as David Hare and Frank McGuinness, whose adaptations of *The Blue Room* (1998) and *Electra* respectively became the talk of the town, both during their runs at the Donmar and then again on Broadway. Many of the Donmar's productions have gone on to have West End runs, including Noël Coward's *Design for Living* (1994), *The Glass Menagerie* (1996), *Company* (1996) and *Boston Marriage*; and two have also transferred to Broadway: *The Blue Room* and Tom Stoppard's *The Real Thing* (2000).

With such a range of innovative writing and directing talent, it's not surprising that the Donmar attracts such an amazing number of star performers – Zoe Wanamaker with her exceptional performances in *The Glass Menagerie*, *Boston Marriage* and the title role in *Electra*, Nicole Kidman in *The Blue Room*, Gwyneth Paltrow in *Proof*, Stephen Dillane in *The Real Thing*, Adrian Lester and Sheila Gish in *Company*, Colin Firth in *Three Days of Rain*, William H. Macy in *American Buffalo*, Jim Broadbent, Colin Firth, Brenda Blethyn and Rachel Weisz – to name just a few.

In November 2002, after his magnificent productions of *Uncle Vanya* and *Twelfth Night*, Sam Mendes took his last bow as Artistic Director, leaving to pursue an independent film and theatre career (his film *American Beauty* took five Oscars in 2000, including Best Director), and Michael Grandage became the

the donmar warehouse

Roger Allam in *Privates on Parade,* 2001

Donmar's new Artistic Director. Through his persistence, vision, hard work and creative brilliance, Mendes leaves a space transformed from a fringe venue into what the *Evening Standard* describes as 'a brilliantly innovative, independent producing theatre, exemplifying the very best that London has to offer'. Now the world eagerly awaits the fruits of the Donmar Warehouse's new theatrical era.

the donmar warehouse
earlham street = wc2

The Theatre Royal, Drury Lane

It is ironic that London's oldest, most historically important and most famous theatre does not echo to the sounds of Shakespeare or other great English playwrights, but to the lusty melodies of the Broadway musical. Ever since *Oklahoma!* wowed British audiences in 1947, Drury Lane's large stage and 2,283 seating capacity has housed the best of American musicals including *Carousel* (1950), *South Pacific* (1951) starring Mary Martin (her son Larry 'J. R.' Hagman was in the chorus), *The King And I* (1953), the record-breaking *My Fair Lady* (1958) with Rex Harrison and Julie Andrews – and again in 2001, with Jonathan Pryce and Martine McCutcheon - *Camelot* (1964), Carol Channing in *Hello Dolly!* (1965), *A Chorus Line* (1976), *Sweeney Todd* (1980), *The Best Little Whorehouse in Texas* (1981) and *42nd Street* (1984). In fact, Americans have found it cheaper to see a hit musical here than on Broadway. Indeed, for most of its 324 years of existence (in four different buildings on the same spot), the name of Drury Lane has been synonymous with popular, spectacular shows.

The first playhouse was erected on the site of a riding yard in 1662, two years after the Restoration. The theatre-loving Charles II granted a patent to the company, under Thomas Killigrew, known as The King's Servants. As they were considered part of the Royal Household, the members of the troupe were entitled to wear the scarlet and gold of the royal livery, and this is still worn by the footmen at Drury Lane today. The entire theatre, seating around 700, was about the size of the present stage. Refreshments were supplied by Mrs Mary Meggs, or 'Orange Moll', a widow

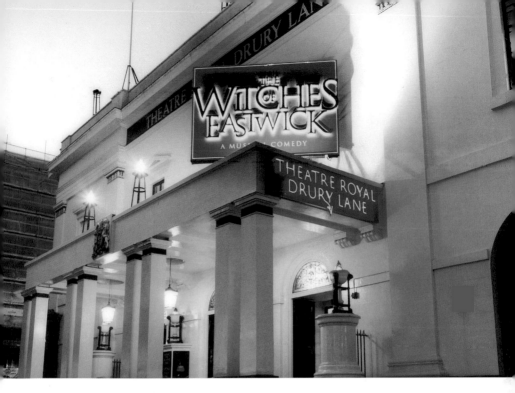

'You are come to act in a wilderness of a place.'
— Mrs Siddons to William Dowton in 1796

who had a licence to hawk her fruits to all customers, except those in the upper gallery who might be inclined to throw them at some unfortunate player. One of 'Moll's' girls, Nell Gwynn, made her stage debut at the age of 15 in John Dryden's *The Indian Queen* in 1665. The King, from the Royal Box, fell in love with Nell at first sight, and took her as his mistress. It is likely that the fire that destroyed the building in 1672 was started by an 'orange girl' searching for fruit with a naked flame under the stairs where it was kept.

Sir Christopher Wren designed the second theatre, the foundations of which can still be traced under the present stage. It was more than twice the size of the first, and prospered with the plays of Dryden, William Wycherley, William Congreve and George Farquhar, the cream of Restoration dramatists. After the deaths of Killigrew and King Charles, the Theatre Royal's prestige suffered until the triumvirate of Robert Wilkes, Thomas Doggett and Colley Cibber, all three fine actors, restored its fortunes in 1711. When Charles Fleetwood, a gambler with no money sense, took over, the theatre was led into near bankruptcy, despite an epoch-making *Merchant of Venice* of 1741 in which Charles Macklin raised the role of Shylock from low comedy to a tragic figure. So impressed was George II that he could not get to sleep either during or after the performance. Macklin was a forerunner of a new school of action which David Garrick was to personify.

Garrick, one of the greatest of English actors, became actor-manager in 1747, and spent the next 30 years at Drury Lane. He introduced better lighting and regular rehearsals and removed the public from the boxes at the sides of the stage. Garrick left the theatre in the hands of the celebrated playwright Richard Brinsley Sheridan, whose first important production was his own *The School For Scandal* in 1777. Two years later, Sheridan's *The Critic* exploited the popular taste for spectacle with remarkable scenic effects and lavish costumes. He engaged the superb tragedienne Mrs Sarah Siddons to play Lady Macbeth and her brother John Philip Kemble to make his London debut as Hamlet. However, by 1791, the building had fallen into such a bad state of decay that it was decided to build another in its place. So down went Wren's edifice, and up went one designed by Henry Holland, of which the *Morning Chronicle* of 1794 wrote, 'At length we have an English theatre worthy of our opulence and taste.' On the night of the opening production of *Macbeth*, with Kemble playing opposite his sister, an iron safety curtain was lowered to assure the audience of their protection from fire. Fifteen years later, the theatre burned down. Sheridan sat watching the conflagration with a glass of wine in his hand. When asked how he could do this so calmly, the playwright retorted, 'Can't a man have a drink by his own fireside?'

Drury Lane, more or less as we know it today, was rebuilt with money raised by the brewer Samuel Whitbread. Designed by Benjamin Wyatt on the elegant neo-classical model of the Grand

Theatre of Bordeaux, it opened in 1812 with an address written by Lord Byron. Over the next few decades, several improvements were made. Gas lighting was introduced in 1817, the splendid portico was added in 1820 and the Russell Street colonnade in 1831. Certain things modern audiences take for granted, such as a centre aisle, stuffed and covered seats and a coffee room, were much welcomed. The impressive Rotunda, magnificent

The renowned David Garrick as Tancred (painted by Thomas Worlidge)

Actors gather in the Green Room, *circa* 1820

Grand Salon and the sweeping staircases date from the early nineteenth century. It was on the latter that George III boxed the ears of the reprobate Prince Regent. This resulted in the staircases being called the King's Side and the Prince's Side, names still to be seen on opposite doors.

The new theatre, under the management of Samuel Arnold, introduced the legendary tragedian Edmund Kean to London audiences. He presented his Shylock, was immediately acclaimed a genius, and remained at Drury Lane, playing many of the great Shakespearean roles for five years, his most successful part being Richard III. Of Kean's death scene as Richard, Hazlitt said he 'had a preternatural and terrific grandeur, as if his will could not be disarmed, and the very phantoms of his despair had a withering power'.

After Kean's departure, opera and spectacle were preferred to straight drama under the reign of Alfred Bunn. In 1879, Augustus Harris, a bronze bust of whom sits above a drinking fountain at the north-east corner of the facade, established the theatre's reputation for elaborately staged melodramas and pantomimes. When Harris, known as 'Druriolanus', died in 1896, his right-hand man, Arthur Collins, continued the tradition with even bigger shows. *Ben Hur* (1902) offered a chariot race with real horses, and other productions contained earthquakes, erupting volcanos and shipwrecks. Sensation was piled on sensation, and the public flocked. Drury Lane was also the home for Henry Irving's last season in 1905, Ellen Terry's stage jubilee a year later, in which all the leading theatrical personalities of the day appeared at a mammoth matinee, and Diaghilev's landmark Ballets Russes. Shakespeare's tercentenary in 1916 was celebrated with a production of *Julius Caesar*, after which Frank Benson, who took the title role, was knighted by George V with a property sword in the Royal retiring room.

After 27 years in the job, Collins handed over to Sir Alfred Butt in 1924, who instigated the policy of big musical shows from the USA such as *Rose Marie* (1925), *The Desert Song* (1927), *Show Boat* (1928) and *The New Moon* (1929). Franz Lehar's *The Land Of Smiles* (1931), featuring Austrian-born tenor Richard Tauber, gave way to Noël Coward's patriotic pageant, *Cavalcade*, which ended with the 250-strong company singing the National Anthem and the audience, on its feet, joining in. The multi-talented Ivor Novello dominated Drury Lane in the 1930s as a leading man, composer and writer of *Glamorous Nights, Careless Rapture* and *The Dancing Years*, each title aptly describing the sort of entertainment that the Theatre Royal provided and continues to provide. Novello, 'the handsomest man in England', also played the soldier-king in a spectacular revival of *Henry V*.

During World War II 'The Lane' became the headquarters of ENSA, the organisation set up to provide shows for the allied forces at home and abroad. In 1940 considerable damage was done to the upper circles by enemy bombs, an explosion rivalling those the theatre had supplied on stage. Restored to its former glory, it reopened to the public on 19 December, 1946 with Coward's musical *Pacific 1860* starring Mary Martin. It flopped and made way for the arrival of Rodgers and Hammerstein's *Oklahoma!*, which ushered in the golden age of Broadway hit musicals, culminating in 1984's *42nd Street*, with a run of 1,824 performances. The longest run at Drury Lane was an amazing 4,263 performances, and it wasn't a Broadway transfer this time but Cameron Mackintosh's home-grown musical hit *Miss Saigon*, starring Jonathan Pryce (1989).

the theatre royal, drury lane

Audiences that come to Drury Lane find themselves wandering around a veritable theatre museum before entering the auditorium. In the large foyer there is a statue of Shakespeare executed in lead by John Cheere. On the walls behind are a handsome Patent Board with a list of all the holders since 1663 and a mahogany War Memorial with the names in gold of the members of the theatrical profession who fell in the Great War. In the stalls and circle rotunda are statues and busts of Garrick, Kean, Novello, Dan Leno, Forbes-Robertson and the first great black American playwright, Ira Aldridge, as well as a John Northcote painting of Kean as Brutus.

Like a few other old London theatres, Drury Lane has its resident ghosts. One, an eighteenth-century gentleman in a long grey riding cloak, riding boots, sword and three-cornered hat, walks through one wall of the upper circle and disappears on the other side. But he only makes his appearance at matinees and when the house is full. He is thought to have some connection with the skeleton found bricked up in one of the walls with a dagger in his ribs. The other ghost, suspected of being that of the illustrious clown Grimaldi who made his farewell appearance at the theatre in 1828, gives bad actors a kick up the backside from time to time. As the standard of performance at Drury Lane is generally high, this is a rare event.

the theatre royal, drury lane
catherine street = wc2b

The Duchess

On the opposite side of Catherine Street from the grandiose Strand and the noble Drury Lane is a small theatre seeking attention with its 'modern Tudor Gothic' facade. Three projecting bays, with a plethora of tiny windows over enamelled panels bearing insignia, give it an elegant air which suits its name – the Duchess. There is not much to catch the eye in the unadorned two-level interior with its hidden lighting effect, enlivened only by two unusual bas-reliefs by the sculptor Maurice Lambert, one each side of the stage. They represent draped figures holding the masks of Comedy and Tragedy above applauding hands. Over the years, hands have applauded plays by J. B. Priestley, Emlyn Williams, Noël Coward and Harold Pinter – and *The Dirtiest Show In Town* and *Oh, Calcutta!*

For most of its existence, the Duchess has been an intimate home for what Priestley called 'the essential Theatre... an institution that cannot safely be despised even by the philosopher'. Priestley, whose *Laburnum Grove* (1933) ran here for 335 performances, managed the theatre from 1934, the year in which two more of his plays were performed. Ralph Richardson, who would be closely associated with the works of Priestley, played an amiable drunkard in *Eden End* and a businessman in *Cornelius*. 'I always see Ralph myself not as a down-to-earth character but as if he is about to float away somewhere,' commented the playwright. Priestley's first play on the concept of time, *Time And The Conways* (1937), ran for over six months; after the war Sybil Thorndike starred in *The Linden Tree* (1947), while *Eden End* was revived in 1948.

Emlyn Williams's links with the Duchess began as an actor in the opening production in November 1929 of a war play called *Tunnel Trench*. He returned as playwright and star in 1935 with *Night Must Fall*, the psychological thriller which contained the

'Ken Tynan had conceived a voyeurs' picnic...called Oh, Calcutta!... Mixing frontery with effrontery it soon found its own public.'
— Raymond Mander and Joe Mitchenson in *Revue*

notorious head in the hatbox. His most popular play, *The Corn Is Green*, ran here from August 1938 until the theatre's closure at the outbreak of war in September 1939. Williams himself played the young Welsh miner who wins a scholarship to Oxford, thanks to his teacher Miss Moffat, a role taken brilliantly by Sybil Thorndike. In 1952, Williams brought his celebrated Dickens recital into the Duchess for a short season.

Although J. B. Priestley and Emlyn Williams were the dominant figures in the theatre's pre-war days, other notable productions were seen here. Nancy Price's People's National Theatre presented Baliol Holloway as Falstaff in *The Merry Wives Of Windsor* and Frank Vosper as Henry VIII in *The Rose Without A Thorn*, both in 1932. In the same year, Jessica Tandy scored a personal success in the all-female play *Children In Uniform*, a translation from the German *Mädchen In Uniform*, set in an oppressive boarding school. It was directed by the Viennese Leontine Sagan, who had filmed it the year before.

During the war years, Noël Coward's 'impossible farce' *Blithe Spirit* (1942) con-

The bronze bas-relief on either side of the proscenium is the only adornment

tinued to break records after being transferred here from the Piccadilly and the now defunct St James. In contrast, the shortest run in theatrical history was recorded at the Duchess in 1930 when a revue failed to complete the first night, the audience retreating before the end! Running considerably longer were post-war hits such as Wynyard Browne's *The Holly And The Ivy* (1950) and Terence Rattigan's drama *The Deep Blue Sea* (1952) with Peggy Ashcroft falling for feckless young Kenneth More and attempting suicide. These dramas were examples of the 'well-made play', soon to be discarded by a new school of British writers, of whom Harold Pinter was one of the best. Producer Michael Codron had the courage to bring Pinter's *The Caretaker* into the heart of the West End, and it paid off. This superb comedy of menace with a splendid cast of three – Donald Pleasence, Alan Bates (replaced by Pinter himself) and Peter Woodthorpe – ran for a year. Some years on, Pinter's double bill, *The Basement* and *The Tea Party* (1970) with Pleasence and

Husky-voiced Joan Greenwood and fruity-toned Donald Sinden lent distinction to Terence Rattigan's *In Praise of Love*

Vivien Merchant and Donald Pleasence in Harold Pinter's *Tea Party* (1970), a teasing black comedy

Vivien Merchant (then the author's wife), and his triple bill, *Other Places* (1985), were seen in the vastly changed climate of British theatre.

Raunchy entertainment became the order of the day at the Duchess when it played hostess to *The Dirtiest Show In Town* (1971) for 794 performances, and the revue which merited the above title, *Oh, Calcutta!* (1974), for six years. The legendary *No Sex Please, We're British* transferred here from the Garrick in 1986 after its long run there; *Run For Your Wife* (1990) completed its nine-year West End run at the Duchess; and *Don't Dress For Dinner* transferred from the Apollo and kept audiences happy for a further four and a half years from 1992.

the duchess

Comedies continued into the 1990s with the highly successful *An Evening With Gary Lineker* by Chris England and Arthur Smith (1991) and Maureen Lipman's one-woman show *Live and Kidding*. On a more serious note came the RSC's brilliant production of Peter Whelan's *The Herbal Bed* (1997) and the Royal National Theatre's productions of *Copenhagen* by Michael Frayn (1999) and *Blue/Orange* by Joe Penhall (2001), all showing that the Duchess is a theatre with the capacity to keep on surprising its audiences.

the duchess theatre
catherine street = wc2b

The Duke of York's

T his elegant, charming and compact Victorian playhouse was built in 1892, the first of the three theatres in St Martin's Lane – at the time literally a lane, with muddy ditches on either side. The New Theatre (now the Albery) sprang up 11 years later, and the Coliseum soon joined them. With the Garrick backing onto the Duke of York's, and the Wyndham's close behind the Albery, they form a neat cluster of theatres between Shaftesbury Avenue and Drury Lane.

The Duke of York's opened as the Trafalgar Square Theatre, but changed to its present name in 1895 after Henry Dana, the manager, received the following letter from the treasurer of the future King George V.

> I am desired to inform you that HRH the Duke of York has no objection to the Trafalgar Theatre being called The Duke of York's Theatre but to say that this permission gives no authority for the use of the word Royal in connexion with the theatre nor may any reference be made such as 'By permission of HRH the Duke of York.'

Nevertheless, it is a right royal building with a theatrical tradition fit for a king.

It was at the Duke of York's on 27 December, 1904 that Peter Pan flew for the first time on stage. Here, too, a year later, 14-year-old Charlie Chaplin played in *Sherlock Holmes*. On returning in the 1950s with his daughter, Victoria, to see a show, Chaplin was given the Royal Box with its Regency-inspired retiring room designed by Cecil Beaton. The theatre has also been graced over the years by, among others, Marie Tempest, Ellen Terry, Isadora Duncan, Edwige Feuillère, John Gielgud, Glenda Jackson and Al Pacino. Peggy Ashcroft (*Jew Süss*, 1929), John Mills (*London Wall*, 1931) and Joan Plowright (*Moby Dick*, 1955)

'Either he must be the whimsical fairy creature that Nina Boucicault made him, or he must be the lovable tomboy of Pauline Chase. There is no other way.'

— J. M. Barrie on the playing of Peter Pan

all began to make their names here. Plowright played the Cabin Boy to actor-director Orson Welles's Ahab in a production the critic Kenneth Tynan described as 'a sustained assault on the senses, which dwarfs anything London has ever seen since, except perhaps, the Great Fire'. And the theatre has its very own ghost. An iron fire-door which once existed is heard to slam shut every night at ten. Some years ago, an old-fashioned iron key with a tag marked 'Iron Door' dropped at the feet of the manager. A female figure dressed in black has been seen to wander through the circle bar. It is said to be none other than the ghost of Violet Melnotte, the owner, known to everyone as 'Madame'.

The theatre, designed by Walter Emden for 'Madame' and her husband Frank Wyatt, was not a success until she let it on a long lease to the influential American impresario Charles Frohman in 1897. Frohman, 'The Napoleon of the Theatre',

brought fame, prestige and money to the Duke of York's. The first long run under his aegis was Anthony Hope's *The Adventure Of Lady Ursula* (1898), in which Evelyn Millard caused a stir by appearing in male attire. In 1900 she also starred in Jerome K. Jerome's *Miss Hobbs* and in David Belasco's

Pauline Chase as Peter Pan – one of J. M. Barrie's favourites in the role

one-act play, *Madame Butterfly*, which accompanied it. Puccini happened to be in the audience one evening, and was inspired to write his opera of the same name four years later. The long and fruitful collaboration between Frohman and James Barrie at the Duke of York's began with *The Admirable Crichton* (1902), a success despite a strike of scene-shifters after the second act on the opening night. Members of the cast, including H. B. Irving (son of Sir Henry), Gerald du Maurier and Irene Vanbrugh, had to move the scenery themselves. *Peter Pan* followed with Nina Boucicault, Hilda Trevelyan and du Maurier as the first ever Peter, Wendy and Hook respectively. Cissie Loftus (1905), Pauline Chase (1906-13) and Madge Titheradge (1914) were the subsequent Peters at this theatre. Hilda Trevelyan continued for some years as Wendy, also proving herself a perfect Barrie heroine in *Alice Sit-By-The-Fire* (1905), alongside Ellen Terry, and as Maggie in *What Every Woman Knows* (1908).

In 1910 Frohman made a brave attempt to mount a repertory season of ten plays, but suffered a heavy financial loss. Among the plays premiered were Galsworthy's *Justice*, Shaw's *Misalliance* and Harley Granville-Barker's *The Madras House*. Five years later, the

Joan Plowright
and Orson
Welles rehearse
for *Moby Dick* in
1955

theatre world on both sides of the Atlantic was stunned by the news that Frohman had drowned on the S.S. *Lusitania*, torpedoed by the Germans. His last words to a survivor were said to have been from *Peter Pan*: 'To die will be an awfully big adventure.'

During the Great War, the theatre's successes were Doris Keane in *Romance* (1915), Renée Kelly in *Daddy Long Legs* (1916) and Mrs Patrick Campbell in *The Thirteenth Chair* (1917). Noël Coward, in his twenties like the century, became the voice of the Bright Young Things. When he was 14, he had appeared as Slightly in the 1913 *Peter Pan*. Now Coward was back with his revue, *London Calling* (1923), in which Gertrude Lawrence sang 'Parisien Pierrot', and two plays, *Easy Virtue* (1926) and *Home Chat* (1927). The latter, despite the casting of two former Peter Pans, Nina Boucicault and Madge Titheradge, was booed on the first night. Coward's connection with the theatre re-emerged years later with *Waiting In The Wings* (1960), featuring a starry geriatric cast, and a 1963 revival of his classic, *Private Lives*.

The 1930s ushered in the Carl Rosa Opera Company, a non-stop season of Grand Guignol (from 2 p.m. to midnight), and the Ballet Rambert and Markova-Dolin dance companies which did so much to popularise ballet in England. The big hit of the 1940s was *Is Your Honeymoon Really Necessary?* (1944), which ran two years. Other long-runners were John Clements and Kay Hammond in *The Happy Marriage* (1952), Flora Robson in *The House By The Lake* (1956), Margaret Lockwood in *And Suddenly It's Spring* (1959), which had its 'first night' for the critics at a matinee, the Kenneth Williams revue, *One Over The Eight* (1961), Donald Pleasence in Jean Anouilh's *Poor Bitos* (1964), *The Killing Of Sister George* (1965), *Relatively Speaking* (1967) – the first of Alan Ayckbourn's multitude of hits – and *The Man Most Likely To...* (1970).

In 1979, Capital Radio bought the building and closed it for refurbishment. It reopened in February 1980 with restored cream and gold decoration, recreating the warm atmosphere of a Victorian theatre while improving the facilities. The quality of

the duke of york's

Glenda Jackson and Brian Cox in Eugene O'Neill's *Strange Interlude*. They had to survive a marathon five hours per performance

productions since then has remained traditionally high, with Glenda Jackson in *Rose* (1980) and *Strange Interlude* (1983), the off-Broadway cast, headed by Al Pacino, in *American Buffalo* (1984), Willy Russell's *Shirley Valentine* (1989), Ariel Dorfman's award-winning *Death And The Maiden* with Juliet Stevenson (1992) and David Mamet's *Oleanna* (1993). In 1996 the Royal Court took up a three-year residence at the Duke of York's. Whilst here they enjoyed a hugely successful two-year run of *The Weir*, which ended its award-winning season in May 2000. *Stones In His Pockets* followed, winning an Olivier Award for Best Comedy, 2001. Violet Melnotte can rest in peace.

the duke of york's theatre
st martin's lane = wc2n

The Fortune

In the shadow of the glorious Drury Lane Theatre, facing its famous colonnade on the stage door side, lies a small theatre that proudly perpetuates the name of a popular Elizabethan playhouse. The architect, Ernest Schaufelberg, based his designs for the exterior on a print of doubtful authenticity of the old Fortune. Like its predecessor as seen in the sketch, it is a square brick building of four storeys, with minimal adornment. The earlier Fortune, situated not far from where the Barbican Centre stands today, had a statue of the Goddess of Fortune over the entrance. This proved rather ineffectual, as the building, the costumes and playbooks went up in flames in 1621. Above the entrance of the present theatre is a nude figure of Terpsichore, the Greek Muse of Dancing. However, the small stage does not lend itself to any but limited displays of the art of dance. What the 440-seat theatre does provide is a cosy intimacy for shows of a diminutive nature. In fact, its biggest successes have been two revues – *At The Drop Of A Hat* (1957) and *Beyond The Fringe* (1961) – with casts of two and four respectively.

The Fortune's principal interest as a building is that it shares its structure with the Scottish National Church. Strangely, it is built over and under the church, whose entrance is cheek by jowl with that of the theatre's. The opening production in November 1924, a play called *Sinners* by Laurence Cowan, the theatre's owner, might have confused churchgoers. There have also been a few plays whose proximity could not have been welcomed by worshippers on the other side of the wall. Nevertheless, it is a rare architectural unity between religion and secularism.

A brass plate in the lobby proclaims, 'There is a tide in the affairs of men, which, taken at the flood, leads on to Fortune.' But it was often 'the slings and arrows of outrageous fortune' that visited this pleasant playhouse in those early days. It was

'Our theatre was miscalled the Fortune... After a very short time we slid into the eternal obscurity of Fatal Fortune.'
— Dirk Bogarde on the failure of *Power Without Glory*, 1947

two years after its opening before there was anything significant to appeal to lovers of the theatre. The influential producer J. B. Fagan changed that by presenting Sean O'Casey's modern Irish classics *Juno And The Paycock* and *The Plough And The Stars* in 1926. A year later the actor Tom Walls, at the time associated with the Aldwych farces, took over the management of the Fortune. Frederick Lonsdale's *On Approval* (1927), a comedy of manners about a trial marriage, ran for over a year, making it the first and last hit here for some time.

The People's National Theatre, run by Nancy Price, its founder and guiding spirit, found its first London home at the Fortune from 1930 to 1931. Their most noteworthy production was the revival of John Galsworthy's first play, *The Silver Box*. After Nancy Price – and her inseparable pet parrot – left the theatre, Sybil Thorndike paid a brief visit in 1932 with two plays. It was then given over to amateur productions until the war, during which it was used by ENSA, the

A 1920s programme cover depicts the proscenium of the then newly built Fortune

114

organisation formed to provide entertainment for servicemen and women.

After the war, the building returned to the professional fold for a brief period. One of the short-lived productions was *Power Without Glory* (1947), a working-class drama featuring two unknown actors named Kenneth More and Dirk Bogarde. It soon closed 'due to lack of star names on the canopy and the excessive competition from the energetic Americans across the street in *Oklahoma!*', according to Bogarde. It was another ten years before fortune smiled on the little theatre with *At The Drop Of A Hat*. Michael Flanders in a wheelchair and Donald Swann at the piano entertained audiences with comic songs and patter for over two years.

In the autumn of 1961 a revue, written and performed on a bare stage by four young men just down from Oxbridge, took an emergent 'Swinging London' by storm. *Beyond The Fringe* was not only instrumental in starting the 'satire industry', but was the springboard for the exceptional future careers of Jonathan Miller, Peter Cook, Alan Bennett and Dudley Moore. The show ran 1,184 performances before transferring to the Mayfair in 1964. Other shows that ran here include *Mr Cinders*, *Double Double*, *Nunsense* and *Dangerous Obsession*.

But the Fortune is most closely associated with *The Woman in Black*, which has become a West End legend. This enigmatic and brilliant play first took up residence in 1989, and the theatre and show celebrated 5,000 performances in July 2001. In the same year, the theatre became part of the hugely successful Ambassador Theatre Group. Bouncer, the Fortune Theatre's cat, must be delighted!

the fortune theatre
russell street = wc2b

The Garrick

I f David Garrick, according to Dr Johnson, had added to 'the gaiety of nations' and 'the public stock of harmless pleasure', then so too has the attractive late Victorian playhouse named after the great eighteenthth-century actor and built exactly 110 years after his death. A copy of the lost Gainsborough portrait of Garrick beside a bust of Shakespeare welcomes one into the theatre at dress-circle level. Cupids holding laurel-decked shields form part of the finely modelled plasterwork on the balcony fronts and from the domed ornamental ceiling held up by caryatids above the boxes hangs a chandelier. The gold leaf of the auditorium was restored in 1986 by the celebrated stage designer Carl Toms. At the same time the distinctive Portland and Bath stone exterior, opposite the statue of Henry Irving, also had a flattering facelift, making the stately colonnade on the first floor come up as good as new.

It was new in 1889 when Walter Emden and C. J. Phipps built it for actor-manager John Hare with the money of W. S. Gilbert, earned from the light operas he wrote with Arthur Sullivan. The construction was delayed when the deep foundations hit an underground river known to the Romans. Today, underground trains run beneath the theatre. A new drama by Pinero entitled *The Profligate*, with Hare, Forbes Robertson, Lewis Wailer and Katie Rorke, inaugurated the building in April 1889. Pinero's connection with the Garrick continued with *Lady Bountiful* (1891) and *The Notorious Mrs Ebbsmith* (1895), the latter living up to its title. During the run of the play, starring Mrs Patrick Campbell and John Hare, a woman named Ebbsmith was found drowned in the Thames, a counterfoil of a ticket for the production in her pocket. Apparently, she had written to a friend that the play had preyed on her mind. In 1896, Hare left the theatre where he had made such a success,

'The proscenium is created by the pilasters that frame the stage boxes; this was a dramatic and simple change.'
— Victor Glasstone

particularly in the role of Benjamin Goldfinch in Sydney Grundy's *A Pair Of Spectacles* (1890), an adaptation from a French farce. In fact, for almost 100 years, until 1987's *When Did You Last See Your Trousers?* (1987), farce established itself as the Garrick's dominant mode.

The twentieth century began well for the Garrick when Arthur Bourchier and his wife Violet Vanbrugh leased it, beginning a splendid line of productions with J. M. Barrie's *The Wedding Guest* (1900). There followed Pinero's *Iris* (1901), Henry Arthur Jones's white-washing *Julia* (1903), Bourchier as Shylock in *The Merchant Of Venice* (1905), Henri Bernstein's *Samson* (1909) and *The Unwritten Law* (1911), a dramatisation of *Crime And Punishment*. Bourchier had an apartment at the top of the theatre with a staircase leading directly to the stage. It is known as the Phantom Staircase because Bourchier's ghost is said

to descend it, sometimes slapping actors on the shoulder in friendly encouragement.

Another husband-and-wife management team, Oscar Asche and Lily Brayton, packed the theatre for the 1911–12 season in which Asche played Falstaff in *The Merry Wives Of Windsor* and Hajj in *Kismet*. Other managements followed in quick succession, and no discernible policy emerged until the 1940s. Between the wars, productions worth mentioning were Austin Page's *By Pigeon Post* (1918), *Cyrano De Bergerac* (1919), Seymour Hicks in *The Man In The Dress Clothes* (1922), Sutton Vane's allegorical drama *Outward Bound* (1923) and Ivor Novello in his own play, *The Rat* (1924). Somerset Maugham preferred to cast Olga Lindo as Sadie Thompson in *Rain* (1925) rather than the more exciting Tallulah Bankhead, who wanted the role. Five years later Tallulah did appear at the Garrick, as another tart with a heart of gold – Marguerite in *The Lady Of The Camellias*.

During a sparse period in the early 1930s, the theatre even resorted to old-time music hall until a play came in which caught the mood of the time, running 391 performances. Walter Greenwood's *Love On The Dole* (1935) dealt with life among unemployed Lancashire cotton workers. It also introduced 23-year-old Wendy Hiller to the London stage, setting her off on a prestigious career. The theatre itself was unemployed from late 1939 until September 1941, when it reopened with a play entitled *Room V* by someone called Peter Wendy. Soon after, some ex-Aldwych farceurs – performers Robertson Hare and Alfred Drayton and writers Vernon Sylvaine and Ben Travers – descended on the Garrick for much of the '40s. In between *Aren't Men Beasts* (1942), *She Follows Me About* (1943) and others, Michael Redgrave was excellent as the timid would-be murderer in *Uncle Harry* (1944), and Beatrice Lillie was hilarious in the revue *Better Late* (1946).

Debonair actor-singer-dancer Jack Buchanan took on the management of the theatre after the war, appearing in Lonsdale's *Canaries Sometimes Sing* (1947) with Coral Browne, and in Vernon Sylvaine's *As Long As They're Happy* (1953). Mainly comedies were presented under Buchanan's distinctive aegis, including Carson Kanin's *Born Yesterday* (1947) with Yolande Donlan, directed by Laurence Olivier; husband and wife Richard Attenborough and Sheila Sim in *To Dorothy A Son* (1951) and Robert Dhéry's French revue, *La Plume De Ma Tante* (1955), which drew mirth-filled audiences for three years. Then came the very English 1958 revue *Living For Pleasure,* starring Dora Bryan, Joan Littlewood's Theatre Workshop production of the Frank Norman/Lionel Bart musical *Fings Ain't Wot They Used To Be* (1960) and the Charles Dyer two-hander *Rattle Of A Simple Man* (1962).

After a closure for redecoration between June 1965 and April 1966, farce re-established itself at the Garrick with the arrival of

Michael Williams and Judi Dench scored another success as Mr and Mrs Pooter in *Mr and Mrs Nobody* (1986), adapted from Grossmith's *Diary of a Nobody*

the garrick

Brian Rix and his team with such plays as *Stand By Your Bedouin*, *Uproar In The House, Let Sleeping Wives Lie, She's Done It Again* and *Don't Just Lie There, Say Something*. Alan Ayckbourn's *Absent Friends* (1975) and Ira Levin's ingenious thriller *Death Trap* (1978) then took the stage briefly before giving way to *No Sex Please, We're British* in 1982, adding another four years to its 11-year run at the Strand. In 1986 the Garrick had great success with Michael Williams and Judi Dench in *Mr and Mrs Nobody* (adapted from George Weedon Grossmith's *Diary of a Nobody*) and later with two Noël Coward plays: *Easy Virtue* (1988) and *The Vortex* (1989) with Rupert Everett. In 1990 the theatre presented short seasons of *Bent*, with Ian McKellen and Frankie Howerd, and in 1991 Brian Friel's acclaimed *Dancing at Lughnasa* transferred from the Phoenix (after the National) for a two-year run. The year 1995 was the start of another very successful run for the Garrick: the Royal National Theatre's production of *An Inspector Calls,* which ran for five years. A second J. B. Priestley classic, *Dangerous Corner*, followed in 2001. In 2002 the Garrick attracted several young Hollywood actors to its stage with an acclaimed production of *This is Our Youth*, US writer Kenneth Lonergan's first play in which Matt Damon, Casey Affleck (brother of Ben) and Summer Phoenix all starred.

the garrick theatre
charing cross road = wc2h

The Gielgud

The noble domed structure that commands the corner of Rupert Street and Shaftesbury Avenue today has been renamed twice in its illustrious history. The theatre was opened in December 1906 as the Hicks Theatre, after actor-manager Seymour Hicks for whom it was built. Thankfully, the name that suggests a theatre for out-of-towners was changed in 1909 to the Globe Theatre. And so it remained until 1994, when it was renamed the Gielgud Theatre, to honour Sir John Gielgud and to ensure that, with the opening of Sam Wanamaker's reconstruction of Shakespeare's theatre in Southwark, there would only be one Globe Theatre in London.

The architect was the omnipresent W. G. R. Sprague, who conceived it as the first of two similar companion theatres, the other being the Queen's on the Wardour Street corner of the block. The classical four-storey facade is decorated with four giant Ionic columns proclaiming the theatre's importance. The auditorium, too, is in grand, even somewhat pretentious style, with bold Corinthian columns framing the boxes. The Louis XVI ornamentation, and further columns, recur throughout the interior. A circular Regency staircase leads to an attractive oval gallery from which patrons can look down on the spacious foyer. Aside from some inevitable refurbishment and slight structural changes, the Gielgud is an extremely well-preserved Edwardian lady.

Seymour Hicks, who would be knighted in 1935, appeared with his wife Ellaline Terriss in the opening production, *The Beauty Of Bath*. (It was a transfer from the Aldwych, the other theatre owned by Hicks, both in association with American impresario Charles Frohman.) Successful early hits at the Gielgud included *Brewster's Millions* (1907), with Gerald du Maurier superb in the title role of the comedy subsequently filmed six

'If the past theatrical decade had to be represented by a single production, this is the one that many good judges would choose.'

— *The Times* on *The Importance of Being Earnest,* 1939

times; George Grossmith and 'Gaiety Girl' Gertie Millar in the Oscar Strauss operetta *A Waltz Dream* (1908); and Henry Ainley and Mrs Patrick Campbell in *His Borrowed Plumes* (1909) by Mrs George Cornwallis-West (the pen name of Lady Randolph Churchill, Winston's American mother). Musical comedies and transfers kept the theatre full until and throughout World War I. In 1917, French music-hall star Gaby Deslys bade farewell to the stage in 'a musical affair' called *Suzette.*

The post-war decade saw the Gielgud under the management of actress Marie Löhr and her producer husband, Anthony Prinsep. Among their achievements were productions of Somerset Maugham's *Love In A Cottage* (1918) and *Our Betters* (1923), A. A. Milne's *The Truth About Blayds* (1921) and *Mr Pim Passes By* (1922), Frederick Lonsdale's *Aren't We All?* (1923) and Noël Coward's *Fallen Angels* (1925), with Tallulah Bankhead and Edna Best as 'those soused sluts' – as one critic called them. On the first night Tallulah, angry with Maugham for not letting her play Sadie Thompson, gazed out of the window and ad-libbed, 'Rain!' It brought the house down. Another funny lady, Jeanne de Casalis, created shock waves by appearing in pyjamas in *Potiphar's Wife* (1927).

Before H. M. Tennant took over the theatre in 1937, the French star Yvonne Arnaud sparkled in J. B. Fagan's *The Improper Duchess* (1931) and in the revival of Fagan's *And So To Bed* (1932). Mlle Arnaud, a favourite with English audiences, had a theatre named after her in Guildford, Surrey in 1965, seven years after her death. In the first year of the Tennant regime, the lovely American actress Ruth Chatterton made her London debut in Maugham's *The Constant Wife*, and Owen Nares and Edith Evans

the gielgud

Gwen ffrancgon-Davies *(left)*, John Gielgud and Edith Evans in the famous 1939 production of *The Importance of Being Earnest*

starred in St John Ervine's *Robert's Wife*. In 1939, John Gielgud directed the classic production of *The Importance Of Being Earnest* with himself as John Worthing, Gwen Ffrangcon-Davies as Gwendolen, Peggy Ashcroft as Cecily and, essaying Lady Bracknell for the first time, Edith Evans in her most popular and famous role. In later years, she began to hate imitations of her celebrated delivery of the line, 'A handbag?' The play was not performed for another ten years. It was a difficult act to follow.

At the beginning of World War II, Evans and Ashcroft, plus Alec Guinness, played in Clemence Dane's *Cousin Muriel* (1940). Plays reflecting the period were Robert Ardrey's anti-isolationist drama *Thunder Rock* (1940) with Michael Redgrave; Robert Sherwood's *The Petrified Forest* (1942), with Owen Nares in his

125

the great theatres of london

last role before his death aged 55; and J. B. Priestley's *They Came To A City* (1943). But it was a comedy, Terence Rattigan's *While The Sun Shines* (1943), that cheered people up for the remainder of the war.

One of the most prestigious of post-war plays at the Gielgud was Christopher Fry's verse drama *The Lady's Not For Burning* (1949). In the cast were Gielgud (who directed), Pamela Brown, Claire Bloom and a youthful Richard Burton. In the role of the drunken tinker was the great Shavian actor Esme Percy, then in his sixties. One night, during his big scene, his glass eye fell out. When a fellow actor stepped forward to pick it up, Percy said, 'Don't step on it, for God's sake. They're so expensive!' The following year Fry's *Ring Round The Moon*, a translation from Jean Anouilh, starred Paul Scofield in the dual role of hero and villain.

Further memorable but contrasting productions took the Gielgud through the '50s: Alec Guinness in *The Prisoner* (1954) and two Graham Greene plays, *The Potting Shed* (1958), with the indefatigable Gielgud, and *The Complaisant Lover* (1959) with Ralph Richardson, Phyllis Calvert and Paul Scofield. The latter returned a year later in his most celebrated role as Sir Thomas More in Robert Bolt's *A Man For All Seasons*.

Comedies were the staple fare in the '70s and early '80s. These included Maggie Smith and Kenneth Williams in Peter Shaffer's *The Private Ear And The Public Eye* (1962), Donald Sinden in *There's A Girl In My Soup* (1966), Tom Courtenay in Alan Ayckbourn's ingenious trilogy, *The Norman Conquests* (1974), Vanessa Redgrave in Coward's *Design For Living* (1982) and a three-year run of Andrew Lloyd Webber's production of the schoolgirl romp *Daisy Pulls It Off* (1983). In 1987 the Gielgud returned to drama with Glenda Jackson and Joan Plowright leading a cast directed by Spain's Nuria Espert in Lorca's *The House Of Bernarda Alba*.

Since then the Gielgud has presented the premiere performance of Peter Hall's brilliant production of Wilde's *An Ideal Husband* (1992), Ayckbourn's *Communicating Doors* (1995), the con-

The award-winning production of Lorca's *The House of Bernada Alba* boasted magnificent sets and lighting by Ezio Frigerio

troversial *Shopping and F***ing* by Mark Ravenhill (1997), as well as Vanessa and Corin Redgrave in Noël Coward's last play, *Song at Twilight* (1999). The Gielgud entered the new millennium in great form with an enormously successful run of *The Graduate* starring, successively, Kathleen Turner, Jerry Hall, Amanda Donohoe, Anne Archer and Linda Gray, and in 2002 *Humble Boy*, with Felicity Kendal, transferred from the Royal National Theatre. The theatre that bears the name of one of Britain's greatest stage actors has good reason to be proud of itself.

the gielgud theatre
shaftesbury avenue = wlv

The Theatre Royal Haymarket

There is no theatre that has more epitomised London playgoing for almost three centuries than the stately Haymarket. Only three London theatres are listed Grade 1 under the 1971 Act on the preservation of buildings of great architectural or historic importance, prohibiting rebuilding or demolition: the Haymarket; the Royal Opera House; and Drury Lane. Of these three national monuments, the Haymarket is the only one where 'straight' plays can be seen, the others being given over exclusively to musicals, opera and ballet. Its graceful John Nash portico, its opulent, well-preserved interior, the premieres of plays by Oscar Wilde, seasons given by theatrical knights and a string of glittering all-star productions have made the Haymarket a byword for elegance and sophistication.

However, this most traditional of West End theatres had a rebellious youth. The first playhouse on the site, just adjoining the present structure, was built without licence or patent in 1720 by a carpenter named John Potter, and called the Little Theatre in the Haymarket. Defying the monopoly which forbade the acting of 'legitimate' drama other than at Drury Lane or Covent Garden, Henry Fielding produced his satire on heroic drama, *Tom Thumb The Great*, here in 1730. Further satires by Fielding attacking both political parties and caricaturing the Royal Family, resulted in the passing of the infamous Licensing Act of 1737, which reinforced the monopoly of the patent theatres and led to the official agency under the Lord Chamberlain for the censoring of all plays. This ended Fielding's career as a dramatist and turned him towards writing novels.

'Mr Oscar Wilde's new play at the Haymarket is a dangerous subject because he has the property of making his critics dull.'

— George Bernard Shaw on *An Ideal Husband*, 1895

When the actor Samuel Foote took over the theatre, he successfully evaded the law by inviting his friends to partake of cups of chocolate with him, and including entertainment in the occasion. In 1766, Foote was thrown during an attempt to ride the Duke of York's unmanageable horse, a result of a practical joke. His leg had to be amputated and the Duke, as compensation, managed to obtain a licence for Foote to perform drama in the summer months when the other two theatres were closed. Thus did London acquire a third Theatre Royal. Foote sold the theatre to George Colman, who carried it into a prosperous period before handing over to his son. Many plays by Colman the Elder and Colman the Younger were performed during their time here, which was marked by two violent incidents. In 1794, at a Royal Command performance, the crowd was so great that 20 people were trampled to death; then, in 1805, hundreds of tailors gathered to protest at a revival of Foote's satire *The Tailors*, which they saw as an offence to their craft. The riot was quelled by troops.

The Little Theatre was closed for a while when Colman the Younger was imprisoned for debt. His brother-in-law David Morris, who took control, left the old building and built the present edifice a little to the south of it. John Nash, one of the principal exponents of nineteenth-century town planning, designed the theatre in 1821 so that its Corinthian portico could be seen from St James Square. The theatre was described by a contemporary as 'in point of architectural beauty the most elegant in London, but for the convenience of seeing and hearing the worst contrived'. This apparently unpleasant auditorium was completely replaced in 1879 when Squire and Mary Bancroft took possession. The changes made were radical. The Bankcrofts created the first picture-frame stage by placing it entirely behind a proscenium arch. This was highlighted by a thick gold painted border. They did away with the pit (the cheap seats near the front) replacing them with the higher-priced orchestra stalls, which caused a riot on the first night. Clearly, audiences were far more vociferous then.

In 1905, the interior was replaced again by that which can still be admired today – a large house of 906 seats in a rich and elaborate Louis XVI style conceived by C. Stanley Peach. Some improvements were made in 1939, including a large and attractive lounge bar which was constructed under the stalls. In 1994 the theatre was completely refurbished inside at a cost of £2.3 million. Joseph Harker's ceiling was restored, the two thousand lead crystals in the central chandelier were cleaned and twenty gilders were employed to work for three months and used over 5,000 books of gold leaf! More recently, and with great difficulty, the theatre has installed an air-conditioning system. Nothing, however, has disturbed its slightly staid, old-world charm.

The great actor-managers of the Haymarket in the nineteenth century were Benjamin Webster (1837–53), J. B. Buckstone (1853–78), whose ghost is said to haunt the theatre, and the Bancrofts (1800–85). Under these three regimes, the Haymarket became the foremost playhouse in London. Famous actors who appeared here were Samuel Phelps in the 1830s as Shylock, Hamlet, Othello and Richard III; William Macready in *Money* (1840); Barry Sullivan as Hamlet (1853); the American Edwin Booth as Shylock (1861), and Edward Sothern repeating his New York triumph as Lord Dundreary in Tom Taylor's *Our American Cousin* (1861). His portrayal of the imbecile lord was so popular that the long side-whiskers he wore became known as 'dundrearies'. Sothern also created the title role in Tom Robertson's *David Garrick* (1864).

In 1887, the theatre passed into the hands of Herbert Beerbohm Tree. His most resounding success was *Trilby* (1895) with himself as Svengali, the profits of which enabled him to build Her Majesty's Theatre just opposite. However, Tree's *Hamlet* of 1892 was a failure, giving rise to Oscar Wilde's comment, 'My dear Herbert, good is not the word.' But when the famous actor-manager produced and played Lord Illingworth in Wilde's *A Woman Of No Importance* (1893), Oscar commented, 'A charming fellow, and so clever: he models himself on me.' On the first night, Wilde arranged the house carefully, placing peeresses next to poets, dowagers beside young men and his wife Constance in a box with Lord Alfred Douglas. There was a slight problem when the Prince of Wales refused to share the Royal Box with his mistress Lillie Langtry. (She had

made her debut at the Haymarket in 1881.) It was on the same night at the Haymarket that a blackmailer caught Wilde at the stage door and offered him, for ten pounds, the original of a love letter the playwright had addressed to him. 'Ten pounds!' cried Oscar. 'You have no appreciation of literature. If you had asked me for fifty pounds, I might have given it to you.' In 1886 another Wilde play, *An Ideal Husband*, had its premiere at the Haymarket. This same play returned to the theatre exactly one hundred years later in a highly acclaimed

Lillie Langtry, mistress to the Prince of Wales, makes her debut at the Haymarket

production directed by Peter Hall, with Martin Shaw as Lord Goring.

After Tree planted himself at his new theatre in 1896, Frederick Harrison and Cyril Maude became the managers, sustaining and extending the tradition of fine plays, casts and settings. Maude gave outstanding performances in J. M. Barrie's *The Little Minister* (1897), Sheridan's *The Rivals* and *School For Scandal* (both 1900); and George Colman the Elder's *The Clandestine Marriage* (1903). Other important productions until the death of Harrison in 1926 (Maude had left in 1905) were Maeterlinck's *The Blue Bird* (1910); the first licensed performance of Ibsen's *Ghosts* (1914), which caused a storm of protest; and Barrie's play of the supernatural, *Mary Rose* (1920).

The highlight of the war years was John Gielgud's repertory season of 1944–45. The plays chosen were *Hamlet, A Midsummer Night's Dream*, Congreve's *Love For Love*, Webster's *The Duchess Of Malfi* and Somerset Maugham's *The Circle*. Gielgud featured in all five plays, while Peggy Ashcroft played Ophelia to his Hamlet and Titania to his Oberon. At the war's end, the sequence of civilised entertainments continued unabated, with the American actress Helen Hayes making her London debut as the mother in Tennessee Williams's *The Glass Menagerie* (1948); Ralph Richardson and Peggy Ashcroft in *The Heiress* (1949); Gielgud in N. C. Hunter's *A Day By The Sea* (1953); and Noël Coward and Margaret Leighton in Shaw's *The Apple Cart* (1954), considered by many to be the finest production of the play.

The Haymarket continued to skim the cream of England's acting establishment: Edith Evans and Peggy Ashcroft appeared in Enid Bagnold's *The Chalk Garden* (1956), and Ralph Richardson in *School For Scandal* (1962), *The Rivals* (1966) and *The Merchant Of Venice* (1967); Alec Guinness was T. E. Lawrence in Terence Rattigan's *Ross* (1960), Trevor Howard starred in Anouilh's *The Waltz Of The Toreadors* (1974), and Maggie Smith triumphed in *The Way Of The World* (1984). In the '80s Hollywood came to the Haymarket in the shape of

Rex Harrison and Diana Rigg headed the cast in a glittering production of Shaw's *Heartbreak House* (1983)

Claudette Colbert in *Aren't We All?* and Christopher Reeve in *The Aspern Papers* (both 1984), Lauren Bacall in *Sweet Bird Of Youth*, Liv Ullmann in Harold Pinter's *Old Times* (both 1985), and, most notably, Jack Lemmon – supreme in Jonathan Miller's quick-fire and powerful production of *Long Day's Journey Into Night* (1986). The '90s saw Robert Lindsay as Cyrano de Bergerac, in a performance celebrating the Queen's 40-year reign, in the presence of Her Majesty (1992), the award-winning *Arcadia* by Tom Stoppard (1994) and *A Streetcar Named Desire*, directed by Peter Hall and starring Jessica Lange (1997). The theatre entered the new millennium in fine form with Helen Mirren in Donald Marguiles's *Collected Stories*, and 2002's highly acclaimed production of *The Royal Family*, starring Dame Judi Dench.

In 1998 the theatre set up 'Masterclass', a charitable trust

Vanessa Redgrave and Joely Richardson in Oscar Wilde's *Lady Windermere's Fan*

providing free theatrical classes and workshops for young people. 'Masters' have included Jeremy Irons, Maureen Lipman and Alan Rickman. Other important developments are 2001's initiative, 'Theatre Royal Haymarket Productions', which aims to create more productions for what has been simply a receiving house, and the appointment of Sir Peter Hall as Advisory Director. All in all, the Theatre Royal, Haymarket has a very noble 282-year history.

the theatre royal, haymarket
haymarket = sw17

Her Majesty's Theatre

'**M**y beautiful, beautiful theatre,' is what Herbert Beerbohm Tree always called Her Majesty's... and with some justification! Today, we can still see this grand old playhouse more or less as the great Victorian actor-manager saw it. However, until the early 1960s its proud dome seemed much higher, for now it is dwarfed by the towering New Zealand House where the Carlton Hotel once stood. The theatre and the hotel were conceived by Charles Phipps in 1897 as an integral architectural unit, facing the Theatre Royal, Haymarket across the street. Of Phipps's theatre interior, still virtually intact, George Bernard Shaw wrote, 'He has had the good sense – a very rare quality in England where artistic matters are in question – to see that a theatre which is panelled, and mirrored, and mantel-pieced like the first-class saloon of a Peninsula and Oriental liner or a Pullman drawing room car, is no place for *Julius Caesar*; or indeed for anything except tailor-made drama and farcical comedy.' In fact, it is luxurious but restrained, inspired by, but not attempting to equal, the classical forms of Ange-Jacques Gabriel's opera house at Versailles. It has similar triple tiers of boxes, framed by marble Corinthian columns with rich entablatures, a decorated proscenium arch and pretty eighteenth-century style paintings on the ceiling.

From 1992 to 1994 the building was completely refurbished – including the replacement of a roof – without losing one performance of *The Phantom of the Opera*.

This consistently successful and attractive theatre has had three predecessors on the same site and five different names. The

'Tree took unofficial but characteristic action by making Her Majesty's serve some of the functions of a National theatre.'

— George Rowell

first playhouse was built by the celebrated dramatist-architect Sir John Vanbrugh in 1705 and named the Queen's Theatre. It was destroyed by fire in 1789 and rebuilt as the King's Theatre in 1791. It became Her Majesty's in 1837 before being burnt to the ground 30 years later. It re-emerged from the ashes in 1877 as the Italian Opera House, and was demolished in 1891 to give way to the present building. This edifice, in the French Renaissance style with an open loggia, was called His Majesty's from 1902 to the accession of Elizabeth II in 1952. But under whatever name, it has made its mark on theatrical history.

It is highly appropriate that the present-day hit musical, Andrew Lloyd Webber's incredibly successful *The Phantom Of The Opera*, should be housed in a theatre whose origins were mainly as an opera house. On this spot was performed Handel's first opera for England, *Rinaldo* (1711), followed by a number of others by the German master who became an English citizen in 1726. There were also English premieres here of Mozart's *La Clemenza Di Tito* (1806), *Cosi Fan Tutte*, *The Magic Flute* (both 1811), *The Marriage Of Figaro* (1812) and *Don Giovanni* (1817); Beethoven's sole opera, *Fidelio* (1832); Gounod's *Faust* (1863); and Bizet's *Carmen* (1878). 'Swedish Nightingale' Jenny Lind made a sensational London debut in 1847 in *Norma* and other operas, and the first complete performance of Wagner's Ring cycle was given at Her Majesty's in 1882. The venue only became a straight theatre in its fourth incarnation.

Under Beerbohm Tree, Her (His) Majesty's was one of the most distinguished playhouses in Europe. He carried on the Irving tradition of sumptuous, romantic productions of Shakespeare using many visual effects. The playwright Ben Travers described the realism of some of the productions: 'In *A Midsummer Night's Dream* he introduced live rabbits. In *Julius Caesar* the actor who played Caesar was made to wear a bladder of ox blood under his toga so that when he was stabbed he bled profusely.' When Tree produced *Macbeth*, he recruited 50 real guardsmen for the battle scene. They used such force that during a dress rehearsal Tree cried, 'Stop. Never hit a backcloth when it's down.'

Between 1888 and 1914, Sir Herbert Beerbohm Tree (he was knighted in 1909) staged 18 of Shakespeare's plays, as well as melodramatic adaptations of *Oliver Twist* (1905), *David Copperfield* (1914), *Faust* (1908) and the first production of Shaw's *Pygmalion* (1914). The story goes that Tree, as Professor Higgins, kept fluffing his lines on the first night. When Shaw asked him to learn them better, Tree replied, 'But I do know my lines. I do!' – to which the playwright responded, 'Oh, I don't

The renowned Herbert Beerbohm Tree in tragic mode

dispute that for a moment, Sir Herbert. I willingly concede that you do know your lines. But you certainly don't know mine.' Nevertheless, *Pygmalion* was Shaw's greatest commercial success, with Tree and Mrs Patrick Campbell's Eliza winning accolades.

In 1904, Sir Herbert instigated a drama school, which eventually became the Royal Academy of Dramatic Art, in rooms in the dome of the theatre. It was moved a year later to its present home in Gower Street. Sir Herbert's wife, Helen Maud Holt, shared his reign at Her Majesty's, and played in most of the productions. (In 1933, aged 70, Lady Tree returned to this theatre in *The Merry Wives Of Windsor*.) Her husband not only ran the theatre, acted and produced, but found time to have three daughters by his wife and six children by his mistress Beatrice May Pinney-Reed, one of whom was the film director Carol Reed. A busy man indeed! This colourful character died in 1917 aged 64. On the corner of the theatre in Charles II Street, there is a bronze tablet commemorating his contribution to the reputation of Her Majesty's.

The phenomenal success of *The Phantom of the Opera*, which has been running since 1986, was foreshadowed by Oscar Asche and Frederick Norton's 'Musical Tale of the East', *Chu Chin Chow*, which occupied the theatre from 1916 to 1921, the longest known run before *The Mousetrap*. It was, according to theatre writer Lynton Hudson, 'a cunning mixture of music, stage realism, and art pantomime, its constantly refurbished "Folies-Bergerian" mannequin parade in frocks remarkable for their bizarre and gorgeous colour schemes'. It made a deep and lasting impression on the 12-year-old John Gielgud who saw it over ten times. 'I was overwhelmed by the production, which fulfilled my most cherished pictorial enthusiasms,' he wrote. The oriental theme was continued in *Cairo* (1921), Somerset Maugham's *East Of Suez* (1922) and James Elroy Flecker's *Hassan* (1923) with incidental music by Frederic Delius.

C. B. Cochran, who produced Noël Coward's operetta, *Bitter Sweet* (1929), was told, 'It has no comedy, and the hero is killed at the end of the second act.' The fashionable first night audience were, according to Coward, 'as responsive as so many cornflour blancmanges'. There was, however, much cheering at the end, mainly due to Cochran applauding and shouting 'Author!', and Noël in the gods, crying 'Cochran!' The show, containing the ravishing 'I'll See You Again' which was composed in a taxi during a long traffic jam, ran two years.

Further illustrious evenings at Her Majesty's offered J. B. Priestley's *The Good Companions* (1931) with John Gielgud as Inigo Jollifant; the legendary music hall comedian George Robey displaying his versatility as Falstaff in *Henry IV Part 1* (1935); Ivor Novello and Vivien Leigh in Clemence Dane's version of *The Happy Hypocrite* (1936), originally a one-act play by Sir

Andrew Lloyd Webber's musical *Phantom of the Opera* opened in October 1986 and became one of the biggest commercial successes the West End has ever seen

her majesty's

Herbert's half-brother Max Beerbohm; and J. M. Barrie's final play, *The Boy David* (1936), written for and performed by Elisabeth Bergner. The war years saw mainly revivals of popular musical comedies before plays returned in 1947 with Peggy Ashcroft and Robert Morley in the latter's play, *Edward My Son*. Two Broadway hits, *The Tea House Of The August Moon* (1954) and *No Time For Sergeants* (1956), were among the few other plays to interrupt the string of musicals that so often filled the 1,261 seats of the theatre.

Alan Jay Lerner and Frederick Loewe's *Brigadoon* (1949) and *Paint Your Wagon* (1953) preceded Leonard Bernstein's landmark musical *West Side Story* (1958), which ran over two years. Also hailing from Broadway were *Bye Bye Birdie* (1961), *Fiddler On The Roof* (1967), starring Topol as Tevye the milkman and running 2,030 performances, *Company, Applause* (both 1972), *Bubbling Brown Sugar* (1980) and the return of *West Side Story* (1984). But now it is the home-grown *Phantom Of The Opera* that continues to attract vast crowds to Her Majesty's. Produced by Cameron Mackintosh, the original cast was led by Michael Crawford and Sarah Brightman. It is the longest-running, most successful production in the theatre's history.

Sir Herbert Beerbohm Tree always disliked long runs, referring to them as 'obstinate successes'. But with *Phantom of the Opera* still playing to capacity audiences, perhaps Her Majesty's present owners, Lord Lloyd Webber's Really Useful Group, might disagree!

her majesty's theatre
haymarket = swly

The Lyceum

On Wellington Street, which runs between Covent Garden and the Strand, stands a magnificent portico. This is the Lyceum – 'The Crown Jewel of the Strand' as it was known in its Victorian heyday. The Lyceum has a truly remarkable history characterised by constant struggle, innovation and transformation. It's amazing that this gutsy theatre has survived into the twenty-first century – so many times has it risen from the ashes (quite literally, on a couple of occasions!).

It all started in July 1771, when the foundation for the very first building was laid in the Strand on part of the gardens of Exeter House. This first theatre was designed by James Payne, and was situated about 100 yards from its present site. It opened in May 1772, and spent its first 30 years as home to an amazing variety of entertainments – as an exhibition hall, for boxing, fencing, concerts, lectures, public debates, travelling curiosities (such as 'Mr Diller and his Philosophical Fireworks'), panorama and phantasmagoria. In 1802, Madame Tussaud held her first waxwork show here.

Then came the first of the fires that was to transform the theatre's history. In 1809 the Theatre Royal, Drury Lane burned down, and the Drury Lane Company arranged to play at the Lyceum until its theatre was rebuilt. This stroke of fate allowed the Lyceum to obtain a proper licence from the Lord Chamberlain for the presentation of plays. When the Drury Lane Company moved back to its new theatre in 1812, the Lyceum held onto this licence for the summer months.

It was decided that this new status required a 'proper' auditorium and in 1815 Samuel Beazley, who was also the architect of the St James Theatre, the colonnade at Drury Lane and London Bridge Station, completely rebuilt the theatre on a scale of great magnificence.

'It became almost a religion to attend the Lyceum, the theatre which had become a temple and a meeting place for the people and the intellectuals alike.'
— J. B. Booth

The history of the Lyceum contains many 'firsts'. It was the first theatre to be lit by gas; the first, in 1817, to experiment at reduced prices with two performances nightly – one at 6.00 p.m., and one at 9.30 p.m; and the first theatre in London to present a one-man show, starring Edmund Kean. However, despite these innovations, the theatre suffered under the licensing laws, which prevented so-called 'minor' theatres from staging drama without a musical interlude. It still managed to play host to Grimaldi, and presented the first performances in England of Weber's *Der Freishutz* in 1824 and Mozart's *Cosi Fan Tutti* in 1828, as well as some Shakespeare.

Fire struck again in 1830, when the theatre, and a large section of Exeter Street, was burnt down. Once again, Samuel Beazley designed a new theatre, which opened its doors on 4 July 1834. It was built slightly to the west of the old building, with the wonderful portico facing the newly created Wellington Street. The new Lyceum was the first theatre in England to incorporate a balcony which projected over the circle and also offered the facility for booking seats in advance. But it wasn't until 1843, when the Licensing Act finally freed all 'minor' theatres from the restrictions which had previously bound them, that the Lyceum was able to get properly into its stride. There were various changes of management for the next 13 years, and the theatre had some successes with burlesques and plays.

In 1856, fire intervened for the third time. Covent Garden went up in flames, and for a while the Lyceum offered the Opera a home, at the time when Adelaide Ristori was enchanting London with his Italian opera.

Innovative director/designer Julie Taymor used masks, puppetry and dramatic designs in her highly original stage version of Disney's *The Lion King*

However, the Lyceum still wasn't having the consistent successes that it needed. And then, in 1871, came the most momentous event in the Lyceum's history. Hezekiah Bateman took over the theatre's management and was persuaded by actor Henry Irving to stage *The Bells*. Irving as Mathias played to overflowing houses for 150 nights (this when 40 to 50 performances was considered a good run). Next year Irving

147

starred in *Charles I*, which ran for 180 nights. By 1878 the actor had taken over the theatre's management. Together with the legendary Ellen Terry, his leading lady, he turned the Lyceum into the most brilliant playhouse in London. Irving's incredible charisma and talent attracted the very best actors, musicians and designers of the time to the Lyceum. All become part of its incredible success. And the public, of every class, came in droves. Irving was knighted in 1895, the first such honour bestowed on an actor.

Sir Henry Irving remained in charge until 1899, presenting one success after another. And then fire intervened again – this time in the theatre's scenery store – destroying almost all of the Lyceum's assets. In the end Irving was forced to sell his control of the theatre to a syndicate. His last appearance at the Lyceum was in 1902, with Ellen Terry at his side, as Shylock in *The Merchant of Venice*. He died shortly after, in 1905.

It was the end of a glorious era, and the Lyceum came very close to being demolished when a new purchaser could not be found. However, it rose again as a music hall, rebuilt by J. Parkinson and designed by Bertie Crewe (Crewe also designed the Phoenix, Piccadilly, Shaftesbury and Saville Theatres). In March 1907 the Lyceum was licensed as a theatre again, and ran successfully for 30 or so years, producing 'popular drama at popular prices' – mostly melodramas and spectacular pantomimes. The annual pantomime became a highly popular star-studded feature, with Ninette de Valois as the *premiere danseuse*. But by 1939 the theatre was struggling again, and was due for demolition to make way for a roundabout. The theatre's final production was *Hamlet*, directed by Ellen Terry's great-nephew, Sir John Gielgud, in June 1939. As the curtain went down, Gielgud proclaimed, 'Long live the Lyceum! Long live Ellen Terry! Long live Henry Irving!'

The intervention of the Second World War saved the Lyceum again – the proposed roundabout was forgotten about. The theatre briefly returned to drama in 1963, with the pantomime *Pinocchio*, but the '60s, '70s and '80s were decades of TV events

the lyceum

and live music – The Who, Bob Marley, The Clash, Iggy Pop and The Kinks all performed here. In 1985 The National Theatre's *The Mysteries* transferred to the Lyceum. At this time, the theatre was described in the *Daily Telegraph* as a 'luscious old playhouse – fluted Tuscan pillars, curved outswelling boxes, plaster figures of maidens and gods, and everywhere balustrades, urns, wrought iron, escutcheons, gilt and Pompeian red – all the long neglect of its Victorian heyday. Everyone asks why can't it all be restored?'

This question remained unanswered until 1994, when the theatre was bought by Apollo Leisure, who restored it to its former opulent glory and introduced state-of-the-art facilities. A triumphant revival of Andrew Lloyd Webber and Tim Rice's *Jesus Christ Superstar* followed, and in 1999 Disney's smash-hit musical *The Lion King*.

The applause that used to greet Sir Henry Irving as he stepped on to the Lyceum's stage was known as the 'Lyceum Roar'. With the successful Lion King in residence, this roar is resounding again. Long live the Lyceum!

the lyceum theatre
wellington street = wc2

The Lyric, Hammersmith

O nce upon a time, an exquisite late Victorian playhouse was designed by Frank Matcham, the most renowned and prolific theatre architect of his day, for the London suburb of Hammersmith. It soon became prosperous and fashionable, despite its remote location, drawing crowds from the West End. The Lyric was, according to one expert, 'one of the best examples of *fin-de-siecle* theatre interiors in greater London – one designed by a master of the art of theatre building'. In 1972, despite public outrage, the theatre was razed to the ground to make room for property development. But the story has a happy ending.

Before the bulldozers could do their destructive work, the Greater London Council ordered that most of the plasterwork of the auditorium be preserved and stored. In 1974, the Hammersmith Council approved plans for a new theatre to be built as part of a modern development in King Street, not far from where the original Lyric stood. This was not to be just another theatre but a complete reconstruction of Matcham's interior, using some of the original decor. The result is a curious but rewarding architectural experience.

The commonplace 1979 building which houses the theatre is located in a mundane suburban shopping centre. At the top of a stairway, one finds a roomy lounge, bar, self-service restaurant and large sun-terrace or patio. Airy and relaxed, the venue provides a pleasant meeting place for people of the area by day and for playgoers by night. Up another flight of stairs and one enters a time warp. There it is: the Lyric Opera House of 1895 with only slight

(*above*) Leading London architect Rick Mather's designs for the Lyric's new front door (2003), restoring the theatre's entrance to its rightful place in the heart of Hammersmith

'The Lyric at Hammersmith... was uncomfortable and smelly, the dressing rooms were wretched, but it had a unique atmosphere.'
— Sir John Gielgud

alterations. The obtrusive pillars have been removed from the stalls and the decorated ceiling has been adapted to incorporate contemporary stage lighting and ventilation. The rococo ornamentation on the boxes and two circles has been retained. The traditional masks of Comedy and Tragedy adorn each side of the slightly enlarged proscenium arch.

Comedy and tragedy have played equal roles during the vicissitudes of the theatre's history. The first structure in Bradmore Grove, known as the Lyric Hall, opened in November 1888 with a French marionette show. Two years later, after reconstruction, it became the Lyric Opera House. In 1895,

A sketch of the period shows the original Frank Matcham exterior of what was then called the Lyric Opera House

the lyric, hammersmith

Matcham was commissioned to redesign the building completely. The tireless new manager, John M. East, produced over 400 shows, acted 120 roles, wrote the spectacular annual pantomimes and invited stars like Lillie Langtry and George Arliss to perform here. Alas, when East left in 1904, the theatre's fortunes plummeted, gaining it the sobriquet of the 'Blood and Flea Pit'. This decline was mainly due to a policy of presenting musty melodramas and the rivalry of the new King's Theatre (designed by W. G. R. Sprague and demolished in 1963) nearby.

In 1918, rescued by Nigel Playfair who redecorated it and changed its name to the Lyric Theatre, it became one of London's most popular and exciting playhouses. A poem of the day went:

No greater name than Nigel Playfair
Occurs in Thespian lore or myth;
'Twas he who first revealed to Mayfair
The whereabouts of Hammersmith.

Many celebrated productions and performers lit up the Playfair years. His first success was John Drinkwater's chronicle play *Abraham Lincoln* (1919), which ran for a year. Athene Seyler and Herbert Marshall starred in *As You Like It* (1920) before the three and a half years of *The Beggar's Opera* (1921), which Gielgud found 'enchantingly pretty, too pretty perhaps, as the squalid satire of the play was lost... But how wonderfully he did it!' Gielgud himself appeared for Playfair here in *The Cherry Orchard* (1925) and as John Worthing in the 1930 Aubrey Beardsley-inspired black-and-white production of *The Importance Of Being Earnest*, opposite his aunt, Mabel Terry-Lewis, as Lady Bracknell. The later and most famous of all Lady Bracknells, Edith Evans, created a sensation as Millamant in Congreve's *The Way Of The World*. She also appeared in *The Beaux Stratagem* (1927) and *The Old Bachelor* (1931). Sir Nigel (he was knighted in 1928) had a penchant for the eighteenth century and revived Isaac Bickerstaff's comic operas *Lionel And Clarissa* (1925) and *Love In A Village* (1928) as authentically as he could. There is a Sickert portrait of Playfair as an over-age Tony Lumpkin in the present Stalls Foyer.

When Nigel Playfair left the Lyric in 1932, brightness left with him. In fact, it was literally dark for most of the period until after the war. Then, once again, playgoers made their way to Hammersmith for exciting productions. Two young actors returned from active service made an impact – Alec Guinness in his own adaptation of *The Brothers Karamazov* (1946) and Richard Burton in Christopher Fry's *The Boy With The Cart* (1950). John Gielgud directed the latter prior to his stunning 1952–53 season of three plays. Gielgud directed Paul Scofield in *Richard II* and *The Way Of The World* with himself as Mirabell, Pamela Brown as Millamant and Margaret Rutherford as Lady Wishfort. The third play was a rare revival of Thomas Otway's Restoration tragedy, *Venice Preserv'd*, directed by a young Peter Brook and starring Scofield and Gielgud.

The Lyric continued to stage diverse and interesting plays for the rest of the decade. Sir Donald Wolfit took on the arduous task of producing and starring in Henri de Montherlant's uncompromising *The Master Of Santiago* and *Malatesta* (both 1957). Challenging, too, were Harold Pinter's first play, *The Birthday Party* (1958), and Ibsen's early work *Brand* (1959). Sandy Wilson's 'high camp' musical, *Valmouth* (1959), was delightfully frivolous and a smash hit.

The internationally acclaimed *Shockheaded Peter*

On 18 October, 1979, the Queen officially opened the newly resurrected Lyric. The premiere production, Shaw's *You Never Can Tell*, continued the great tradition of the theatre's previous life. The theatre, which is funded by the Arts Council, has a flexible 110-seat studio underneath the main auditorium and offers lunchtime music, art exhibitions and children's matinees. Among its productions that have transferred to the West End – a sure sign of acclaim – have been Michael Frayn's *Make And Break* and *Noises Off*, *Charley's Aunt*, *Miss Julie*, *Kean* and *The Seagull*. Under the current management, the Lyric has regained its place as a true London original. The boldly programmed repertoire mixes sharp classical revivals with theatrically innovative contemporary work, and attracts a notably young and varied audience. Recent successes have included plays by Marivaux, Kleist and Maugham, the internationally acclaimed *Shockheaded Peter* and a string of strikingly designed Christmas shows, giving a new twist to the theatre's distinguished history.

**the lyric, hammersmith
king street = w6**

The Lyric, Shaftesbury Avenue

The Lyric, the oldest of the six surviving theatres in Shaftesbury Avenue, blends into a block of buildings in the Renaissance style that stretches from Rupert Street to Great Windmill Street, with only its canopy and sign betraying its function as a theatre. However, the C. J. Phipps interior, redecorated extensively but tastefully in 1932 by Michel Rosenauer, dispenses the charm and atmosphere of a late Victorian playhouse. Giant Corinthian columns frame the boxes, attractive plasterwork decorates the large arch over the proscenium and a handsome pale green and gold circular ceiling encloses the auditorium.

It was built for Henry Leslie, who made a fortune out of the comic opera *Dorothy* by B. C. Stephenson and Alfred Cellier at the Prince of Wales Theatre. Its eight hundred and seventeenth performance opened the Lyric in December 1888. *Doris*, by the same authors, followed in 1889. As befitting the theatre's name, operettas were the principal fare into the 1920s. Many of the early ones featured Marie Tempest, who only forsook singing for straight acting in 1899. W. S. Gilbert, who had quarrelled with Arthur Sullivan, delivered *The Mountebanks* (1892), music by Cellier, and *His Excellency* (1894), music by F. Osmond Carr.

The legitimate drama was strongly represented by the great Italian actress Eleonora Duse, making her debut in England in *La*

'It is fortunate that Phipps's interior (although altered) was not then completely devastated for the sake of fashion.'

— John Earl, *Curtains!!!*

Dame Aux Camellias, *Fédora* and *A Doll's House* in 1893. La Duse refused to wear make-up, and was able to blush or pale at will. Three years later, a play with a religious theme brought people to the Lyric who had never before entered a theatre. It was *The Sign Of The Cross* by Wilson Barrett, who himself played the Roman patrician converted to Christianity by his love for a Christian girl. Barrett claimed in private that he was a believer only as far as the box-office was concerned, and continued to present plays of a similar nature, making him the forerunner of Cecil B. De Mille who filmed *The Sign Of The Cross* in 1932.

Not long after Duse appeared here, two of the greatest French actresses arrived in seasons of French plays – Rejane in 1897 and Sarah Bernhardt in 1898. Loïe Fuller danced through nearly 200 performances of *Little Miss Nobody* (1898), and Evie Greene in *Florodoro* (1899) saw the theatre move profitably into the new century. In 1902 Forbes Robertson, considered the greatest Hamlet of his time, repeated the role (he was to play it into his 60s), also taking on Othello and Kipling's *The Light That Failed*. His Desdemona in the former was Gertrude Elliott,

The programme cover for the opening hit, *Dorothy*, in 1888

whom he later married despite his affair with Mrs Patrick Campbell. Lewis Waller, known as 'the high priest of dignified tushery' appeared between 1906 and 1910 in *Othello, Monsieur Beaucaire, Robin Hood, Henry V* and *The Rivals.*

Musical entertainments such as Oscar Strauss's *The Chocolate Soldier* (1910), *The Girl In the Taxi* (1912), *Love And Laughter* (1913) and *Mam'selle Tralala* (1914), the latter three with Yvonne Arnaud, led up to the wartime hit *Romance* (1915) starring Doris Keane. In 1919, she went on to play the female lead in *Romeo And Juliet* with the septuagenarian Ellen Terry as the Nurse. John Gielgud, Terry's grand-nephew, recalled, 'She could hardly remember a word, and Basil Sydney and Leon Quartermaine, who were playing Romeo and Mercutio respectively, whispered every line in her ear, and then she said the line herself and it sounded as if she had just thought of it.'

It was back to musical comedy with *Lilac Time* (1922) and *The Street Singer* (1924) before Tallulah Bankhead, the darling of the 'bright young things', drew the crowds in *The Gold Diggers* (1926), *Garden Of Eden* (1927), *Her Cardboard Lover* (1928) and *Let Us Be Gay* (1929). A dazzling sequence of stars and productions epitomising the best in commercial theatre followed: Leslie Howard (just prior to his Hollywood debut) in *Berkeley Square* (1929); J. B. Priestley's ingenious *Dangerous Corner* (1932); Robert Sherwood's high comedy *Reunion In Vienna* with Alfred Lunt and Lynn Fontanne (later replaced by Noël Coward and Yvonne Printemps) in 1934, as well as Edna Ferber and George S. Kaufman's *Theatre Royal* (the English title of *The Royal Family*), which starred Madge Titheradge, Marie Tempest and Laurence Olivier, directed by Coward. Olivier, playing a flamboyant character based on John Barrymore, slipped and fractured two ankle bones while jumping over a banister rail.

Olivier returned with his friend Ralph Richardson in Priestley's 'farcical tragedy', *Bees On The Boatdeck* (1936), which sank after four weeks. Vivien Leigh came to a matinee with Ivor Novello and sat prominently in a box, making Olivier upstage everyone in order to impress the woman he loved. Many years later Leigh herself (now Olivier's wife) held the stage at the Lyric in Coward's *South Sea Bubble* (1956). Critic Harold Hobson wrote, 'Vivien Leigh is the splendour of the production. Her performance shines like the stars, and is as troubling as the inconstant moon.' When she left the cast to have a baby (she subsequently miscarried), the play lost money.

Plays that had good runs without a dependence on big names were Rattigan's *The Winslow Boy* (1946), *The Little Hut* (1950) and the musicals *Grab Me A Gondola* (1956), *Irma La Douce* (1958) and *Robert and Elizabeth* (1964). However, stars such as the Lunts in *Amphitryon 38* – S. N. Behrman's adaptation of Giraudoux (in 1938) – and in Rattigan's *Love In Idleness* (1944); Deborah Kerr in *The Day After The Fair* (1972); Alec Guinness in *Habeas Corpus* (1973); Jessica Tandy and Hume Cronyn in *The Gin Game* (1979), and Glenda Jackson in *Summit Conference* (1982) did no harm to ticket sales. In the latter, a then unknown Gary Oldman had a role. Other future stars were Antony Sher in *John, Paul, George, Ringo... And Bert* (1974), and Bob Hoskins in *Happy End* (1975). In contrast, 90-year-old Ben Travers, master of the Aldwych farce, provided a new hit play called *The Bed Before Yesterday* (1975) in which Joan Plowright (Lady Olivier) and Helen Mirren appeared. Sher returned to the Lyric 23 years later to play Cyrano de Bergerac in the RSC's 1997 production.

John Moffitt, Helen Mirren and Joan Plowright in the hit comedy, *The Bed Before Yesterday* (1975) by Ben Travers

Five Guys Named Moe won the Laurence Olivier Award for Best Entertainment in 1991

Joe Orton's black comedy *Loot* (1984), which features a coffin on stage throughout, was playing to full houses when the lead actor, Leonard Rossiter, tragically died of a heart attack during a performance. The Lyric recovered from the shock and was soon filled with Lerner and Loewe's melodies in *Gigi* (1985) and Clarke Peters's all-singing, all-dancing *Five Guys Named Moe* (which ran for five years from 1990). After a musical revival of *Ain't Misbehavin'*, the Australian dance sensation *Tap Dogs* in 1995 and a transfer of Andrew Lloyd Webber and Alan Ayckbourn's musical *By Jeeves* in 1996, the Lyric returned to drama with a series of leading actresses: Janie Dee in Alan Ayckbourn's *Comic Potential*; Fanny Burney's *A Busy Day* with Stephanie Beacham and Sara Crowe; *Brief Encounter* with Jenny Seagrove; and Eugene O'Neill's masterpiece, *Long Day's Journey Into Night*, starring Jessica Lange. In 2002, after David Warner's return to the stage in *The Feast of Snails*, the Lyric lived up to its name again with a lively revival of the Andrew Lloyd Webber musical, *Daisy Pulls It Off*.

the lyric, shaftesbury avenue
shaftesbury avenue = wlv

The National Theatre

The National Theatre on London's South Bank, overlooking the Thames, opened in 1976. Despite its relatively young status in this location, the theatre has already built up an impressive and vibrant history – a history that actually goes back to the beginning of the last century, when the dream of a state-owned theatre, especially designed for a permanent company, was first discussed. It was a book by critic William Archer and dramatist Harley Granville-Barker, *A National Theatre; Scheme And Estimates*, that sparked off the debate in earnest. In 1913, the first of many proposed sites was acquired in Gower Street for a National Theatre. Another was in South Kensington where George Bernard Shaw 'turned the first sod'. On Friday, 13 June, 1951, Queen Elizabeth (the late Queen Mother) laid the foundation stone of the new building in front of the main entrance to the newly constructed Royal Festival Hall. The site shifted a little further along the South Bank where construction began a mere 18 years later. Meanwhile, the National Theatre Company was set up in 1962 under the directorship of Sir Laurence Olivier, and was housed 'temporarily' at the Old Vic Theatre for almost 13 years.

Finally, the long-awaited building, designed by Sir Denys Lasdun at a cost of £20 million, took its place proudly beside the Royal Festival, Queen Elizabeth and Purcell Concert Halls, the Hayward Gallery and the National Film Theatre as part of an arts centre of international repute, unrivalled in London even by the impressive Barbican Centre inaugurated in 1982. It is certainly situated in one of the most attractive parts of the great capital,

'I think Lasdun's work is triumphant. He has divested concrete of its brutality. It is slender, delicate, and in beautiful geometric patterns. I think the theatre is a masterpiece.'
— Peter Hall

looking out on a splendid reach of the Thames, curving past Somerset House towards St Paul's Cathedral, a scene not all that different from those painted by Turner and Canaletto.

This panoramic view of the noble and busy river can be appreciated from the many jutting terraces, both open and closed, that form an integral part of the bold, unadorned, functional concrete structure. The National Theatre itself is best seen by walking across Waterloo Bridge towards the lights that spell out the day's events, beckoning potential customers over the water. On entering the building, either from the river walk or from the bridge, one is welcomed by the roomy and relaxing foyers, a restaurant, seven bars, five buffets and excellent bookshops. Before each performance, live music is played in the Ground Floor foyer. The building is open all day and members of the public are encouraged to use it as a social centre whether they see a play or not. In 1996, an Arts Council Lottery Fund award allowed the National to develop and expand its foyers, with a new entrance created to include the box-office and bookshop. Although a fairly large building, now housing three theatres, it has an intimacy lacking at the Barbican, London's other large government-subsidised theatre.

Of the four auditoria, the largest and most radical is the Olivier, so called after the company's first artistic director and England's most famous actor. Sadly, Sir Laurence never performed in the theatre that bears his name. Seating 1,160 people, it is fan-shaped with sharply raked seats in the stalls, slightly raised balconies on either side and an upper circle all bearing down on the large apron stage, most suitable for epic theatre of which the opening production in October 1976 was a supreme example. It was a spectacular rendering of Christopher Marlowe's rarely performed masterpiece, *Tamburlaine The Great*, with Albert Finney powerful in the title role.

It was Finney as Hamlet (transferred from the Old Vic) who opened the 890-seat Lyttelton Theatre seven months previously. Named after the National's first chairman Oliver Lyttelton (Lord Chandos), it is of conventional design with an adjustable proscenium stage, part of which can be lowered to form an orchestra pit.

The Cottesloe is a small (approximately 400 seats), simple, flexible, rectangular room with two tiers of galleries on three sides, which can be used for theatre in the round if necessary. This theatre was named after Lord Cottesloe, the chairman of the South Bank Theatre Board. It provides an essential space for experimental or chamber theatre, or as a try-out venue for plays that might transfer to one of the two larger houses. It opened on Saturday 1 March, 1977, the first occasion on which all three main theatres were in use simultaneously.

The fourth theatre, created as part of the National's Transformation season in 2002, is the smallest and most intimate of them all – the Lyttelton Loft, which seats 100 people.

The aims of the National Theatre are to present 'a diversity of repertoire embracing classic, new and neglected plays from the whole of world drama; to present these plays to the very highest standards; to do experimental work, and work for children and young people; to give audiences a choice of at least six different productions at any one time; to take current productions regularly to the regions and abroad; to use fully the unique advantages of the building so that the public is continuously offered, in addition to plays, all kinds of other events.' On the whole, this manifesto has been admirably adhered to. As principal evidence of this, a look at what has been offered over three decades should suffice.

Among the many outstanding productions of classics, both ancient and modern, the National has given us Trevor Nunn's *The*

Broadway came to the South Bank with *Guys and Dolls*. The Salvation Army prayer meeting is here about to begin...

Merchant of Venice (1999); Alan Bennett's *The Wind In The Willows* (1990); Howard Davies's 1988 production of *Cat On A Hot Tin Roof*; Peter Hall's lucid and exciting production of *Coriolanus* (1984), starring Ian McKellen and using members of the audience as extras; and Paul Scofield and Ben Kingsley in *Volpone* (1977). American classics have been represented by Richard Eyre's out-Broadwaying-Broadway production of *Guys And Dolls* (1982), which transferred to the West End for a commercial run, and 2000's superb production of *All My Sons* by Howard Davies, which Arthur Miller acclaimed as the best performance ever of his play. The NT's policy of commissioning established writers to translate and adapt foreign masterpieces has also paid off well. These have included versions of Molière's *Don Juan* (1981) by John Fowles; Chekhov's *Wild Honey* (1984) and Tolstoy's *Fruits Of Enlightenment* (1979) by Michael Frayn; and the vigorously rhythmic and masked Aeschylus trilogy, *The Oresteia* (1981), strikingly adapted by Tony Harrison.

Neglected plays given new life have included 1996's acclaimed version of Ibsen's *John Gabriel Borkman*; Kyd's *The Spanish Tragedy* (1984), the work that most influenced *Hamlet*; Granville-Barker's *The Madras House* (1977); and Maugham's *For Services Rendered* (1979). Some of the new plays presented have been 2002's multi-award-winning *Gagarin Way* by Gregory Burke; *Amy's View*, by David Hare (1997); Tom Stoppard's *Arcadia* (1993); Alan

James Hazeldine in Howard Davies's revival of Arthur Miller's modern classic, *All My Sons* (2000)

Bennett's *The Madness of George III* (1991); Howard Brenton and David Hare's brutally funny exposé of Fleet Street, *Pravda* (1985), starring the brilliant Anthony Hopkins; Peter Shaffer's universally acclaimed *Amadeus* (1979), which was first revealed at the Olivier with Paul Scofield as Salieri; Harold Pinter's *Betrayal* (1978); and Alan Ayckbourn's *Bedroom Farce* (1977).

In 1999 Trevor Nunn, the NT's current director, launched a new ensemble of actors with Shakespeare's *Troilus and Cressida*, and two years later the theatre celebrated its twenty-fifth anniversary on the South Bank. In 2002 Transformation – a five month season with reduced ticket prices presenting 13 world premieres - introduced new generations of theatre makers and theatre audiences to one of the best theatres in the world. On 9 March 2002 the National Theatre company staged an astounding and record-breaking 28 performances in 14 different theatres country-wide and in the USA.

And so the noble aims which the National Theatre set for itself over 25 years ago are more than being fulfilled. London's premiere theatre company really has established a triumphant reputation the world over.

the royal national theatre
upper ground, south bank = se1

The New Ambassadors

King: What do you call the play?
Hamlet: *The Mouse-trap*.

Hamlet's sub-title for 'The Murder of Gonzago' lent its name to the Agatha Christie whodunnit which would occupy this dainty and diminutive theatre for over 21 years. From 25 November, 1952 to 25 March, 1974, until it moved a few yards across Tower Court to the St Martin's where it still runs, *The Mousetrap* and the Ambassadors were synonymous. It is a pity, in a way, that many plays and players did not have the opportunity to appear in one of London's most intimate and pretty playhouses during that marathon run.

The Ambassadors and the St Martin's were conceived by their architect, W. G. R. Sprague, as companions born at the same time in 1913, but World War I interrupted the construction of the latter for three years. The Ambassadors is smaller and lower than its neighbour, both conveniently situated opposite the renowned Ivy Restaurant, favourite haunt of the theatrical elite. The theatre has an unfussy classical facade, crowned with a parapet and balustrade decorated with ball-shaped ornaments. Less restrained is the elegant Louis XVI auditorium, the walls of which are festooned with ambassadorial crests. For political reasons these were painted out at the outbreak of war in 1914, and they only reappeared in 1958. A beautiful chandelier shines down from the circular ceiling onto the 453 seats below. The horseshoe-shaped single balcony is reached by a few stairs up from ground level, while the stalls are actually underground.

'In a little theatre like the Ambassadors, to have sitting together five or six people who don't laugh or applaud is demoralising.'

— Charles B. Cochran

Charles B. Cochran recognised that the charming atmosphere and compact size of the Ambassadors would lend itself perfectly to 'intimate' revue when he took a lease on the theatre at the beginning of the war. Here, the great impresario introduced England to what was then a new genre of entertainment from Paris. *Odds And Ends*, starring French actress and singer Alice Delysia, was aimed at more sophisticated audiences than those attending the spectacular revues of the music halls. After 400 performances, it was followed by further Cochran 'miniature revues' called *More (Odds And Ends)* and *Pell Mell*, also with Delysia, between 1915 and 1917. The French connection was continued in 1917 with the presentation of two translated plays, Anatole France's *The Man Who Married A Dumb Wife* and Eugene Brièux's *The Three Daughters Of Monsieur Dupont*.

Many productions of quality were staged during the regime of H. M. Harwood from 1919 to 1932, including his own plays. It was at the Ambassadors that West End audiences first applauded Ivor Novello (in *Deburau*, 1921), 24-year-old Hermione Gingold (in Lord Dunsany's *If*, 1921), Margaret Lockwood in *Family Affairs* (1934) and 22-year-old Vivien Leigh in Ashley Duke's *The Mask Of Virtue* (1935). Miss Leigh created a great impression, as did America's Paul Robeson in Eugene O'Neill's *The Emperor Jones* (1925). When Sydney Carroll took over as manager in 1932, he continued Harwood's good work by presenting revivals of *The Rivals*, *The Country Wife* (1934) and *The Soldier's Fortune* (1935). The last hit before World War II was Margaret Rutherford in *Spring Meeting* (1938).

Hermione Gingold returned to the scene of her adult debut as a fully fledged performer in the vastly successful *The Gate Revue*

(1939), named after the little theatre in Villiers Street, bombed in 1941, from where the show derived. The first revue, which had a young Michael Wilding in the small cast, was followed by *Swinging The Gate* (1940), *Sweet And Low* (1943), *Sweeter And Lower* (1944) and *Sweetest And Lowest* (1946), all with the inimitable Gingold. In 1949, she and Hermione Baddeley used the first major revival of Noël Coward's *Fallen Angels* as a joint showcase for their comic personalities.

A very young Richard Attenborough and his wife, Sheila Sim, as Trotter and Mollie in the original cast of *The Mousetrap* (1952)

the great theatres of london

Nobody ever imagined that a competent little thriller, adapted by Agatha Christie from her own short story *Three Blind Mice*, would enter the record books as the World's Longest Run. The small theatre, the able direction of Peter Cotes, the gripping old-fashioned murder yarn and the snowball effect of a long run helped *The Mousetrap* on its way to becoming a seemingly permanent tourist attraction. Richard Attenborough and his wife Sheila Sim were in the first of generations of casts. When the theatre was finally liberated from *The Mousetrap*, it took some years to catch the habit of success again. This came triumphantly with the transfer of the Royal Shakespeare Company's hit

Lindsay Duncan and Alan Rickman as the sexually decadent and scheming protagonists of *Les Liaisons Dangereuses*, adapted from Laclos's intriguing novel

the new ambassadors

production of Christopher Hampton's *Les Liaisons Dangereuses* (1986) which ran for four years. From 1996 to 1999 the Royal Court leased the theatre for their Royal Court Upstairs, while premises in Sloane Square were renovated. They extended the circle upstairs to create a new theatre, and converted the downstairs into a bar and studio space – and staged landmark productions such as *Shopping and F***ing* by Mark Ravenhill and *East is East* by Ayub Khan-Din. In 1999, when the Royal Court returned to Sloane Square, the theatre was bought by the Ambassadors Theatre Group and renamed the New Ambassadors Theatre. Since then it has continued to present high quality drama with productions like *Krapp's Last Tape*, starring John Hurt, Marie Jones's award-winning *Stones In His Pockets*, Berkoff's *Women, One For the Road,* by and starring Harold Pinter, and David Mamet's acclaimed *Boston Marriage*, from the Almeida.

the new ambassadors theatre
west street = wc2h

The New London

The New London Theatre, built in 1973, lies in the heart of the historic Drury Lane. The very names of the streets surrounding it – Kean, Kemble, Macklin, Betterton, Garrick and Dryden – echo with theatrical history. On the site of the large glass structure, which could pass for a bank or office block, once stood a public house called The Great Mogul, frequented by Nell Gwynn who lived nearby.

In the mid-nineteenth century, the Mogul began to provide entertainment before becoming the renowned Middlesex Music Hall where artistes such as Dan Leno and Marie Lloyd charmed Victorian audiences. Rebuilt by Frank Matcham in 1911, it continued as the New Middlesex Music Hall throughout the Great War, the last of its kind to have a Chairman, the performer who introduced the acts from below the footlights. In 1919, it was taken over by George Grossmith and Edward Laurillard, redecorated and renamed the Winter Garden. Leslie Henson (father of the National's Nicky Henson) returned to the stage from the army to star in the opening production, *Kissing Time*, a musical play by P. G. Wodehouse and Guy Bolton. He continued his association with the theatre in *A Night Out* (1920), an adaptation of Feydeau's farce *L'Hotel Du Libre Echange*, which re-emerged as *Hotel Paradiso* at the Winter Garden in 1956 starring Alec Guinness. Henson also appeared in *Sally* (1921) by Guy Bolton and Jerome Kern, *The Cabaret Girl* (1922) by Bolton, Wodehouse and Kern, and *Primrose* (1925) by Grossmith, Bolton and George Gershwin. Further musical comedies were *Tip Toes* (1926) by Fred Thompson, Bolton and Gershwin, and Sophie Tucker in Vivian Ellis's *Follow A Star* (1930), Rudolf Friml's operetta *The Vagabond King* (1927) and Gracie Fields in the revue *Walk This Way* (1932).

(facing page) Cats – and more cats. It ran and ran...

174

'The New London is a theatre of the future. It is a theatre that moves; stage, seats, lights — even the walls can be made to change their position.'
— Opening press release, 1973

The lights were out at the Winter Garden for most of the 1930s, coming on again with *Peter Pan* (1942) in which Alastair Sim was Captain Hook for the first time, a role he was to play on and off for 26 years. The theatre was slightly damaged by a bomb shortly after Jack Buchanan and Elsie Randolph appeared in *It's Time To Dance* (1943), but it kept open just the same. Joan Temple's *No Room At The Inn* (1946), which dealt with the wartime evacuation of children, had a surprisingly good run at a theatre noted for much lighter subjects. When *Witness For The Prosecution* (1953) had been running a year, it was one of three Agatha Christie hits in the West End, *The Mousetrap* (at the Ambassadors) and *Spider's Web* (at the Savoy) being the others.

Peter Ustinov *(foreground)* and Brian Bedford in *The Unknown Soldier And His Wife*, which officially opened the theatre in January, 1973

the new london

Hollywood star Tyrone Power, who played in the film version of *Witness For The Prosecution*, was dashing as Dick Dudgeon in Shaw's *The Devil's Disciple* (1956). In 1959, the Winter Garden closed its doors forever.

The theatre stood as a hollow shell until 1965, when it was flattened to make room for a complex, incorporating shops, apartments, restaurants… and the New London theatre, designed by Michael Percival. The result is a different environmental experience from the playhouses of yesteryear. Taking on many of the experiments of theatre architecture carried out on the Continent, it gets away from the concept of a fixed space. By having a third of the floor of the auditorium built to revolve, and walls as movable panels, its shape can change from that of an amphitheatre to theatre in the round, from a studio to its utmost capacity of 907 seats, which can be raised or lowered.

The first performance here was a TV recording of Marlene Dietrich's one-woman show in November 1972, two months before the New London opened officially with Peter Ustinov's *The Unknown Soldier And His Wife*, an anti-war play featuring the author and his eldest daughter Tamara Ustinov. Also in 1973, the 25-year-old unknown Richard Gere (prior to his meteoric movie career) played Danny Zuko in the 1950s nostalgia musical *Grease*. Other shows came and went until Andrew Lloyd Webber's music, Trevor Nunn's direction, Gillian Lynne's choreography and T. S. Eliot's minor verse came together to create the legendary *Cats*, which opened in 1981 and has since become the longest-running British musical. But 'even magical things must come to an end' as the slogan went before *Cats'* emotional last performance on 11 May 2002. The question now is, what next for the New London? *Cats* is going to be a hard act to follow…

the new london theatre
drury lane and parker street = wc2

The Old Vic

There is no theatre in London whose history is more imbued with the character of one person than the venerable Old Vic. The spirit of this theatre was embodied by an irritating, God-intoxicated, 'undereducated', unmarried, bespectacled woman who hardly ever saw a play through. Yet Lilian Baylis probably exerted the most profound influence on the performing arts in Britain than anyone else in the twentieth century. And she did it from her tiny office in the theatre she loved and seldom left, away from the mainstream of the West End. It is not too fanciful to argue that without her instinct, indefatigability and religious zeal there would be no National Theatre, Royal Ballet or English National Opera, neither would English acting have acquired the international reputation it enjoys today.

Reputed to have prayed, 'Lord God, please send me a good actor, but send him cheap,' Lilian Baylis was tight-fisted with money but generous with art. She didn't seem to care that patrons would catch their feet in the holes of the carpets as long as there was quality on stage. Such was the prestige and joy of appearing here that the greatest actors would accept miserably low salaries. She treated everyone the same; there were no stars in her heaven. Baylis used to cook bacon and sausages on a gas ring in the wings between, and sometimes during, performances. When Robert Atkins, one of the leading actors and producers in the company, advised her to go out and see what was happening in other theatres, Baylis replied, 'Not keen on plays, dear. Don't know what they're about.'

Tyrone Guthrie, who would become a leading light as producer at the Old Vic, describes a visit he paid to the theatre in 1929 to see Gielgud's Shylock. 'The old house was shabby, even grubby. Rather rude and angry crones shoved a programme into

*'It smells and feels like a theatre, and is
able to transform a collection of human beings
into that curious, vibrant instrument for an
actor — an audience.'*

— Sir John Gielgud

your hands… But the house was packed, and the enthusiasm of the unspoilt, intelligent audience was infectious…the Old Vic audience, one felt, was composed of people who you could die to please, who wanted their horizons enlarged, who would come out to meet new ideas and new challenges… For the first time in my life I saw new social possibilities in the theatre.'

How did the Old Vic, as critic Ivor Brown wrote, 'become more truly Shakespearean in spirit than any regular professional theatre since the age of the poet himself?' The first hundred years of its existence gave little indication that it would ever become so. In 1816 it was proposed that a theatre be built in Lambeth on the South Bank of the Thames. It was to be named the Royal Coburg in honour of Prince Leopold and Princess Charlotte, who headed the list of subscribers. The architect was Rudolph Cabanel of Aachen, and the foundation stone and other materials came from the recently demolished Savoy Palace at the foot of Waterloo Bridge, not far from the site. However, building progressed slowly due to lack of funds until Joseph Glossop, stage-struck son of a wealthy Soho merchant, put up the money and became manager when it eventually opened in May 1818.

Owing to the state of the roads and its unfashionable location, the Royal Coburg soon developed into the home of lurid melodramas for the local population. According to a contemporary writer, it was 'the very haunt and refuge of the melodramatic muse… where murder bares her red arm'. Nevertheless, none other than Edmund Kean acted here for a season in 1831, under the management of George Davidge who insisted that the Monday night working-class audiences were succeeded in the middle of the week by 'the better classes, the play-going public generally'. In 1833, a redecoration and a change of name – it became officially the Royal Victoria, but known ever since as the Old Vic – did not disguise the fact that it was still a 'Blood Tub', the name given to a theatre staging crude melodramas at very cheap prices. In 1871, it was newly baptised the New Victoria Palace before closing down in 1880. In December of that year, the whole history of the disreputable building was altered.

Emma Cons, a doughty social reformer and the first woman member of the London County Council, bought it and changed the entire interior and the name – to the Royal Victoria Hall and Coffee Tavern. With William Poel as manager, it was used for concerts, operas and scenes from Shakespeare. At the close of the nineteenth century, Miss Cons sent for her 24-year-old niece, then a music teacher in South Africa, to come and assist her. Lilian Baylis, whom Hugh Walpole called a 'first-class Cockney from South Africa', was born in London and went out to the colony with her family in her teens. Although she had had little previous connection with the theatre world, the management passed to her in 1912. Two years later, she began the bold experiment of presenting all of Shakespeare's plays in the First Folio at popular prices. This was achieved with the help of epoch-making producers like Harcourt Williams, Robert Atkins, Ben Greet and Tyrone Guthrie and performers such as Sybil Thorndike, John Gielgud, Laurence Olivier, Ralph Richardson, Peggy Ashcroft, Edith Evans, Charles Laughton, Michael Redgrave, Flora Robson, Alec Guinness and James Mason. In 1923, the production of *Troilus And Cressida* completed the cycle of Shakespeare plays, making the Old Vic the first theatre in the world to achieve this. It must also be noted that opera and ballet performances were being given at the same time until a second house was found at Sadler's Wells in 1931.

Lilian Baylis, 'The Magnificent Tyrant' according to James Agate, died in 1937. After a bomb severely damaged the building in 1941, the theatre was closed for the duration of the war. In

The young Ralph Richardson was a delightful Bottom in *A Midsummer Night's Dream* (1931)

November 1950, the Old Vic Company, after a glittering sojourn at the New Theatre (later renamed the Albery), returned home under the directorship of Michael Benthall. From 1953 to 1958, Benthall followed in Baylis's footsteps by embarking on a 'Five Year Plan' to stage all 36 of Shakespeare's plays in the First Folio once again, beginning with Richard Burton as Hamlet and ending with John Gielgud, Edith Evans and Harry Andrews in *Henry VIII*. Both Burton and the aristocratic-looking John Neville were 'matinee idols' of this period, alternating the parts of Iago and Othello in a 1956 production. Neville broke new ground by playing Hamlet in a white shirt and jeans in 1958.

In 1963, this unofficial national theatre company was disbanded, and the Old Vic became the 'temporary' home (for 13 years) of the newly formed National Theatre under Laurence Olivier, who directed the inaugural production of *Hamlet* starring Peter O'Toole and Michael Redgrave. If, as Voltaire states, 'History is nothing more than a tableau of misfortunes', then the history of the National Theatre at the Old Vic can only be described as a tableau of triumphs. John Dexter and William Gaskill were associate directors and Kenneth Tynan the literary manager, while Olivier's own contribution was tremendous. In addition to his administrative duties, he played 13 roles including Astrov in *Uncle Vanya* (1963), in a cast that boasted Redgrave, Thorndike, Joan Plowright and Fay Compton, as well as Solness in *The Master Builder* and an extraordinarily magnetic pitch-black Othello, both in 1964 and both with Maggie Smith. Among the new plays introduced here were Peter Shaffer's *The Royal Hunt Of The Sun* (1964) and *Equus* (1973), Tom Stoppard's *Rosencrantz And Guildenstern Are Dead* (1966) and *Jumpers* (1974), John Arden's *Armstrong's Last Goodnight* (1964) and Trevor Griffiths' *The Party* (1973).

The first Old Vic production following the departure of the National Theatre in 1976 was *The White Devil* with Glenda Jackson. The following year, the Old Vic became the home of the Prospect Theatre Company directed by Timothy West, with productions including *Hamlet* with Derek Jacobi. The finances of

the theatre were precarious, and in 1982 it was put up for sale. Bought by Canadians Ed and David Mirvish, the Old Vic was restored to its former Victorian splendour. The stone and stucco facade and arched side wall in Waterloo Road were redecorated, and the auditorium with its lyre-shaped balconies was enlarged by 130 to 1078 newly upholstered seats. It was under the Mirvish management that one of the great British

Laurence Olivier (seated) gave one of his many great performances in Strindberg's *The Dance of Death* (1967). Geraldie McEwan was his wife, Robert Lang her brother

theatre directors, Jonathan Miller, was made artistic director. Between 1987 and 1990 he directed 17 productions at the Old Vic, collecting five Olivier Awards, including one for *Candide* as Best Musical. At the end of 1997 the Mirvishes announced their decision to sell, and the fate of this historic theatre lay in the balance again. Rumours circulated about plans for a themed pub or - worse – a lap-dancing club. But at the eleventh hour, following pleas from the Government, a non-profit-making trust was formed to buy and save the theatre. The Trust, initially chaired by Alex Bernstein with director Stephen Daldry, actor Kevin Spacey and impresario Sally Greene, undertook to raise the money required and to implement an artistic policy to place the Old Vic once again at the forefront of British Theatre.

Peter O'Toole won great acclaim for his performance in the title role of *Jeffery Bernard Is Unwell*

Since the acquisition of the freehold in 2000, the theatre has been doing just that. The first production under the Trust's ownership was the Almeida's phenomenally successful *The Iceman Cometh*, directed by Howard Davies and starring Kevin Spacey. Subsequent successes have included a new production of *Amadeus* with David Suchet, directed by Sir Peter Hall, a revival of *Jeffrey Bernard is Unwell,* starring Peter O'Toole and directed by Ned Sherrin, Frank McGuinness's new play *Dolly West's Kitchen* and Adventures in Motion Pictures' new production of *The Car Man*, choreographed by Matthew Bourne. In 2002 it was announced that theatre-lover Elton John was to be the new chairman of the Old Vic Theatre Trust – no better figure to help raise funds for renovations and keep the Old Vic in the position it deserves, as one of the greatest theatres in London.

the old vic
the cut, waterloo road = sel

The Palace

'The World's Greatest Artistes Have Passed And Will Pass Through These Doors' is engraved in stone above the stage door of the Palace. The claim is not an idle one, because 'artistes' of the calibre of Sarah Bernhardt, Marie Tempest, Anna Pavlova, Maurice Chevalier, Max Miller, Evelyn Laye, Cicely Courtneidge, Jack Hulbert, Ivor Novello, Jean-Louis Barrault, Laurence Olivier, Judi Dench and Natalia Makarova have played at the Palace, one of London's most glorious monuments to musical theatre.

This High Victorian edifice was built for Richard D'Oyly Carte in 1891 as the Royal English Opera House, to encourage the writing and production of home-grown operas. But to D'Oyly Carte's mortification, only the opening production, *Ivanhoe*, Arthur Sullivan's sole attempt at grand opera, was forthcoming from an English composer. He had to follow it up with André Messager's *The Basoche* from France. After its short run, and a Sarah Bernhardt season during which she played Sardou's Cleopatra, the impresario, who had brought Gilbert and Sullivan together, admitted defeat and sold the building to Augustus Harris in 1892. Harris immediately abandoned any idea of presenting operas here, and renamed the building the Palace Theatre of Varieties.

Although its days as an opera house were short-lived, the theatre retains the air and structure of such a place. In fact, Andrew Lloyd Webber and Tim Rice's rock opera *Jesus Christ Superstar* (1972) and the current musical *Les Misérables*, which began its incredible run in 1985, have been perfectly at home here. Of the latter, Alain Boublil, who wrote the original text, says, 'this book (Victor Hugo's) is already a spoken opera…', and the composer Claude-Michel Schonberg writes, 'after the libretto was written… I decided, when faced with such an epic story, to

'The only theatre architecture of the last sixty years in London, or for that matter the provinces, which climbs into the regions of a work of art.'
— John Betjeman, 1952

employ a real operatic structure using a mixture of romantic nineteenth-century music with a contemporary mood – I am an opera fan so this exercise was very enjoyable for me.'

The building, occupying a whole block, partly in Shaftesbury Avenue, was designed by C. H. Holloway and decorated by T. E. Colcutt. The striking and unusual Francois I terracotta frontage (restored in 1989) facing Cambridge Circus has three bays filled with dozens of tiny arched windows, and at each corner domed towers rise above the parapet. Inside, a grand marble staircase leads up to the circle bar, also in marble, and down to the extremely attractive Palace Brasserie, looking as it might have done in the last century. The auditorium, seating 1,450, has

ornate gold mouldings and mirrors, and the deeply projecting galleries were said to be unparalleled at that time by any theatre in Europe. However, in 1959 John Betjeman wrote, 'Alas, the veined marbles which were so elegant and essential a part of its interior decoration have lately been defaced by a coat of plum-coloured paint.' Fortunately, when Andrew Lloyd Webber's Really Useful Company took over the building in 1982, this paint was scraped off to reveal that the marble and the Mexican onyx panels were undamaged. The Palace is gradually being returned to its former glory in an ongoing project of restoration without affecting performances

Many of the glories of the music hall performed here in variety bills for some years before revues became all the rage. American star Elsie Janis made a hit in *The Passing Show* (1914) in which Clara Beck sang 'I'll Make A Man Of You', one of the most famous recruiting songs of the Great War. In the sequel, *The Passing Show Of 1915*, Basil Hallam introduced the song 'Gilbert The Filbert' before he was killed at the front. Other revues of the period were *Bric-A-Brac* (1915) with Gertie Millar, *Vanity Fair* (1916), *Airs And Graces* (1917) and *Hullo, America!* (1918) in which Elsie Janis partnered Maurice Chevalier. A semi-Pierrot group called *The Co-Optimists*, of whom Stanley Holloway was a founding member, had a good run in 1924.

The tradition of musical comedy at the Palace began in earnest, or rather in frivolity, with Vincent Youmans's *No, No, Nanette* (1925), which ran for 655 performances. Then came *Princess Charming* (1926), *The Girl Friend* (1927), Jerome Kern's *The Cat And The Fiddle* (1932), *The Gay Divorcee* (1933), Cole Porter's *Anything Goes* (1935) and Rodgers and Hart's *On Your Toes* (1937), which returned triumphantly 47 years later. In between these musicals was a Charles B. Cochran revue, *Streamline* (1934), in which Tilly Losch danced exotically, Gilbert and Sullivan were burlesqued, and Florence Desmond played 'The first British mother to fly over the North Pole with her baby'.

From 1938 to 1945 the Palace was almost exclusively occupied by that madcap married couple Cicely Courtneidge and

Jack Hulbert in *Under Your Hat* (1938), *Full Swing* (1942) and *Something In The Air* (1943). They made way for two operettas based on the works of Johann Strauss (*Gay Rosalinda*, 1945) and Edward Grieg (*Song Of Norway*, 1946). During the long run of the latter, the theatre came under the management of Tom Arnold and Emile Littler. Over a year into the run of Ivor Novello's *King's Rhapsody* (1949), its composer-star collapsed and died aged 58.

Coincidentally, the great German playwright Bertolt Brecht, Novello's antithesis, died at the same age in 1956 in East Berlin while his Berliner Ensemble was paying a visit to the Palace on the invitation of impresario Peter Daubeny. Before they left for England, Brecht had told the Ensemble to remember that, as English audiences did not understand German, they were to play it 'quick, light and strong', to dispel any idea the English had that German drama was heavy. Daubeny also brought over other foreign troupes in the 1950s, including the Renaud-Barrault company and Jean Vilar's Theatre Nationale Populaire. The last in a short period of straight plays at the Palace was the transfer from the Royal Court of John Osborne's *The Entertainer* (1957) starring Laurence Olivier with his future wife, Joan Plowright (taking over from Dorothy Tutin), playing his daughter. From then on it was musical entertainment all the way.

Imports from Broadway with British casts were Frank Loesser's *Where's Charley?* (1958) with Norman Wisdom, two Rodgers and Hammerstein hits, *Flower Drum Song* (1960) and *The Sound Of Music* (1961), which ran six sentimental years, and *Cabaret* (1967) with Judi Dench. Among the great big flops were *Two Cities* (1969), a musical derived from the novel *A Tale Of...*, and Betty Grable in *Belle Starr* (1970). Also showing lovely legs was drag artist Danny La Rue, wearing an array of gorgeous gowns for two years in the revue *At The Palace* (1970). Then came *Jesus Christ Superstar* (1972) which, according to Andrew Lloyd Webber, 'kept two then young British lads off the surrounding streets for nine years!' *On Your Toes* (1984) starred Russian ballerina Natalia Makarova, and was directed by 97-year-

Crowd scene in the Cameron Mackintosh production
of *Les Misérables*

old George Abbott, before the Royal Shakespeare Company
brought in *Les Misérables*. Now in its seventeenth year, and
counting, it is the theatre's longest running production.
Nicknamed 'The Glums' by its director Trevor Nunn, *Les
Misérables* has kept the Palace happy for many years.

the palace theatre
shaftesbury avenue = wlv

The Palladium

Life Begins At Oxford Circus And Round About Regent Street, the title of a 1935 Crazy Gang show at the London Palladium, just about summed up what lovers of the music hall felt when approaching this enormous edifice of entertainment. For a variety act to have played the Palladium was equal in theatrical mythology to playing a two-a-day at Broadway's Palace Theatre. A list of all the famous stars who have appeared here would make up a 'Who's Who' of show business.

Until 1865 there stood on the spot a large mansion that belonged to the Dukes of Argyll and Marlborough (hence the names of the two streets that bound the Palladium). After it was demolished a firm of wine merchants built what was known as the Corinthian Bazaar. (The present safety curtain shows what it looked like.) From 1871 to 1887, the building was occupied by Charles Hengler's Circus and then for some years it functioned as a 'Real Ice Skating Rink'. When a syndicate led by the promoter Walter Gibbons (later knighted) acquired the site at a time when business was booming at such places as the Palace, the Hippodrome and the Coliseum, it was decided that a music hall should be built. The architect of the latter two theatres, Frank Matcham, built the Palladium's facade by incorporating parts of the former circus building. With its six giant Corinthian columns on tall pedestals and statues at the centre and either side of the roof it could pass for a neo-Baroque temple, but for the canopy and the neon sign – one of the first to light up a theatre.

The vast, richly adorned and gilded auditorium with its two cantilevered balconies became familiar to millions on TV from the mid-1950s on, with a weekly variety show called *Sunday Night At The London Palladium*. MCs over the years included Tommy Trinder, Norman Vaughan, Bruce Forsyth and Jimmy Tarbuck. The formula was revived for a new generation in 1987

'The Palladium ... attracts a large number of shoppers who patronise the performances before they go home.'

— Ronald Mayes, *The Romance of London Theatres*, 1930

with *Tarbuck's Friends* – who included Howard Keel, Shirley Bassey, Tom Jones and Bruce Forsyth. Bruce himself performed a one-man show at the Palladium for a week in 1991, and on his seventieth birthday in 1998 the theatre staged a special *Sunday Night At The London Palladium* show with Diana Ross.

Those who have had the pleasure of going to this theatre can testify to the surprising intimacy and atmosphere of the place. This People's Palace can claim, with a seating capacity of over 2,300, to be the largest live theatre in London, discounting only the Coliseum – slightly bigger but now an opera house. *The Era* of 1910 noted: 'Perhaps the most unique feature is the box-to-box telephone that has been installed. It will therefore be possible for the occupants of one box, recognising friends in another box, to enter into conversation with them.' Alas, this little convenience no longer exists, and waving and shouting from the paired boxes in arched niches on each level must suffice.

the palladium

The Palladium opened on 26 December 1910 with a variety bill topped by Nellie Wallace, 'The Essence of Eccentricity', Ella Shields and 'Mr Martin Harvey and his full company' in a one-act play called *Conspiracy*. Subsequent programmes mixed farce, ballet, opera, melodrama, song and comedy in two shows each evening and two matinees a week. Variety it was called and variety it was! All the most famous artistes of the music hall appeared here in the first few years: Albert Chevalier entertained with his Cockney coster songs like 'My Old Dutch', and George Robey was elected 'The Prime Minister Of Mirth'. One bill had Thomas Beecham (whose father was an investor in the company running the theatre) conducting operatic excerpts between the comic turns.

In 1912 Charles Gulliver took over the management from Gibbons. Gulliver went in for spectacular revues such as *Whirl Of The Town* (1915), *The Palladium Minstrels* (1921), *Rockets* (1922) and *Whirl Of The World* (1923). The latter starred Nellie Wallace, Tommy Handley – later to come into his own on radio during World War II – and Nervo and Knox, who would return with the Crazy Gang in the 1930s. Revues alternating with the annual pantomime continued until 1928 when George Black reintroduced variety. Black, a theatre manager from the North of England, was the outstanding figure in music hall between the wars.

George Black's opening variety bill featured Gracie Fields, 'The Lancashire Lass making her first Palladium appearance', and Dick Henderson (father of comedian Dickie Henderson), alongside Ivor Novello and Phyllis Monkman in a one-act play entitled *The Gate Crasher*. In 1930, the Royal Variety Show, in aid of the Entertainment Artists' Benevolent Fund, was instigated at the Palladium, the theatre used more often than any other for this annual event. It was also host to the Christmas presentation of J. M. Barrie's *Peter Pan* until 1938. The Peters were Jean Forbes-Hamilton (1930–34 and 1938), Nova Pilbeam (1935), Elsa Lanchester (1936) and Anna Neagle (1937).

The Crazy Gang shows became another Palladium institution from 1932. The three pairs of comedians – Bud Flanagan and Chesney Allen, Charlie Naughton and Jimmy Gold, and Jimmy Nervo and Teddy Knox – brought back the low comedy tradition of 'the halls'. Their outrageous routines kept Londoners laughing in lavish productions, always containing one number with the unprepossessing sextet in drag, until 1938. Some titles were *Okay For Sound* (1936), *London Rhapsody* (1937) and *These Foolish Things* (1938).

The war years were filled with revues: *The Little Dog Laughed* (1940); *Best Bib And Tucker* (1942) starring Tommy Trinder, a favourite Buttons in the pantomime *Cinderella* here for some years; and Irving Berlin's *This Is The Army* (1942) in which the composer himself sang 'Oh, How I Hate To Get Up In The Morning'. On George Black's death in 1946, Val Parnell took over the management and Moss Empires the ownership.

Apart from the Christmas pantos, often running well into the new year, Parnell introduced variety bills topped by big American stars from 1948. Jack Benny, Ethel Merman, Danny Kaye, Bob Hope, Bing Crosby, Fats Waller, Duke Ellington, Frank Sinatra, Tony Martin, Cyd Charisse, Phil Harris, Betty Garrett and Liberace were some of the names to appear on the Palladium's programmes. In 1964, Judy Garland, who had triumphed here in the 1950s, returned with her 18-year-old daughter Liza Minnelli. Judy dominated the show, and Liza's inexperience was cruelly exposed. But in 1973, now a star in her own right, Liza earned a standing ovation from the Palladium audience.

Although the Palladium kept variety alive long after it was said to be dead, there came a time when it had to ring down the curtain on what had been the mainstay of the theatre for most of its history. But *nil desperandum*... musicals were there to save the day. Yul Brynner played his most famous role in *The King And I* (1979), a role replayed by Jason Scott Lee, with Elaine Paige, in 2000. Michael Crawford risked his neck every night for two years in *Barnum* (1981), Tommy Steele attempted to follow Gene Kelly's footwork in *Singin' In The Rain* (1983 and again in 1989); George

the palladium

Yul Brynner played the King of Siam for the umpteenth time in
The King and I (1979). The governess was Virginia McKenna

Hearn and Denis Quilley camped it up in the opulent *La Cage Aux Folles* (1986); Jason Donovan, then Phillip Schofield stopped hearts in a new production of *Joseph and the Amazing Technicolor Dreamcoat* (1991); Sam Mendes directed *Oliver!* with Jonathan Pryce as Fagin in 1994 – the Palladium's longest-running show, with 1,385 performances – and in 2002 Michael Ball took to the air in the Sherman brothers' best-loved musical, *Chitty Chitty Bang Bang*, all in the best Palladium tradition.

the palladium theatre
argylle street = wla

The Phoenix

Champagne corks and flashbulbs popped as London's glitterati poured into the Phoenix Theatre on its opening night, 24 September, 1930. It was not only a special evening because of the launching of Sidney Bernstein's new playhouse, but it was also that most fashionable of premieres – a 'Noël Coward First Night'. *Private Lives*, his brittle and now classic cocktail and dressing-gown comedy, was unveiled, starring the author and Gertrude Lawrence. The pair sparkled as ex-marrieds Elyot and Amanda on honeymoon with their dull spouses, played by the attractive Adrienne Allen and a devastatingly handsome 23-year-old named Laurence Olivier. Few theatres could have had a more glamorous beginning.

Coward wrote *Private Lives* as a vehicle for Lawrence and himself in just four days, while recovering from flu in Shanghai. Of their first love scene on the balcony, Coward's biographer Cole Lesley wrote, 'Gertie and Noël looked so beautiful together, standing in the moonlight, that no one who saw them can ever forget; and they played the scene so magically, lightly, tenderly, that one was for those fleeting moments brought near to tears by the underlying vulnerability, the evanescence, of their love.' The much-revived play got generally good reviews, but Ivor Brown in *Weekend* commented, 'Within a few years, the student of drama will be sitting in complete bewilderment before the text of *Private Lives* wondering what on earth these fellows in 1930 saw in so flimsy a trifle.' Despite full houses, the play closed after three months when it went to Broadway with Jill Esmond, whom Olivier had just married, replacing Adrienne Allen.

In 1936, Noël and Gertie returned to rescue the Phoenix from a bad patch with his programme of nine one-act plays under the title of *Tonight At 8.30*. In one of them, *Hands Across The Sea*, Coward took off Lord and Lady Mountbatten, but sent Lord

'Private Lives *was decked in a glorious sheen of success... and, in addition, was chosen to open the Phoenix Theatre, a smart new ornament to London's theatreland.'*

— Cole Lesley

Louis tickets for the first night. Mountbatten was not amused. 'It was a bare-faced parody of our lives... absolutely outrageous and certainly not worth six free tickets!' (Coward made amends with his 1942 war film, *In Which We Serve*.) On 12 September, 1952, Coward attended *Quadrille*, the Victorian comedy he had written for the Lunts, with gorgeous sets and costumes by Cecil Beaton. It was six days after he had heard that Gertie Lawrence had died of cancer of the liver. He found it difficult to sit through the first night in what he and Gertie used to refer to as 'our theatre'.

Seventeen years later, on 16 December, 1969, the owners of the Phoenix, Gerald and Veronica Flint-Shipman, helped organise a midnight matinee in honour of Coward's seventieth birthday. Coward entered his box on the stroke of midnight, and friends on stage and in the audience, including Princess Margaret, rose to their feet to sing 'Happy Birthday'. A few days before, he had opened the swanky Noël Coward Bar in the foyer, the first thing that greets one on entering this pleasing theatre. A collection of paintings and photos associated with Coward line the walls. He died in 1973, the year that Vanessa Redgrave, Jeremy Brett and John Stride appeared here in a successful revival of *Design For Living*, the play Coward wrote for himself and the Lunts in the 1930s.

The atmosphere of the 1930s still permeates the Phoenix with its Art Deco fittings, mirrored corridors and patterned ceilings conceived by the innovative Russian director and designer Theodore Komisarjevsky (briefly Peggy Ashcroft's second husband). In contrast to the modern, the classical is represented by the painted panels, by Vladimir Polunin, showing reproductions of works by Tintoretto, Titian and Giorgione. The exterior of the Charing Cross Road entrance is also classical in style with its four rather jaundiced columns. This entrance is awkwardly separated from the main entrance in Phoenix Street (next to a newly built cinema) by an unappetising apartment block.

The carefree early days of the theatre receded as the Munich crisis loomed. In 1938, Michel St Denis produced Bulgakov's *The White Guard* and Shakespeare's *Twelfth Night*, both with Michael Redgrave and Peggy Ashcroft, to acclaim. They were followed by a timely revival of Elmer Rice's *Judgement Day* (1939), about the Reichstag trial. The highlight of the war years was John Gielgud's production of *Love For Love* (1943) with himself as Valentine and Yvonne Arnaud as Mrs Frail. The critic W. A. Darlington noted that 'the crowds who flocked to see it

The breakfast table scene from Coward's immortal *Private Lives* (1930) with *(from left to right)* Adrienne Allen, Noël Coward, Gertrude Lawrence and Laurence Olivier

were not impelled by a sudden realization of Congreve's excellence as a writer, but by his bawdiness'. It might be remembered that Arnold Bennett called Noël Coward 'the Congreve of our day'. Gielgud returned after the war as Leontes in *The Winter's Tale* (1951) and Benedick in *Much Ado About Nothing* (1952). During the former, Hazel Terry (Fred Terry's granddaughter) accidentally set herself alight and was doused by a fellow actor, the playwright John Whiting. Gielgud remarked before making his entrance, 'I hear cousin Hazel caught fire. The Terrys have always been combustible.'

Failing to catch fire here was Thornton Wilder's 'history of the world', *The Skin Of Our Teeth* (1945), starring Vivien Leigh and presented by her husband Laurence Olivier. This eminent theatrical couple appeared together in Terence Rattigan's Coronation year offering, a Ruritanian tale called *The Sleeping Prince* (1953) – filmed in 1957 as *The Prince And The Showgirl* with Olivier and Marilyn Monroe. Rattigan, on much better form, had been here previously with his double bill of *The Browning Version* and *Harlequinade* with Eric Portman and Mary Ellis in the vastly contrasting pieces. Paul Scofield made a great impact in *Hamlet*, Graham Greene's *The Power And The Glory* and T. S. Eliot's *The Family Reunion* from 1955 to 1956. There was a touch of Hollywood in the 1976 'Phoenix Theatre Season' of four plays – Rock Hudson and Juliet Prowse in *I Do I Do*, Glynis Johns and Louis Jourdan in *13, Rue De Lamour*, Lee Remick in *Bus Stop* and Douglas Fairbanks Jr in *The Pleasure Of His Company*, and in 1992 Dustin Hoffman's memorable Shylock, directed by Sir Peter Hall. This production, and the young Kenneth Branagh's season (1988), with Branagh himself in *As You Like It*, showed that Shakespeare could still be a West End attraction.

The '80s and '90s have seen their share of award-winners - Alan Bleasdale's Elvis musical, *Are You Lonesome Tonight?* (Musical of the Year, 1985) and Brian Friel's *Dancing at Lughnasa* (1991 Olivier Award for Best Play). The Phoenix also continues its tradition for long runs: from *Canterbury Tales* (1968, for five years) to Tom

Stoppard's *Night and Day* (1978 for two years) and the longest run
of all – *Blood Brothers*, the Willy Russell musical, which transferred
from the Albery in late 1991.

the phoenix theatre
charing cross road = wc2h

The Piccadilly

In the souvenir programme that accompanied the opening of
the Piccadilly Theatre in April 1928, it was stated that if all
the bricks used in its construction were placed end to end in
a straight line, they would stretch from London to Paris. This was
another way of saying that the theatre was a huge construction,
one of the largest built in London in the twentieth century.
Designed by Bertie Crewe and Edward A. Stone for the
impresario Edward Laurillard, its 1,400-seat auditorium aimed
for space and comfort. There were elongated bars on the three
levels and beautifully equipped Ladies' Salons with rows of
dressing tables and mirrors to assist any necessary facial
refurbishment. The fittings and decoration in green and gold
were carried out in the modernist Art Deco style by Marc-Henri
and Laverdet, as the French designers Marc-Henri Levy and
Gaston Laverdet were known. The attractive four-storey Portland
stone facade curves gracefully round the corner on which the
theatre stands, vaguely influenced by John Nash's classical
frontages in Regent Street only a few yards away.

Evelyn Laye, reputedly the most popular musical comedy
actress of the time, starred in the first production here, Jerome
Kern's *Blue Eyes*, which ran four months before transferring. For
the next year, the theatre was used by Warner Brothers for the
showing of 'talkies', starting with Al Jolson's second film, *The
Singing Fool*. Live theatre returned in November 1929 with a
revival of *The Student Prince*. A very mixed batch of productions
ensued, failing to give the Piccadilly any distinctive personality or
policy.

Up to the outbreak of war, the theatre played host to Cicely
Courtneidge in a revue entitled *Folly To Be Wise* (1931), Robert
Donat and Ernest Thesiger in James Bridie's *A Sleeping
Clergyman* (1933) and Gwen ffrangcon-Davies in *The Barretts Of*

'In May 1973 success arrived at last with Gypsy starring Angela Lansbury.'
— Mander & Mitchenson

Wimpole Street (1935). The character of the Piccadilly was epitomised in a *mélange* called *Choose Your Time*. It consisted of a continuous programme of variety turns, a swing band, newsreels, cartoons and *Talk Of The Devil*, a short play with Yvonne Arnaud and John Mills.

In 1941, Noël Coward's *Blithe Spirit* had its premiere here. The hugely popular 'supernatural' comedy, starring Cecil Parker, Fay Compton, Kay Hammond and Margaret Rutherford as the eccentric clairvoyant Madame Arcati, soon transferred to the St James's (since demolished) and the Duchess to complete an amazing 1997 performances. After touring with *Macbeth* (1942), John Gielgud brought it to the Piccadilly for a few 'exhausting, and not very successful' months. (Incidentally, Ernest Thesiger played the First Witch.) The bad luck said to attend 'the Scottish play' lingered on into 1943, when the theatre was damaged by a flying bomb attack.

In 1945, the year of its reopening, Coward's revue *Sigh No More* was seen. It featured Joyce Grenfell, Cyril Ritchard and Coward's close friend Graham Payn, for whom he wrote the song 'Matelot'. Edith Evans and Godfrey Tearle tackled *Antony And Cleopatra* (1946), and John Van Druten's *The Voice Of The Turtle* (1947) was coldly received. Short runs and transfers occupied the Piccadilly until the interior was completely redecorated in a streamlined, rather anonymous manner in 1955, the red plush seating being reduced to number 1,150.

In the five years leading up to the acquisition of the theatre by Donald Albery (against stiff competition from Bernard Delfont) four comedies stood out: Peter Ustinov in his own *Romanoff And Juliet* (1956); Richard Attenborough, John Clements, Kay Hammond and Constance Cummings in *The Rape Of The Belt*

Paul Thornley and Derek Griffiths in *Noises Off*, the hit comedy by Michael Frayn

(1957) by Cummings's husband Ben W. Levy; *Hook, Line And Sinker* (1958) with Joan Plowright and Robert Morley; and the real-life married couple Clements and Hammond in *The Marriage Go Round* (1959).

It was American drama and musicals that gave the Piccadilly some prestige in the '60s and '70s – Edward Albee's scabrous *Who's Afraid Of Virginia Woolf?* (1964), Claire Bloom in *A Streetcar Named Desire* (1974) and Henry Fonda in his solo performance as Clarence Darrow (1975). The Royal Shakespeare Company brought productions here while waiting for the Barbican to open, including the hit *Educating Rita* (1981) with Julie Walters. The 1990s were a decade of variety, with dance – notably the award-winning *Swan Lake* presented by the contemporary ballet company, Adventures in Motion Pictures; plays – a season directed by Sir Peter Hall; in 1999, a return to the musical – the award-winning *Spend, Spend, Spend* starring Barbara Dickson; and comedy – Michael Frayn's smash-hit comedy *Noises Off*. And the Piccadilly sails on…

the piccadilly theatre
denman street = wlv

The Playhouse

On the corner of the junction between Northumberland Avenue and the Embankment, almost tucked beneath Charing Cross Railway Station, stands a lovely theatre with a pretty glass canopy. The story goes that the original theatre was built on this site not because the speculator, Sefton Parry, was a theatre-lover but because he believed that the South-Eastern Railway would have to acquire the ground, at a large profit to Sefton, for an extension scheme to Charing Cross Station. Thankfully, the hoped-for extension never happened, and the theatre is now 120 years old, and thriving.

The first building was designed by architects Fowler and Hill in the French renaissance style, with an elevation of Portland stone, ornamental carving and statues over the main entrance and internal decorations of ivory and gold. The auditorium ceiling featured medallion portraits of famous poets and a handsome glass chandelier, and the stage had damask draperies and curtains. To this day, the theatre retains its beautifully painted canvas act drop (the last in London).

In March 1882, the Avenue Theatre (as it was first known) opened with a revival of *Madame Favart* by Offenbach. It was the first of a long series of French comic operas, given under several managements, which filled the theatre until 1890. Then George Alexander, before the historic era of his management of the St James's Theatre, was manager of the Playhouse for a year. His first production was a great success called *Dr Bill*. In 1894 the theatre had another big hit, with Shaw's *Arms and the Man*, in a season given by the actress Florence Farr. Florence was sponsored by Miss Horniman, a tea heiress, in what is believed to be the first example of commercial sponsorship in the theatre. The opening night of Shaw's production – his very first West End play – was a great success, with Oscar Wilde and W. B. Yates on the guest list.

'The best West End theatre for comedy.'
— Jon Naismith, Producer, BBC Radio 4

Apparently, when Shaw took the stage at the end to take a bow, amongst the cheering came a single 'boo' from the gallery. Shaw responded: 'My dear fellow, I quite agree with you, but what are we two amongst so many?' The Playhouse's auditorium has always been a favourite with actors for its intimacy with the audience.

From 1898 until 1900 the highly popular actor Charles Hawtrey had a run of 544 performances with Ganthony's *A Message From Mars* – quite phenomenal at that time. Other significant productions were Somerset Maugham's early play, *A Man of Honour*, and R. C. Carton's *Mr Hopkinson*, with James Welch. In 1905 Cyril Maude took over the management, leaving the Haymarket where he had been established for some years. He set about reconstructing the theatre. The work was almost completed when on 5 December, 1905 part of Charing Cross Station collapsed onto the theatre. Six people were killed, 26 injured and the theatre badly damaged. After some delay, rebuilding work started. Most of the original exterior was retained, but a completely new interior was constructed, and decorated in rich brown and gold. The new theatre was renamed the Playhouse and it opened on 28 January, 1907. Cyril Maude continued as manager until 1915, presenting a long series of successes. His family's association with the theatre is commemorated today by a stucco cameo of his son John above the foyer bar.

(above) George Bernard Shaw

the playhouse

Frank Curzon then took the theatre, with Gladys Cooper as leading lady. She joined him in management in 1917 and together they were responsible for a series of light, popular shows. In 1927 Gladys became the sole lessee, and there followed a golden period for the Playhouse, with presentations of several plays by Maugham with distinguished casts that included Laurence Olivier, Ivor Novello, Gerald du Maurier, Noël Coward and Raymond Massey.

In the 1930s the Playhouse staged the acclaimed *Libel!* (1934), the professional debut of Alec Guinness, and during 1938 and 1939 the actress and theatre manager Nancy Price ran her People's National Theatre here. On the outbreak of World War II, the theatre closed. It reopened during the war with the Old Vic Company's staging of three productions, including an early play by Peter Ustinov, *Blow Your Own Trumpet*. After the war, the theatre had successes with Bridget Boland's *Cockpit, The Perfect Woman* (1948) and Agatha Christie's *Murder at the Vicarage* (1949), with Thora Hird.

A recording of *The Goon Show*

211

the great theatres of london

The theatre left the fold in 1951, and was converted to become a BBC radio recording studio. These years were rich with classic comedy – the *Goon Shows* and *Hancock's Half Hour* were presented here, to delighted and packed houses. In 1972 very first episode of *I'm Sorry, I Haven't a Clue* was recorded, and in 2002 the cast and crew were welcomed back to the Playhouse for their historic thirtieth anniversary show.

The BBC left the theatre in 1975, and for the next 25 years the Playhouse changed hands many times. The first new proprietor was Robin Gonshaw, who formed a public company to reopen the Playhouse as a theatre, restoring the auditorium to the original 1907 decor of Maude's era, while refitting the backstage area. The theatre reopened in October 1987 with the musical *Girl Friends*. Shortly afterwards, the politician, novelist and playwright Jeffrey Archer bought a controlling interest in the theatre, and the Playhouse staged various productions featuring Ian McKellen, Donald Sinden, Leo McKern, Jackie Mason and Patricia Routledge. In 1991 the Peter Hall Company made the theatre their new home, with Shakespeare's *Twelfth Night*, Tennesee Williams's *The Rose Tattoo*, starring Julie Walters, and Molière's *Tartuffe* with Felicity Kendal, Paul Eddington and John Sessions. In the same year, an award-winning production of Ibsen's *Hedda Gabler*, directed by Deborah Warner, was presented. In 1992 the legendary Ray Cooney, actor, playwright and producer, bought the Playhouse and presented the highly popular *It Runs in the Family* – a farce written by, directed by and starring Ray Cooney!

Then in 1996 the theatre changed hands again, and had hits with Thelma Holt's *A Doll's House* (subsequent winner of four Tony Awards in New York), *HRH,* starring Amanda Donohoe and Corin Redgrave, and *The Wood Demon* by Chekhov. Two years later, the Almeida Theatre chose the playhouse to produce its own work in the West End for the very first time, with two outstanding plays: *The Judas Kiss* with Liam Neeson, and *Naked* with Juliette Binoche. Since then there have been the critically acclaimed Jackie Mason in his one-man show *Much Ado About*

J. B. Priestley's thriller *An Inspector Calls* has won 19 major theatre awards

Everything, a record-breaking run of *Thunderbirds F.A.B.* and currently the National Theatre's *An Inspector Calls*, which has been running at the Playhouse since September 2001. The success of these last two productions shows that the Playhouse really has established itself again in the West End. In this new, more stable atmosphere, the management have introduced the West End's first theatre crèche, the restaurant has been refurbished, and there are plans for an outdoor café and possibly a theatre bookshop.

The Playhouse has sometimes suffered as a result of being seen as 'out of the way'. So, while we all have good reason to be grateful to the South-Eastern Railway for not building their extension to Charing Cross 120 years ago, we also have good reason to be grateful today to Westminster County Council, whose beautiful new footbridge over the Thames leads pedestrians right up Northumberland Street, straight towards the Playhouse Theatre.

the playhouse theatre
northumberland avenue = wc2

The Prince Edward

For the last 24 years crowds have been making their way past sex shops, pubs and restaurants in the lively, cosmopolitan, rather sleazy area of Soho to a brown-brick building in the shape of an Italian palazzo on the corner of Greek and Old Compton Streets. Behind the sturdy square facade, decorated unostentatiously with four pillars, is the gorgeously plush interior, the result of 1990's daringly impressive refurbishment costing £3.5 million. In fact, the Prince Edward simply reeks of the sleek satisfaction that comes from having had the smash-hit musical *Evita* (1978) here for eight fat years, followed by *Chess* (1986), booking over a year ahead, and 1993's Broadway hit *Crazy For You*, with its three-year run. But this money-making did not come about overnight. Despite the hits of the past 20 or so years, the theatre itself has had an extremely chequered career.

This chameleon of a structure has been variously a theatre, a cabaret-restaurant, a servicemen's club, a trade show cinema and the home of Cinerama. It has staged musicals, revues, variety, pantomimes, floor shows and ballet. It has also had three names. On the spot where it was built in 1930 stood a vast draper's shop known as The Emporium. Although Royalty and other nobs patronised it, it began losing trade in the 1920s and was demolished. The building that arose on the site was the first of four new theatres opened in London in 1930. All of them – the Cambridge, the Phoenix, the Whitehall and the Prince Edward – went for the latest in interior decoration, much of which was what we now call Art Deco. The interior designers, Marc-Henri and Laverdet, went for rectilinear patterns and René

'To Evita this evening at the Prince Edward... It's the cult of kitsch again, inert, calculating, camp and morally questionable. I felt out of step with popular taste...'

— Sir Peter Hall (Diaries)

Lalique amber glass to frame the proscenium arch. Alas, this has vanished now.

Coincidentally, the theatre that finally came into its own with *Evita* kicked off with another Latin American señorita. The popular Broadway operetta of the 1920s, *Rio Rita*, was chosen as the opening production. Unfortunately, the show that Ziegfeld presented so successfully in the USA failed to take off in the UK. Other short-lived musical comedies followed with only *Nippy* (1930), starring Binnie Hale, managing to get beyond 100 performances. Not even the wonderful black American cabaret artiste Josephine Baker, the toast of Paris, could fill the theatre in 1933. Non-stop revue from 2 p.m. to midnight was tried until the management, admitting defeat, leased the building for the use of trade film shows.

However, thanks to a syndicate which included the theatre's architect, E. A. Stone, it opened in April 1936 as the London Casino, having been converted skilfully, and at a cost of £25,000, into a cabaret-restaurant. A dance floor and stairways from the stalls to the dress circle were constructed. Business boomed as people flocked to dine, dance and watch spectacular stage shows such as *Folies Parisiennes*. But the party was over in 1940, when the London Casino had to close down during wartime and became the Queensbury All-Services Club.

Tom Arnold and Emile Littler changed it back into a theatre, again called the London Casino. *Pick-Up Girl* (1946) retained the air of naughtiness, dispelled by a revival of Ivor Novello's operetta *The Dancing Years* (1947). A mish-mash of variety, ballet, pantomimes and musicals continued for the next few years.

the prince edward

These included the French-style 'Les Girls' show, *Latin Quarter* (1949), Cicely Courtneidge in a revue called *Over The Moon* (1953), and *Wish You Were Here*, a musical set in a holiday camp and the last stage production before the arrival of Cinerama Holiday in 1954. A flashing sign proclaimed the newest big-screen fad, and *How The West Was Won* (1962) as well as *2001: A Space Odyssey* (1968) were shown here.

In 1974, the Delfont Organisation took over the ownership, redecorated the building and used it as a cinema but for the occasional annual pantomime. Reverting to its original name, the Prince Edward opened its doors to *Evita* in 1978, and it was a case of 'Don't cry for me any more'. Andrew Lloyd Webber and Tim Rice's politico-rock musical, with a sensational Elaine Paige, an unknown, in the title role, put British musicals firmly on the map. Eight years later Elaine Paige starred again in *Chess*, and then again, in 1989, in Cole Porter's *Anything Goes*. Tim Rice collaborated with members of the pop group Abba and RSC director Trevor Nunn to create *Chess*. Those same Abba members, Benny Andersson and Bjorn Ulvaeus, have written the Prince Edward's latest show, *Mamma Mia*, a musical based on the songs of this best-loved pop group. Looks like the perfect recipe for another smash hit for the Prince Edward.

the prince edward theatre
old compton street = wlv

The Prince of Wales

I f a vote were to be taken on the best location for a theatre in the West End, the key position on the corner of Coventry and Oxendon Streets, where stands the Prince of Wales, would surely win. The crowds of revellers streaming between Piccadilly Circus and Leicester Square cannot fail to see the dominating, once-white artificial-stone building with its huge sign and belfry-like tower. Its favourable position has certainly helped to fill its 1,139 seats since it was built in 1937.

The first theatre on the site, called simply the Prince's, was designed by C. J. Phipps as an exotic affair with a Moorish style foyer and smoking room. It opened in January 1884 with Herbert Beerbohm Tree in W. S. Gilbert's 'Fairy Comedy', *The Palace of Truth*. Tree also appeared in a free adaptation of Ibsen's *A Doll's House* called *Breaking A Butterfly* and in Charles Hawtrey's farce *The Private Secretary*, both in the year of the theatre's inauguration. In 1885, Tree played Joseph Surface to Lillie Langtry's Lady Teazle in *School For Scandal*. 'The Jersey Lily' returned for a season of plays in 1886, the year the Prince's, coincidentally, changed its title to the Prince of Wales, named after the actress's intimate friend. The success of the comic opera *Dorothy* (1887), which ran a year, led the producer, Henry J. Leslie, to build the Lyric, Shaftesbury Avenue from its profits. The appearance of the 'wordless play' *L'Infant Prodigue* from France, with mimes Jane May and Zanfretta, led to the establishment of the first Pierrot troupe in England.

According to the dictionary definition, musical comedy is 'a popular type of light entertainment which derives from a fusion

'A curious medley of song, dance and nonsense ...and the very vaguest attempt at satirising the modern masher.'

Sunday Times on *In Town*, 1892

of burlesque and light opera'. Thus George Edwardes's *In Town* (1892) has the distinction of being considered the first true musical comedy. Another example of the new genre as presented by Edwardes was *The Gaiety Girl* (1893). Apart from musical comedy, Mrs Patrick Campbell and Forbes Robertson performed in Maurice Maeterlinck's symbolist drama *Pelléas et Mélisande* with incidental music by Fauré. Marie Tempest, having deserted Edwardes and musical comedy, played in three adaptations from novels: *English Nell*, from Anthony Hope; *Peg Woffington*, from Charles Read; and *Becky Sharp* from Thackeray's *Vanity Fair*, all between 1900 and 1901. Edwardes's musical comedies returned from 1903 to 1910; 'Man-about-town' Charles Hawtrey appeared in comedies from 1912 to 1918, and Beatrice Lillie, Gertrude Lawrence, Jack Buchanan and Jessie Matthews featured in André Chariot revues from 1918 to 1926. Things deteriorated somewhat in the 1930s as the Prince of Wales resorted to 'Non-Stop Revue' which was only halted by the demolition of the theatre in 1937.

The foundation stone of the new house, which opened in October 1937, was laid by Gracie Fields. The architect, Robert Cromie, conceived a large two-tier theatre with the circle front within 21 feet of the orchestra. The auditorium has a slightly cavernous feel, but the enormous stalls bar has room for an impressive archive of playbills of the many shows that have played here. Among them were the successes under the management of George Black in the 1940s. He introduced comedian Sid Field to London audiences in *Strike A New Note* in 1943. Field also shone in *Strike It Again* (1944), *Piccadilly Hayride* (1946) and finally *Harvey* (1949), Mary Chase's Broadway hit about an amiable

Linda Baron was the mature Belle Poitrine in the musical version of Patrick Dennis's *Little Me* (1984)

drunk with an imaginary giant white rabbit as a friend. Sadly, Field died at the age of 46 during its long run. *Harvey* returned to the Prince of Wales in 1975, when Hollywood star James Stewart repeated his New York stage role of Elwood P. Dowd, the drunk, which he had also played on the screen in 1950. Another legendary movie star, Mae West, appeared here briefly in *Diamond Lil* in 1948.

For much of the 1950s the theatre was given over to traditional variety shows, featuring Benny Hill, Frankie Howerd and Norman Wisdom, until *The World Of Suzie Wong* (1959) – called by critic Kenneth Tynan 'The World Of Woozey Song' –

the great theatres of london

arrived for a run of almost three years. American comedies and musicals were to be the principal fare from then on. Neil Simon's first play, *Come Blow Your Horn* (1962), had a good run, but it was Barbra Streisand's dynamic presence in *Funny Girl* (1966) that had the queues collecting in Coventry Street. Streisand was

Cameron Mackintosh's musical adaptation of *The Witches of Eastwick* hit the London stage in 2000

the prince of wales

some months pregnant at the time (by her then husband Elliot Gould), so the show's run was limited. Other imports were the splendid *Sweet Charity* (1967) starring Juliet Prowse, *Promises Promises* (1969), *Same Time Next Year* (1976), *I Love My Wife* (1977) and *Little Me* (1984). Home-grown productions included *The Good Old Bad Old Days* (1972), directed, starring and written (with Leslie Bricusse) by Anthony Newley, *Underneath The Arches* (1982), a tribute to Flanagan and Allen, and *Allo Allo* (1986), a comedy derived from the television series about the French Resistance which vast sections of the population found irresistible. The 1990s was a decade of musical hits, with *Copacabana* (1994), *Smokey Joe's Café* (1996) and *West Side Story* (1999). Now the smash-hit musical *The Full Monty* (2002), based on the highly popular film, is outstripping the West End competition.

the prince of wales theatre
coventry street = wlv

The Queen's

In the heart of 'theatreland', on the corner of Shaftesbury Avenue and Wardour Street, stands the modern glass-fronted, red-brick, five-storey building that houses the Queen's Theatre. If one wonders, while contemplating the pleasing but unexceptional 1959 facade, what the 1907 playhouse once looked like, then one has only to walk a few yards to the Gielgud Theatre on the Rupert Street corner of the block. They were designed by W. G. R. Sprague as near-identical twin theatres. Today, they could not be more dissimilar.

Some people may agree with John Earl's views on the Queen's 'outdated, un-theatrelike, and even heartless' exterior, but few can fail to be charmed by the red, white and gold auditorium, with its domed ceiling and Louis XVI-style plaster ornamentation, which creates an elegant Edwardian atmosphere. The reason why the Gielgud's exterior remains little altered from its inception in 1906, while its twin resides in a modern shell, is that a German bomb fell on the unfortunate Queen's in September 1940, destroying much of the facade and the back of the stalls. It is ironic that the first London theatre casualty of the war was a theatre which had had fewer theatrical bombs than most.

However, the Queen's took some years to make its reputation. The opening production, *The Sugar Bowl* (1907), a comedy with Edmund Gwenn, was a flop, allowing Shaw's *The Devil's Disciple* to transfer from the Savoy. H. B. Irving took over the management in 1909, appearing in a number of his famous father Henry's renowned barnstorming parts such as *The Bells*, *Louis XI* and *The Lyons Mail*. But in 1913 blood and thunder gave way to 'Tango Teas' for which the stalls were transformed into a dance floor with tables placed around it so that the patrons could partake of tea and dance the fashionable tango – all for half-a-crown.

*'No doubt in 1957 the restoration of the facade...
was seen as exciting and new. Now it looks outdated,
un-theatrelike, and even heartless.'*
— John Earl in *Curtains!!!*

When the strains of the tango had died away, the sound of
applause returned to the building for the American Jewish comedy
Potash And Perlmutter (1914) and its sequel *Potash And Perlmutter
In Society* (1916). In the '20s, the theatre welcomed Alfred Savoir's
Bluebeard's Eighth Wife (1922), Fred and Adele Astaire in *Stop
Flirting* (1923), Owen Nares and Fay Compton in J. M. Barrie's
The Little Minister (1924) and Edmund Gwenn and Yvonne
Arnaud as Mr and Mrs Pepys in *And So To Bed* (1926).

From 1929, the stage of the Queen's held a dazzling array
of stars and stars-to-be that elicits the inevitable phrase 'the
good old days'. Cedric Hardwicke (knighted in 1934) appeared
as Magnus in *The Apple Cart* (1929) and Mr Barrett in *The
Barretts Of Wimpole Street* (1930) with Gwen ffrangcon-Davies as
Elizabeth; Edith Evans was in *The Apple Cart, Heartbreak House*

the queen's

(1932) and *Once In A Lifetime* (1933); and Marie Tempest, Sybil Thorndike, Margaret Rutherford, Ursula Jeans and Rex Harrison were assembled for Robert Morley's first play, *Short Story* (1935). But it was John Gielgud's presence that dominated the Queen's from 1937 to the outbreak of war.

He made his first appearance in the West End here in his debut performance of *Hamlet*, transferred from the Old Vic in 1930, with Donald Wolfit and Martita Hunt as Claudius and Gertrude. To see a 25-year-old Prince of Denmark was a novelty for audiences used to middle-aged actors tackling the role. It did well even though two other *Hamlet*s were playing in London at the same time. (Henry Ainley at the Haymarket, and Alexander Moissi, in German, at the nearby Gielgud Theatre – then called the Globe.) Gielgud returned in 1937 in a play especially written for him by Emlyn Williams, titled – curiously to our modern ears – *He Was Born Gay*. It ran for 12 nights. Putting that behind him, he brought in a season of four plays for eight months starting in September of the same year. Gielgud not only played Richard II to Michael Redgrave's Bolingbroke, Shylock to Peggy Ashcroft's Portia, Vershinin in *Three Sisters* and Joseph Surface in *School For Scandal*, but also directed the first two.

In addition to the leading actors, Harry Andrews, Dennis Price and Alec Guinness had small parts in all four productions. Redgrave and his wife Rachel Kempson appeared as Charles Surface and Maria in Tyrone Guthrie's *School For Scandal*, little knowing that their one-year-old daughter Vanessa would appear on the same stage with her father in Robert Bolt's *The Tiger And The Horse* (1960), triumph in Ibsen's *The Lady From The Sea* (1961) and as Nina in *The Seagull* (1964), and star with her sisters Lynn and Jemma in the acclaimed *Three Sisters* and *Matador* (1990).

Immediately after this exhausting but rewarding season, Gielgud stepped into modern dress to play opposite Marie Tempest in Dodie Smith's family saga *Dear Octopus* (1938). Dame Marie did not get on with the author, and when Smith took a curtain call on the first night with the company, the actress turned her back on her in full view of the audience. The first night also coincided with Chamberlain's return from Munich. The year's run was broken by the declaration of war, and the Queen's closed down. It reopened in December 1939 with the optimistically titled revue *All Clear* starring Beatrice Lillie, followed by Daphne du Maurier's *Rebecca* with Owen Nares, Celia Johnson and Margaret Rutherford. It was during the successful run of the latter that the bomb fell.

The devastated theatre stood dark and deserted for almost 20 years, a sad reminder of the Blitz, before architects Bryan Westwood and Hugh Casson restored it. It reopened in July 1959, appropriately enough with John Gielgud giving his Shakespeare recital, *The Ages Of Man*. In the same year, the year of his knighthood, Sir Michael Redgrave returned in *The Aspern Papers*, his own adaptation of the Henry James story. Anthony Newley sang 'What Kind Of Fool Am I?' as Littlechap in the allegorical musical *Stop The World I Want To Get Off* (1961) for over a year before moving with it to Broadway.

The big theatrical event of 1966 was the return of Noël Coward to the West End after a 13-year absence. He starred alongside Irene Worth and Lilli Palmer in a trio of new plays which he gave the omnibus title of *Suite In Three Keys*. Although Coward's health was poor and he often 'dried', he felt 'a warmth and a genuine love emanating from the front of the house at every performance'. It was his final stage appearance. 'The Master' died not long after his friend Marlene Dietrich's successful one-woman show at the Queen's and Gielgud's starry production of *Private Lives* with the then married couple, Maggie Smith and Robert Stephens, both in 1972.

The '70s and '80s were successful decades for the Queen's, with Alan Bates in *Otherwise Engaged* (1975), Alec Guinness in *The Old Country* (1978), Tom Courtenay in *The Dresser* (1980), Charlton Heston in *The Caine Mutiny Court Martial* (1985) and Alan Bennett's *Single Spies* (1989). In the same year came a brilliant production of *Shadowlands*, starring Nigel Hawthorne, as C. S. Lewis, and Jane Lapotaire; Hawthorne also directed and starred in

the queen's

The young Vanessa Redgrave was Nina in Chekhov's *The Seagull* in 1964. Twenty-one years later, she graduated to Arkadina, co-starring with her daughter Natasha Richardson as Nina

The Clandestine Marriage (1994). Acclaimed director Thelma Holt has had two successful Shakespeare productions at the Queen's – *Much Ado About Nothing* with Mark Rylance (1993) and *Macbeth* with Rufus Sewell (1999). In 2000, the Queen's became a Really Useful Theatre when Lord Lloyd Webber and Bridgepoint Capital purchased Stoll Moss Theatres Ltd. Under this new management it opened with a sell-out production of *The Seven Year Itch* starring Daryl Hannah. In 2002 the theatre staged a highly acclaimed South African production of *The Mysteries* – all demonstrating that the Queen's is a venue of continuing quality.

the queen's theatre
shaftesbury avenue = wlv

The Royal Court

The Establishment-sounding Royal Court Theatre, with its noble brick and stone Italian Renaissance frontage, brazenly stares out on the leafy confines of trendy Sloane Square and the fripperies of the King's Road, Chelsea – a surprising locality in which to find the most radical of all of the great theatres of London, and one that changed the face of British drama in the late 1950s.

In 1956, the year of the Suez Crisis, Britain was forced to re-examine its role on the world stage; youth culture burst onto the scene, and so did the production of *Look Back In Anger* at the Royal Court. 'An angry play by an angry young author... neurotic, exaggerated and more than slightly distasteful,' railed the *Daily Mail*, typical of most of the reviews. One critic's voice came through loud and clear – Kenneth Tynan in the *Observer* wrote, 'I doubt if I could love anyone who did not wish to see *Look Back In Anger*. It is the best young play of its decade.' Whatever one thought of 27-year-old John Osborne's choleric, wittily rhetorical shout against aspects of British society, it advanced the careers of its author, the director Tony Richardson and the actors Kenneth Haigh, Alan Bates and Mary Ure (Osborne's wife-to-be); it gave rise to a movement labelled 'Angry Young Men', and was a landmark in the counterblast against the complacency of the commercial theatre.

The English Stage Company was formed in 1956, with Arts Council subsidy, 'to stage and encourage new writing' under the artistic direction of George Devine (pronounced Deveen). Living up to this pledge, Devine presented a multitude of new works by

'If more plays like tonight's Look Back In Anger
*are produced, the "Writer's Theatre"
at the Royal Court must surely sink.'*
— *Birmingham Post,* 1956

British writers in the nine years he was at the Court. His
achievement was extraordinary. After his death in 1966, the
tradition was admirably continued by his successors, William
Gaskill, Stuart Burge and Max Stafford-Clark. Among the many
notable productions presented over the years have been Osborne's
Luther (1961), *Inadmissible Evidence* (1964) and *A Patriot For Me*
(1965); Arnold Wesker's *Chicken Soup With Barley* (1958), *Roots*
(1959), *I'm Talking About Jerusalem* (1960) and *Chips With
Everything* (1962); John Arden's *Serjeant Musgrave's Dance*
(1959); Ann Jellicoe's *The Knack* (1962); David Storey's *The
Contractor* (1969), *In Celebration* (1969) and *The Changing Room*
(1971); Christopher Hampton's *The Philanthropist* (1970) and

(above) Julie Covington and Tom Wilkinson in *Tom And Viv* (1984), Michael Hastings's searing play about T. S. Eliot's first wife, confined to an asylum

(left) John Osborne's *Look Back In Anger* (1956) changed the face of British theatre forever. Here, Jimmy Porter (Kenneth Haigh, right) vents his spleen on his wife, Alison (Mary Ure), while friends Cliff and Helena (Alan Bates, Helen Hughes) look on.

Savages (1973); David Hare's *Teeth 'n' Smiles* (1975); Mary O'Malley's *Once A Catholic* (1977), Nigel Williams's *Class Enemy* (1978), Michael Hastings's *Tom And Viv* (1984); and Caryl Churchill's *Cloud Nine* (1980), *Top Girls* (1982) and *Serious Money* (1987).

Modern foreign greats have not been neglected either, and Brecht, Beckett, Genet, Ionesco and Sartre have been well represented. Even the theatrical knights from the 'other' theatre have not been able to resist the pull of the Royal Court. Sir Alec Guinness played in Ionesco's *Exit The King* (1964) and *Macbeth* (1966); Sir John Gielgud (with Sir Ralph Richardson) in David Storey's *Home* (1970), Charles Wood's *Veterans* (1972) and as Shakespeare in Edward Bond's *Bingo* (1973); and Sir Laurence Olivier in Ionesco's *Rhinoceros* (1960) directed by Orson Welles. After seeing *Look Back In Anger*, Olivier asked Osborne to write a play for him. The result was *The Entertainer* (1957), a triumph in all departments and a turning point in the great actor's career.

Archie Rice, the fifth-rate comedian Olivier played in *The Entertainer*, says, 'Don't clap too hard, lady, it's an old building.' In fact, the present building dates from 1888, although there had been a theatre of the same name on the south side of Sloane Square. After that was demolished in 1887, another, designed by Walter Emden and Bertie Crewe, went up on the east side next to the Metropolitan railway station (now Sloane Square tube). Originally a three-tier theatre with a 642-seat capacity, its interior was reconstructed in 1952, closing off the old gallery and reducing the seating to 401. Further redecorations in 1980 enlarged it somewhat. In 1971, a rehearsal room became the 80-seat experimental Theatre Upstairs. However, by 1994 this historic theatre was threatened with closure as its major structures disintegrated. It closed for redevelopment for four years from 1996, and with great technical difficulty a new theatre emerged from the old, managing to reflect its architectural late-Victorian origins while creating better backstage conditions, updated technical systems, improved audience circulation and a modern front of house. While work was in progress the Theatre Downstairs moved to the Duke of York's, and the Theatre Upstairs relocated to the New Ambassadors. In February 2000, the refurbished theatre at Sloane Square opened again, with both auditoria named after the Jerwood Foundation – the Jerwood Theatre Downstairs and the Jerwood Theatre Upstairs.

Arthur Wing Pinero was the playwright most associated with the Royal Court in its earliest days. His successes here included *The Cabinet Minister* (1890), *The Amazons* (1893) and, particularly, *Trelawny Of The 'Wells'* (1898), which recalled his days as an actor. Also popular was *Under The Clock* (1893), a precursor of intimate revue, in which 22-year-old Seymour Hicks and Charles Brookfield impersonated various theatrical luminaries of the day. But the Court's reputation for advanced drama was established when J. E. Vedrenne and Harley Granville-Barker managed the theatre from 1904 to 1907, presenting a remarkable range of plays, 11 of them by George Bernard Shaw, whose wide renown dates from this memorable season. If the spirit of Shaw haunts any theatre, it would surely be the Royal Court. *You Never Can Tell, Man And Superman* and *The Doctor's Dilemma* proved there was a public for intellectual theatre. Not unlike today's Court audience, people came to be stimulated mentally and enjoyed being lectured at. It was Harley Granville-Barker's experience here which led him to espouse the cause of a national theatre.

Shaw returned to the Court, under J. B. Fagan's stewardship, with *Heartbreak House* (1921), his first play since before the war. When Barry Jackson became manager in 1924, he had the courage to present Shaw's mammoth five-part *Back To Methuselah* over four nights. Among Jackson's other achievements were Eden Phillpott's *The Farmer's Wife* (1924), which ran almost three years, and modern dress productions of *Macbeth* and *The Taming Of The Shrew* (both 1927). Twenty-one-year-old Laurence Olivier played small roles in the Shakespeare plays. For most of the latter, he had to sit in a stage box in full view of the audience. According to Olivier, he spent much of the time trying to make Ralph Richardson, who played Tranio, laugh. Every

East is East by Ayub Khan-Kin

night he would pull faces and make gestures to no avail. One night, he did absolutely nothing but stare at Ralph who promptly 'corpsed'. Olivier also appeared in Elmer Rice's expressionist fantasy *The Adding Machine* (1928).

The Royal Court was closed (except for a short period as a cinema) between 1932 and 1952. It then marked time for a few years before the historic arrival of the English Stage Company, which has always invited controversy. There was uproar in some quarters at Edward Bond's *Saved* (1965), which depicted a baby being stoned to death, and the same author's *Early Morning* (1968), which presented Queen Victoria having a lesbian affair with Florence Nightingale. Only on one occasion has the Court been seen to give in to outside pressure. This concerned the last-minute withdrawal of Jim Allen's *Perdition* in 1987, concerning the Holocaust, on the grounds that 'it might offend too many people'.

Under the artistic direction of Stephen Daldry, the theatre flourished throughout the '90s. Key productions were *Oleanna* by David Mamet (1993), *Mojo* by Jez Butterworth, *Blasted* by Royal Court protégé Sarah Kane (1995), *The Beauty Queen of Leenane* by Martin McDonagh (1996) and the notorious *Shopping and F***ing* (1997) by Mark Ravenhill. The same year also saw the stage premiere of *East is East* by Ayub Khan-Din, which became a highly successful film two years later, and *The Weir* by Conor McPherson. In 2000 writer Sarah Kane's *4.48 Psychosis* was performed to great acclaim a year after her death. Under Ian Rickson, the theatre staged *Boy Gets Girl* by Rebecca Gilman (2001) and in 2002 *The Night Heron* by Jez Butterworth. And so the Royal Court Theatre, back home in Sloane Square, continues its grand tradition of daring, enlightened drama by exciting new writers.

the royal court
sloane square = swlw

The Royal
Opera House

Opera houses are generally grandiose, luxurious palaces erected to stage the most expensive theatrical art form ever devised – and the Royal Opera House, Covent Garden can take its place among the world's best. Although less monumental than the Paris Opera or La Scala, its ambience of opulence and enchantment and a sense of occasion are created immediately in the sumptuous lobby. The splendid Grand Staircase on the left rises, between huge allegorical paintings, towards the famous Crush Bar – a great hall with 20-foot-high paintings adorning the walls, beneath a sparkling chandelier. All this even before one enters the majestic auditorium, substantially as it was when new in 1858. From the Orchestra Stalls, Stalls Circle and Grand Tier, the horseshoe-shaped levels move up to the Balcony Stalls and the Valhalla of the Amphitheatre close to the shallow, aquamarine dome. Looking down from this vertiginous height towards the stage, with its famous crimson velvet curtains bearing the Queen's monogram, one notices, above the proscenium, a rustic scene in which Orpheus plays his lyre. Along the gold tier-fronts stand a bevy of bare-breasted maidens behind rows of claret-shaded candelabra. From 1996 to 1999 the Royal Opera House underwent a massive programme of development and refurbishment. The auditorium and original foyers were renovated; the magnificent nineteenth-century glass and iron Floral Hall – the roof of which was destroyed in the 1950s – was restored and incorporated into the main theatre building as the new main audience circulation space, and a new building, which houses additional public areas, new rehearsal studios for the

'A very English place for grand occasions! An odd and endearing mixture of red velvet plush and drawing-room intimacy.'
— Max Loppert

Royal Ballet and Opera and better backstage facilities was constructed.

The first theatre, on the site of what had been a convent garden (hence the name), was built in 1732 for John Rich, who held the patent which permitted only the two Theatre Royals, at Drury Lane and Covent Garden, to perform 'legitimate' theatre legitimately. It was originally, therefore, mainly devoted to drama, though three of Handel's operas, *Alcina* (1735), *Atalanta* (1736) and *Berenice* (1737), had their premieres here. Rich, who was constantly in litigation, and who killed a fellow actor in a fight over a wig, managed the theatre until his death in 1761. John Beard, his son-in-law, took over and presented mainly operas until he was succeeded by Thomas Harris in 1774 when plays became the order of the day. Oliver Goldsmith's *She Stoops To Conquer* (1773) and Sheridan's *The Rivals* (1775) had first performances here. In May 1789 Charles Macklin, playing Shylock in *The Merchant of Venice*, made his last appearance but, being as old as the century, he failed to complete the performance. In contrast, a tragedian aged only 13 made his London debut in 1804. Master Betty, known as the young Roscius, played the great Shakespearean roles and caused a sensation. Parliament even adjourned in order to see his Hamlet. This freakish success ended a year later when his attempt at Richard III was hissed off the stage.

In September, 1808, a fire in which 23 firemen were killed destroyed the building and Handel's organ and scores with it. A mere 12 months later a new theatre, modelled on the Temple of Minerva at the Acropolis, stood in its place. Owing to the cost of rebuilding, seat prices were raised. This action caused riots and disturbances for 61 nights until finally actor-manager John Philip Kemble was forced to lower them again. Kemble's sister, Sarah Siddons, bade farewell to the stage with Lady Macbeth in 1812, and Kemble retired in favour of his younger brother Charles in 1817. Charles Kemble was one of the first actor-managers to bring some historical accuracy to costumes and sets, beginning in 1823 with *King John*, designed by James Robinson Planche. Planche was also the librettist of Weber's *Oberon* (1826), 'the most important English romantic opera'.

In March 1833, Edmund Kean, playing Othello, was taken ill during a scene with Iago, played by his son, Charles. Falling into Charles's arms, Kean cried, 'Oh God! I am dying... speak to them for me.' The greatest actor of the age had made his last exit. One of Kean's rivals was William Charles Macready, who assumed the management of Covent Garden in 1837. He introduced a new calcium light that was to revolutionise stage lighting. 'It was the application of the limelight', wrote Edward Fitzgerald, 'that really threw open the realms of glittering

A contemporary engraving of the tragedienne Rachel at Covent Garden in 1841

fairyland to the scenic artist.' Macready's reign was marked by internal dissension. The remarkable Madame Vestris took over in 1839, and the French actress Rachel made a memorable appearance in *Horace* in 1841. In 1856, fire once again consumed the Theatre Royal.

On 15 May, 1858, the Royal Italian Opera, the building we know today, opened. Sir Edward M. Barry created an imposing structure in the Roman Renaissance style with a raised Corinthian portico. The statues by Rossi on either side of the facade, and the Flaxman bas-reliefs along the front, survive from the 1809 building. Managed by Frederic Gye, the new premises were given over entirely to operas sung in Italian, regardless of their provenance. Opera at that period was more a social than an artistic event and, as before, the lights remained on during performances so that the gentry could see and be seen. Berlioz was once refused entry because his evening coat did not match his trousers.

Things improved when Augustus Harris took over in 1888. As operas were now given in their original language and in English, the 'Italian' was dropped from the name of the house. Harris introduced Edouard and Jean de Reszke and Nellie Melba to London, the latter making her debut in *Lucia di Lammermoor* (1888) and continuing to appear in almost every season here until 1914. Adelina Patti sang 25 consecutive seasons in over 30 roles at around £200 a performance.

In the orchestra pit, Gustav Mahler conducted Wagner's Ring cycle in 1892 and, in 1908, Hans Richter conducted the first Ring in English. Thomas Beecham, backed by his father (Joseph, of pills fame), launched his first season in 1910 with the British premiere of Richard Strauss's *Elektra*. After World War I, during which the opera house was used as a furniture warehouse, Bruno Walter became chief conductor. He concentrated mainly on Wagner, Mozart and Strauss, and his *Der Rosenkavalier* of 1924 (with Lotte Lehmann and Elisabeth Schumann) was a landmark. Beecham returned to take over the baton from 1932 to 1939. Between the wars Italian opera, excepting Puccini's works, was somewhat neglected. For example, not a note of Verdi was heard here for six years.

In 1946 the Covent Garden Opera Company was formed, subsidised by the Arts Council, and would share the house with the Sadler's Wells Ballet Company run by Ninette de Valois. (Both companies became Royal later.) The infant opera company had stormy beginnings, with music director Karl Rankl clashing with the director of productions. The latter was Peter Brook, then only 24 years old, who produced an erotic *Salome*, with sets by Salvador Dali, in 1949. Erich Kleiber contributed greatly to the development of the company between 1950 and 1953. He conducted the first British performance of Alban Berg's *Wozzeck* in 1952. In the same year, Maria Callas made her Covent Garden debut in *Norma*, her grandest tragic role. Highlights of Rafael Kubelik's tenure (1955–58) were Birgit Nilsson's Brunhilde in the Ring (1957), *The Trojans* – given in its entirety for the first time on a single evening, also in 1957 – directed by John Gielgud, and Visconti's production of *Don Carlos* (1958), conducted by Giulini.

English performers, and operas, began to attract attention in the 1950s. There were world premieres of works by native

David Hockney designed *L'Enfant et Les Sortilége*

composers such as Benjamin Britten (*Billy Budd*, 1951; *Gloriana*, 1953), William Walton (*Troilus and Cressida*, 1954) and Michael Tippett (*The Midsummer Marriage*, 1955). The wonderful contralto Kathleen Ferrier gave her last ever performance, while in considerable pain, in Gluck's *Orfeo ed Euridice* in 1953. She did not complete the second performance, and was soon dead. In 1959, Australia's Joan Sutherland became a star overnight in *Lucia di Lammermoor*.

Georg Solti took over in 1961, with such triumphs during his regime as *Fidelio* (1961), conducted by Klemperer; *Tosca* (1964) with Callas and Gobbi in a Zeffirelli production, the second act of which is preserved on film for posterity; *Pelléas et Mélisande* (1969); and *Tristan und Isolde* (1971).

Under Colin Davis (1971–86) there were many great nights at the opera, mention of two or three must suffice – *The Marriage Of Figaro* in 1971, which brought an unknown young Maori

Mikhail Baryshnikov and Antoinette Sibley in MacMillan's *A Month In The Country* (1985)

the royal opera house

soprano named Kiri Te Kanawa to fame; *La Fanciulla del West* (1980) with sets by James Bond film designer Ken Adam; and Berg's *Lulu* in 1981. Bernard Haitink became Music Director in 1987. Highlights of his triumphant 15-year tenure included the first performances at Covent Garden of Borodin's *Prince Igor* and Janacek's *Katya Kabanova*, a tour of Japan with an all-Mozart programme, restagings of the Wagner repertory, Luciano Pavarotti singing in a revival of *Tosca* (2001), Placido Domingo in *Die Frau Ohne Schatten* (2001) and Bryn Terfel as Don Giovanni (2002).

Developing parallel to the Royal Opera has been the Royal Ballet, much-travelled and world-renowned. Its reputation took root when the company unveiled the great Margot Fonteyn in *The Sleeping Beauty* to New York audiences in the 1950s. Aside from the traditional classical repertoire – sometimes rechoreographed, as with Rudolph Nureyev's version of *The Nutcracker*, the company's choreographers have enriched the programme with new works too numerous to mention. Examples include John Cranko's *Pineapple Poll*, Frederick Ashton's *Symphonic Variations* and Kenneth MacMillan's *Anastasia*, created for the exciting Canadian-born ballerina, Lynn Seymour. Guest choreographers have included the cream of America – Balanchine, Jerome Robbins, Glen Tetley. All have been served by superlative dancers, among them Fonteyn, Michael Somes, Nadia Nerina, David Blair, Merle Park, Donald Macleary, Antoinette Sibley, Anthony Dowell, Lesley Collier, Wayne Eagling and Stephen Jefferies. Svetlana Beriosova, Nureyev himself and his natural successor Mikhail Baryshnikov have also enhanced this great company.

the royal opera house
floral street = wc2e

Sadler's Wells

The world of tutus and tights, pirouettes and *pas de deux* is conjured up for most people when Sadler's Wells is mentioned, mainly because of the years between 1931 and 1940 that the Vic-Wells (later the Sadler's Wells) Ballet Company spent at the building where the hitherto undreamed-of English Ballet was born. Until then, dancers had to change their names to foreign ones to gain acceptance. It was here, in the north London suburb of Islington, far from the madding West End crowds, that a permanent ballet company was formed. It was created by the formidable Lilian Baylis of the Old Vic, who spent five years raising the money to build the theatre after demolishing the old one, and rapidly went from strength to strength, so that the 'Wells' became known throughout the land. Installed since 1946 at the Royal Opera House, Covent Garden, the company has perpetuated the name in its official title – the Sadler's Wells Royal Ballet.

In 1998, the sixth theatre on the Sadler's Wells site was opened, replacing the functional brick building which had existed since World War II. The new Sadler's Wells Theatre, with its soaring glass facade, is an inspirational modern creation designed by the Arts Team at RHWL, with consultant architects Nicholas Hare Architects. It is as impressive and creative inside as it is outside, with a flexible auditorium adjustable to seat either 1,000 or 1,600 people, a sprung stage, double the previous size, and advanced computer-controlled stage and lighting technology.

The name Sadler's Wells derives from the medicinal spring that was discovered in the grounds of a Mr Thomas Sadler in the year 1683. (The original well can be found under a trap door at the back of the stalls.) The land, then in the open country, became a popular pleasure garden where people could watch various

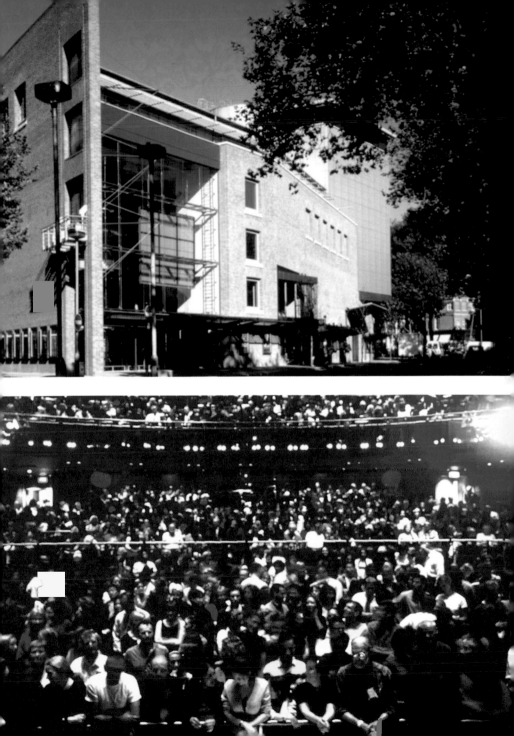

'A bold, handsome, welcoming theatre – its glass facade invites the passer–by to come in... with spacious public areas and a splendid stage, up to the minute in technology...'

— *Financial Times*, 1998

entertainments and take the waters. A wooden 'Musick House' was erected where concerts and masques could be given. It stood for nearly a century, until a stone theatre was built in its place in 1765 by Thomas Rosoman, who became manager. Tom King, the well-known Drury Lane actor and creator of the role of Sir Peter Teazle, succeeded him in 1772, remaining for ten years until Henry Siddons (the actress Sarah Siddons's husband), in association with dramatist-actor-composer Charles Dibdin and his two sons, took over. In 1801, a small boy called Master Carey performed here; he would become Edmund Kean in adulthood.

'Nautical Drama' drew the crowds to Islington from 1814, when a tank of water, 90 feet long and three feet deep, was placed on the stage in order to simulate naval battles. Swimmers manipulated scale-model ships while cannons fired in plays called *The Siege of Gibraltar* and *Naval Triumph; Or, The Tars Of Old England*. However, with the breaking of the monopoly of the Patent Theatres which prevented legitimate drama being given other than at the Theatres Royal in 1843, a new era dawned at Sadler's Wells. The superb actor-manager Samuel Phelps took a lease on the near-derelict building in 1844 where, in the following 18 years, he produced almost all of Shakespeare's plays, thus making it 'a place for justly representing the works of our great dramatic poet', as Phelps rightly claimed. The location which started as a spa became an oasis of culture.

But 'Oh! What a fall was there!' when Phelps retired in 1862. The theatre was used as a skating rink and a prize-fighting venue before it was closed for repairs in 1878. A year later it was bought by Mrs Bateman, the widow of the owner of the Lyceum. On her death in 1881, it passed into her daughter Isabel's hands. Unfortunately, the theatre developed into the home of crude melodrama where the 'gallery contained the most villainous, desperate, hatchet-faced assembly of ruffians to be found in all London'. No wonder Miss Bateman left the stage to take Holy Orders. The 'Wells' later became a music hall, then an early cinema before closing down in 1906 where it lay, like Aurora in *The Sleeping Beauty*, until Lilian Baylis hacked her way through the tangled financial undergrowth to kiss it into life again.

At first, drama, ballet and opera alternated between the Old Vic and Sadler's Wells. The opening Shakespeare season of 1931–32, in which John Gielgud played Malvolio, Benedick and King Lear, and Ralph Richardson was Sir Toby Belch, Petruchio, Bottom and Henry V, ran two weeks at the 'Vic' and one at the 'Wells'. But this proved too expensive and in 1935 only opera and ballet were given, while drama remained at the Vic. With the help of Nicolas Sergueyev from the Russian Maryinsky, the ballet company, under Ninette de Valois (born Edris Stannus in 1898), was able to build up a classical repertoire that included *Giselle*, *Swan Lake*, *Coppélia* and *The Nutcracker*, and new ballets were commissioned from British choreographers. Frederick Ashton delivered *Facade* (1931), *Apparitions* (1936), *Les Patineurs* (1937) and *Horoscope* (1938), while de Valois choreographed *Job* (1931), *The Rake's Progress* and *Checkmate* (both 1935), most of them still performed. When the leading dancers Alicia Markova (Alice Marks) and Anton Dolin (Patrick Healey-Kay) left to form their own company, Margot Fonteyn (Peggy Hookham) and Robert Helpmann stepped into their ballet shoes. The opera company took a little longer to gain wide recognition, but under the baton of Laurence Collingwood, and with singers such as Joan Cross, Edith Coates, Tudor Davies and Henry Wendon, and a growing repertoire strong on Wagner and Verdi sung in English, it soon blossomed.

In 1938, the year after the parsimonious Baylis died, improvements were carried out by enlarging the stage and building new dressing rooms and a rehearsal room. However, in 1940 the theatre was damaged by a bomb and performances were held at the New Theatre (now the Albery) during the war. Only the opera company returned to its home at Sadler's Wells in 1945 with an historic reopening, the world premiere of Benjamin Britten's *Peter Grimes* with Peter Pears in the title role and Reginald Goodall in the pit. It heralded a new dawn of English opera. Over the years, especially under Norman Tucker from 1948 to 1966, the Sadler's Wells opera grew into a real ensemble, members of which were conductors Alexander Gibson and Colin Davis, producers Denis Arundell, Wendy Toye, Basil Coleman and Glen Byam Shaw, and singers who became internationally famous such as Amy Shuard, David Ward, Peter Glossop, Donald McIntyre, Norman Bailey and Rita Hunter. In 1959, the doubtful acoustics were improved by a canopy suspended over the proscenium.

After the company moved to the Coliseum in 1974 to become the English National Opera, the theatre fell on less exciting times. But under the leadership of Ian Albery, who arrived as Chief Executive and Producer in 1994, Sadler's Wells has really thrived again, with ground-breaking productions like Adventures in Motion Pictures' all-male *Swan Lake* in 1996. Today, in its

A venue for international art, The Wells presented the Japanese Noh Theatre in 1983

sadler's wells

Random Dance's modern masterpiece, *Nemesis*

inspirational new home, it is a dance and lyric theatre of world stature. In the two years since the new Sadler's Wells opened, it has attracted top international choreographers such as Matthew Bourne and Pina Bausch, companies like the Ballett Frankfurt, Mikhail Baryshnikov's White Oak Dance Project, Sankai Juko and Kabuki, as well as the Welsh National Opera, the Royal Ballet and the Royal Opera. In 2001 it was announced that the Random Dance Company (led by the brilliant Wayne McGregor) was to become the Sadler's Wells' Resident Company. Islington's Angel is obviously keeping a good eye on the 'Wells'.

sadler's wells theatre
rosebery avenue = ec1

St Martin's

They make an odd couple, the sober St Martin's and the more frivolous New Ambassadors, a few yards from each other, separated in space by Tower Court and in time by World War I. The pre-war New Ambassadors has a richly adorned interior while the post-war St Martin's avoided fancy plasterwork, opting for the polished wood of the balustraded balcony fronts and Doric columns on pedestals at balcony level, making it seem less intimate than the 550-seat capacity would suggest. Classicism is maintained by the six giant Ionic columns, framing three storeys of large windows, on the stone facade. Links between the two theatres are their common architect, W. G. R. Sprague, the fact that Charles B. Cochran was a lessee of both at their beginnings, and *The Mousetrap*, which ran for 22 years at the Ambassadors, then moved next door to the St Martin's in 1974 for a further interminable run – in 2002 celebrating a record-breaking 50 years!

The theatre that started off on a light note in August 1916 with Gaiety Girl Gertie Millar in Cochran's *Houp La!* soon plunged into the gloom of Eugene Brieux's *Damaged Goods* in the same year. The play, a study of sexually transmitted disease, caused a sensation. After a couple of musical comedies, the theatre returned to 'serious' business with 62-year-old Sir Frank Benson as Hamlet (1920). The director Tyrone Guthrie noted that 'He'd been a very handsome man and proud of his fine physique. It was sad to see this rouged, gaunt ruin of masculine beauty pretending to be Hamlet.'

When the St Martin's was brought under the management of Alec Rea and Basil Dean in 1920, an enterprising series of modern plays was produced. Among the more established writers, John Galsworthy was represented by *The Skin Game*

'Alfred Butt instructed his lieutenants to get the pick of my girls from the St Martin's, even if they cost double the salary of the ordinary chorus girl.'
— Charles B. Cochran, 1925

(1920), *Loyalties* (1922) and *The Forest* (1924); Karel Capek's satire on modern regimentation, *R.U.R.* (1923), made an impact, as did Frederick Lonsdale's *Spring Cleaning* (1925), which had people raising their hands in horror at a 'street walker' being among the dramatis personae. Less controversial was Noël Coward's cardboard Ruritanian drama, *The Queen Was In The Parlour* (1926), with Madge Titheradge, Herbert Marshall and Lady Tree.

Clemence Dane's first play, *A Bill Of Divorcement*, which dealt with the problem of divorce on grounds of insanity, featured a promising young actress called Meggie Albanesi in the role that first brought Katharine Hepburn film fame. Sadly, Miss Albanesi died two years later aged 24, her death being commemorated by a plaque in the foyer of the theatre. Another young actress, 17-year-old Hermione Baddeley, scored a triumph as Florrie Small in Charles McEvoy's study of East End slum life, *The Likes Of Her* (1923). The Great War was the subject of *The White Chateau* (1927) written by Reginald Berkeley while recovering from wounds he received at the front.

The St Martin's continued its policy of dramas on contemporary issues into the 1930s with John Gielgud directing his first modern play, Rodney Ackland's *Strange Orchestra*. Unfortunately, Mrs Patrick Campbell left, after rehearsing for some weeks, because her dog was in quarantine. Of *The Green Bay Tree* (1933) by Mordaunt Shairp, featuring Hugh Williams and Frank Vosper, the critic of the *Star* wrote, 'If the object was to arouse powerful detestation of two abominable people a kind

of success may be concluded, but that is all.' The play is possibly
the first contemporary drama on the subject of homosexuality,
although the word itself is never used.

The first production of J. B. Priestley's oft-revived Yorkshire
comedy, *When We Are Married* (1938), was given here, directed
by Basil Dean. The author himself took over the role of Henry
Ormonroyd, the pickled photographer, when Frank Pettingell
was injured in a road accident. He played it for several nights to
great applause. Its run was terminated by the outbreak of war.
Productions came and went like buses for some years until
Edward Percy's murder tale, *The Shop At Sly Corner* (1945), ran
863 performances.

Successes in the '50s and '60s were Joyce Grenfell in the revue
Penny Plain (1951), American actress Geraldine Page in *The*

The Mousetrap lives on

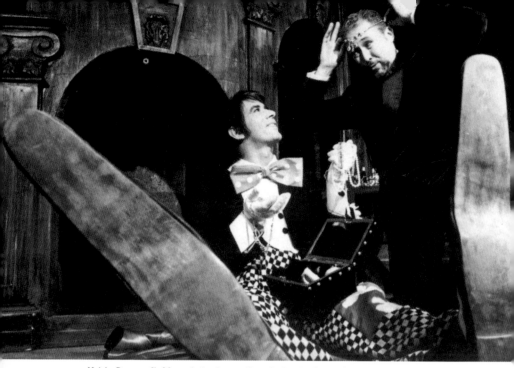

Keith Baxter (left) and Anthony Quayle in Anthony Shaffer's ingenious *Sleuth* (1970)

Rainmaker (1956), two plays by Hugh and Margaret Williams, *Plaintiff In A Pretty Hat* (1957) and *The Grass Is Greener* (1958), *Guilty Party* (1961), *Where Angels Fear To Tread* (1963), from E. M. Forster's novel, and Eric Portman in *The Creeper* (1965). In preparation for the long years of *The Mousetrap*, Keith Baxter, Anthony Quayle and 'many others' starred in Anthony Shaffer's clever thriller *Sleuth* (1970) for three years. *The Mousetrap* was transferred here on 25 March, 1974, and continues making theatrical history as it enters its 50th year. In 1994 Sir Peter Saunders sold the management of *The Mousetrap* and with it the lease of the St Martin's Theatre to Mousetrap Productions Limited, and the theatre underwent major redecoration to a design by Carl Toms. In 1999, the set of *The Mousetrap* was completely replaced – only the clock on the mantelpiece now remains from the set and props of 1952! Presumably, the news of

st martin's

'whodunnit', despite the play having been seen by over ten million people, has still not reached the eager crowds buying their tickets at the St Martin's.

**st martin's theatre
west street = wc2h**

The Savoy

The Savoy Theatre, built for impresario Richard D'Oyly Carte from the profits he accrued from Gilbert and Sullivan's light operas, was the very model of a modern major theatre when it opened in October 1881. As *The Times* stated, 'This is the first time that it has been attempted to light any public building entirely by electricity. What is being done is an experiment, and may succeed or fail.' At the opening production, the one hundred and seventieth performance of *Patience*, the electric lights were 'cheered to the very echo'. People have been cheering at the Savoy ever since.

D'Oyly Carte, who had instigated the partnership of W. S. Gilbert and Arthur Sullivan, dreamed of building his own theatre in which to stage their works. A suitable site was found close to the Thames Embankment within the grounds of the old Savoy Palace Hotel, and a theatre, designed by C. J. Phipps, was constructed within a few months. Not only by the 'application of electric light for theatrical purposes' was the Savoy in advance of other theatres of the day. Not for D'Oyly Carte the 'Gingerbread School of Decorative Art' with its elaborate ornamentation and paintings of cherubs and the like. The decoration was composed of cleaner lines and delicate colouring.

The first years were given over almost exclusively to Gilbert and Sullivan's works, which became known as the Savoy operas: *Iolanthe* (1882), *Princess Ida* (1884), *The Mikado* (1885), *Ruddigore* (1887), *The Yeomen Of The Guard* (1888) and *The Gondoliers* (1889) all had first performances here. During the run of the latter, the irascible Gilbert (lyrics) quarrelled with Sullivan (music) and they refused to work with each other again. Sir Arthur, therefore, collaborated with Sydney Grundy on *Haddon Hall* (1892) before the celebrated duo were reconciled. Their thirteenth operetta together, *Utopia Limited* (1893), failed by

'The new Savoy Theatre is the first really outstanding example of modern decoration applied to a public place on a commercial basis.'
— Country Life, 1929

trying to hit too many targets in Victorian England at once. Their last work as a team was *The Grand Duke* (1896), also a failure. It marked the end of an era, but not the end of Gilbert and Sullivan at the Savoy. There were seasons of revivals in 1929–30, 1932–33, 1961–62, and two weeks in 1975 celebrating the centenary of their first success, *Trial By Jury*. Full-length portraits of Gilbert and Sullivan stand in the theatre today as a memento of their splendid reign.

In contrast to the melodious music of Sullivan and the witty libretti of Gilbert were Harley Granville-Barker's epoch-making Shakespeare productions between 1912 and 1914. John Gielgud recollected in *A Midsummer Night's Dream*, 'the gold-painted fairies, the swaying green curtains to suggest the wood, the hanging canopy overhead – a kind of chandelier of white and green – and the slim tall figure of Oberon, my cousin Dennis Neilson-Terry. I recall also the slightly bewildered reactions of the audience.' The simple and abstract staging, in contrast to Tree's lavish productions at His Majesty's, received much abuse. Granville-Barker's wife, Lillah McCarthy, played Helena, Viola in *Twelfth Night* and Hermione to Henry Ainley's Leontes in *The Winter's Tale* of whom critic W. A. Darlington commented, 'my first experience of really passionate acting, and it convinced me once and for all that the theatre's first concern was with emotion.'

Between the wars, Gertrude Page's Paddy *The Next Best Thing* (1920) ran for over two years, while Noël Coward's second play, *The Young Idea* (1923), featuring himself, ran only eight weeks causing Coward to remark, 'London is outraged at the play coming off, everyone is talking about it and it's doing me a lot of good.' Playwright John Van Druten first came to prominence with *Young*

Woodley (1928), a study of a schoolboy's infatuation with his teacher's wife, which had unaccountably been banned until then. In 1929 a first play by a then unknown playwright, R. C. Sherriff, a moving and realistic portrayal of men in the trenches called *Journey's End*, was an immediate success. It led to the Hollywood careers of both the director James Whale and the actor Colin Clive. Laurence Olivier, who had created the role of Captain Stanhope in Sunday performances, opted to play in *Beau Geste*, which flopped. After *Journey's End* transferred, the whole of the interior and part of the exterior of the theatre was rebuilt.

The main entrance was shifted from the Embankment side (where the old Phipps facade is still visible) to the courtyard of the new Savoy Hotel. In keeping with the hotel's frontage of stainless steel with its knight in shining armour above the entrance, the theatre decked itself in silver splendour. The interior, designed by Frank A. Tugwell and Basil Ionides, was an Art Deco delight. Many exquisite details on doors, seats and

Paul Eddington, Jan Waters and Patricia Routledge in Michael Frayn's hilarious look at theatre folk, *Noises Off*

walls, a glass screen in the Circle Bar, a group of Egyptian maidens round a large vase and golden Japanese scenes on either side of the stage gave it all an air of chic. Winston Churchill, a constant visitor, would always have a seat in the Royal Box. This was built out for him slightly, thus obscuring a few seats on the side of the circle. When his hearing deteriorated, he would sit in the front row.

The hits of the World War II years were Kaufman and Hart's wicked comedy, *The Man Who Came To Dinner* (1941), in which Robert Morley played Sheridan Whiteside. (The actor's son, critic Sheridan Morley, was named after the character.) Coral Browne also appeared, and would later star in *My Sister Eileen* (1943), *The Last of Mrs Cheyney* (1944) and *Lady Frederick* (1946). Post-war, Margaret Lockwood appeared in Agatha Christie's *The Spider's Web* (1954) for over two years, and in *Subway In The Sky* (1957). Noël Coward renewed his acquaintance with the Savoy with his musical *Sail Away* (1962) in which Elaine Stritch as Mimi Paragon first made herself known to British audiences. *High Spirits* (1964), a musical adaptation of Coward's play *Blithe Spirit* by Hugh Martin and Timothy Gray, limped along for three months, but the Savoy would soon have a string of long runs with plays like *Alibi For A Judge* (1965), two William Douglas Home comedies, *The Secretary Bird* (1968) and *Lloyd George Knew My Father* (1972) with Ralph Richardson and Peggy Ashcroft (afterwards replaced by Celia Johnson) and the controversial *Whose Life Is It Anyway?* with Tom Conti in 1978. Michael Frayn's farce of the theatre, *Noises Off* (1982), ran for over four years.

Then in February 1990, disaster struck – a fire ravaged the auditorium. Three years later, the auditorium and public areas had been faithfully restored to the 1929 vision of Tugwell and Ionides, and the theatre triumphantly reopened with a Royal Gala performed by the English National Ballet, in the presence of HRH The Princess of Wales. Since then, the Savoy has gone from strength to strength with productions such as *The Importance of Being Oscar* with Simon Callow, Edward Fox in *A Letter of*

Gilbert and Sullivan's *Mikado* enjoyed a new audience in 2002 at the Savoy

Resignation and Coward's *Hay Fever* with Geraldine McEwan. The new millennium saw the triumphant return of the D'Oyly Carte season with *The Mikado*, as well as Donald Sutherland's return to the stage in *Enigmatic Variations*. Since then, the D'Oyly Carte Opera Company has returned again to its spiritual home, with acclaimed performances of *The Mikado*, *Iolanthe* and *The Yeomen of the Guard*.

the savoy theatre
savoy court, the strand wc2r

The Shaftesbury

On 19 July, 1973, just as the Shaftesbury Theatre was about to celebrate the two thousandth performance of the 'flower children' musical *Hair*, part of the ceiling of the auditorium fell in. It seemed as though the theatre's days were numbered as the threat of turning it into an office block loomed over its little roof tower. Would demolition workers really knock down Bertie Crewe's stone frontage that had dominated the corner at the junction of Shaftesbury Avenue and High Holborn since 1911? Would anyone have the heart to wreck the florid interior, with its eight bow-fronted boxes framed by giant Ionic columns? Would a hammer be taken to the life-size statues representing Comedy, Tragedy, Poetry and Music that sit over each upper box? How could the bas-relief of reclining women and Roman soldiers over the proscenium be shattered without compunction? Members of the entertainment industry and Equity, the actors' union, fought a vigorous campaign to keep the theatre open by organising protest marches and getting petitions signed. Happily, in March 1974, the Department of the Environment gave in to the pressure and placed the Shaftesbury on the Statutory List of Buildings of Special Architectural or Historic Interest. Like one of the heroines in the melodramas for which it was built, this pretty Edwardian theatre was saved from a terrible fate in the nick of time.

Under the management of the brothers Walter and Frederick Melville, the New Princes Theatre (as it was originally called until it became the Princes in 1914) housed a series of popular melodramas that have since come to dust. Seymour Hicks's three-year reign began in 1916 with a revival of *Bluebell in Fairyland*. In 1919, Charles B. Cochran took over for a while, the year the great soprano Maggie Teyte appeared in André Messager's light opera *Monsieur Beaucaire*. The Princes also played host to the

*'This particular theatre, because of the ambience
of the auditorium... provides an intimate
relationship between performer and audience,
so necessary for comedy.'*
— Ray Cooney

D'Oyly Carte Opera Company when the Savoy was unavailable. Seasons of the works of Gilbert and Sullivan were presented here in the 1920s, '40s and '50s. In fact, the large auditorium of 1,250 (now 1,305) seats has always been suitable for operettas, musicals and ballets. Diaghilev's Russian ballet performed here in 1921 and 1927, and Sadler's Wells Opera and Ballet Company in 1944.

Among the straight plays were *Daniel* (1921), in which Sarah Bernhardt made her final London appearance; *Alf's Button* (1924), a fantasy written by the theatre critic W. A. Darlington; and *Macbeth* (1926), starring Sybil Thorndike and Henry Ainley as the murderous Scottish couple. A gas-pipe explosion in a nearby street interrupted the run of George Gershwin's *Funny Face* (1928), featuring Fred and Adele Astaire and Leslie Henson. Due to 'the impassability of the roadway to vehicular traffic', the theatre was closed for some weeks. In 1929, Firth Shephard blew in as manager, remaining until 1946. The shows under his aegis included Sardou's *Diplomacy* (1933), two adaptations from stories by Edgar Wallace, *The Frog* (1936) and *The Gusher* (1937), and John O'Keeffe's 1791 comedy *Wild Oats* (1938). Although the theatre suffered some bomb blasts in 1940 and 1941, it managed to remain open during the war years.

Ironically, it was in the post-war days that the Princes was dark more often than not. Bright spots were *His Excellency* (1950) with Eric Portman; Michael Redgrave and Peggy Ashcroft in *Antony And Cleopatra* (1953) from Stratford-on-Avon; the American musicals *Pal Joey* (1954) and *Wonderful Town* (1955), and a British one, *Summer Song* (1956), based on the music and life of Dvorak. When the partnership of Charles Clore and EMI bought the theatre in 1962, it was redecorated and renamed the Shaftesbury. Frank Loesser's Broadway hit musical *How To Succeed In Business Without Really Trying* (1963) did for the box-office what the title suggests. In contrast Lionel Bart's Robin Hood musical, *Twangi* (1965), ran for a mere 43 performances. After that, Eric Sykes and Jimmy Edwards in *Big Bad Mouse* (1966) kept the coach parties happy for over a year before the advent of *Hair* in 1968.

Hair was the musical that gave voice to hippiedom, to the anti-Vietnam war and Civil Rights movements, and that opened the day after theatre censorship officially ended, thus allowing audiences the sight of full frontal nudity, both male and female.

After its escape from the bulldozers, the Shaftesbury continued to present musicals, notably Neil Simon and Marvin Hamlisch's *They're Playing Our Song* (1980). The theatre had another facelift in 1986, and again in 1989. It now has a bright and attractive lobby with an array of flowers placed in small alcoves, and the auditorium is a delightful wedding cake of pink and white. It was two years earlier that the Theatre of Comedy company, founded by writer-director Ray Cooney and supported by 30 leading actors, writers and directors, bought the theatre and renamed it, officially, the Shaftesbury Theatre of Comedy.

Among the many highly successful productions presented by the company are founder Ray Cooney's *Run For Your Wife,* Shaw's *Pygmalion* with Peter O'Toole and *See How They Run* (which won founder member Maureen Lipman an Olivier Award). More awards came thick and fast through the '90s: Ray Cooney's *Out of Order* (1990) won the 1991 Olivier Award for Comedy of the Year; the controversial *Kiss of the Spider Woman* won the *Evening Standard* Award for Best Musical 1992, then went on to collect seven Tony awards on Broadway; *Tommy*, by Pete Townsend (1996), won three Olivier Awards, including Outstanding Musical Production; and in 1998 the Shaftesbury was chosen as the London venue for the multi-award-winning musical *Rent*. In 1997 the theatre provided a home for the Royal

The seminal American 'hippy' musical *Hair* made its English home at the Shaftesbury

the shaftesbury

Opera whilst the Royal Opera House Covent Garden underwent major redevelopment. Six operas were performed, including new productions of *Il Barbiere di Siviglia* and the Olivier Award-winning *Paul Bunyan*, directed by Francesca Zambello. Since then, there has been Charles Aznavour's new musical *Lautrec* and the sumptuous *Napoleon*. All in all, a history to be very proud of.

the shaftesbury theatre
shaftesbury avenue = wc2h

Shakespeare's Globe

London's very first playhouse, erected in London in April 1576, was simply called The Theatre. When it was pulled down in 1597, its timber was taken across the River Thames and used to build the Globe – Shakespeare's famous 'wooden O'. The original Globe Theatre was built on the south bank of the Thames in 1599 by an architect named Peter Street, especially for William Shakespeare's company of players. Shakespeare's players (The Chamberlain's Men – later, in 1603, The King's Men) were led by Richard Burbage – the first Hamlet, Lear and Othello, and one of the first in a long line of actor-managers who ran, and often owned, the theatres in which they performed. This noble tradition was echoed in the twentieth century by Sam Wanamaker, actor and director, whose determination and vision created today's modern Globe, and it continues with actor Mark Rylance, the present Artistic Director of the Shakespeare's Globe Theatre.

When the original Globe was built, the South Bank was London's playground – characterised by brothels, bear-baiting and theatre-going. Shakespeare and his contemporaries presented their plays at the Rose, Swan, Hope and Globe theatres – and the Globe was the most popular of them all. But in 1613 a spark from a stage cannon set fire to the thatched roof of the theatre and it was burnt to the ground. A second Globe was built on the same foundations with a tiled roof, and probably a more ornate interior. In 1616 Shakespeare died, and in 1642 the Globe was closed by the Puritans. Two years later, the theatre was destroyed and its foundations buried to make way for tenement buildings.

'...an atmosphere that reflects the ethos of the Globe – informal, infectiously friendly and compellingly inviting.'
— *Time Out* magazine

And there it lay for four hundred years. Then, in 1949, fleeing the artistic oppression of the US's McCarthy era, actor/director Sam Wanamaker came to London and settled there, devoting the rest of his life to realising his vision of bringing Shakespeare's Globe back to life and revitalising world-wide interest in Shakespeare's plays. Central to this vision was the rebuilding of the Globe Theatre as it was in Shakespeare's time, for which Wanamaker tirelessly campaigned to raise money.

In 1970 he established the Globe Playhouse Trust, dedicated to the experience and international understanding of Shakespeare in performance and the celebration of the fact that the greatest dramatic poet in the English language lived in the cradle of English theatre, on Bankside by the River Thames. In the same year, Southwark Council offered the Trust a 1.2-acre site beside the River Thames – a site only 200 yards from the original position of the Globe. This wasn't acquired until 1989, when the foundations of the original building were discovered under a Georgian terrace and Southwark Bridge Road.

shakespeare's globe

Theo Crosby was the architect of Shakespeare's Globe, and he began designs for the site in 1986. Archaeological excavations, panoramas, maps, building contracts, contemporary accounts and remaining buildings each contributed to the body of knowledge that informed the reconstruction. There are no plans or construction drawings that clearly depict the form of the original theatre itself, so its design and construction were quite a challenge. Theo Crosby died in 1994, shortly after the death of Sam Wanamaker. Sadly, neither man had a chance to see their dream fully realised. Since 1994, Crosby's work has been continued by John Greenfield, who first joined the project in 1987, the same year that the site was cleared for ground-breaking and the six-metre-deep foundations were laid.

In 1993 the construction of the theatre itself began on the newly laid Piazza. The next summer, under the supervision of master craftsman Peter McCurdy, the walls were built using traditional methods and traditional components – handmade bricks, lime plaster and 168,000 metres of oak laths. The roof used 6,000 bundles of Norfolk water reed, making the Globe the first thatched building to be built in central London since the Great Fire of 1666.

In 1995, there was a Workshop Season for the new Globe Theatre Company, and in the same year, with funding from the National Lottery, the Globe Theatre was completed, including foyer areas, a restaurant and a café. The theatre is a beautiful, organic building, and its setting is wonderful. Right on the bank of the Thames, it looks towards St Paul's Cathedral across a river spanned by the graceful lines of the Millennium Bridge. To its left is the Tate Modern. The area is full of vibrant landmarks of twenty-first century London, part of a celebration of arts, culture and architecture. On 12 June 1997, in the presence of HM the Queen and HRH Prince Philip, Patron of the Shakespeare Globe Trust, the theatre opened officially with a production of *Henry V*.

The theatre season runs each year from May to September, and audiences at the Globe sit in the gallery or stand informally as 'groundlings' in the yard, just as they would have 400 years

Mark Rylance as Posthumus in *Cymbeline*, 2001

ago. If it rains, the groundlings get wet! But that doesn't seem to put audiences off – each year numbers have been rising, and the theatre's fifth anniversary season was the Company's best attended yet, with nearly a quarter of a million people.

The Globe Theatre Company, under the artistic direction of Mark Rylance, has so far produced 15 of Shakespeare's plays. The three productions of 2001 (*Macbeth, King Lear* and *Cymbeline*) were particularly highly acclaimed. They have also presented the work of Shakespeare's contemporaries: Thomas Middleton, with *A Chaste Maid in Cheapside* (1997) and *A Mad World, My Masters* (1998); Fletcher and Beaumont, with *The Maid's Tragedy* (1997); Richard Brome, with *The Antipodes* (2000); and Thomas Dekker, with *An Honest Whore* (1998). New plays are also commissioned to exploit the theatre's unique audience/actor relationship. Resident playwright Peter Oswald's *Augustine's Oak* (1999) and

shakespeare's globe

his version of the epic comedy *The Golden Ass* (2002) were both written especially for the Globe.

The theatre also welcomes international theatre companies. In 1997 it staged *Umabatha*, the Zulu *Macbeth*; in 1998 the Cuban Company Teatro Buendia's version of *The Tempest*; in 1999 the Annette Leday/Keil Company's *Kathakali King Lear*; in 2002 Grupo Galpao's Brazilian *Romeo & Julieta*; and in 2002 the Japanese play *The Kyogen of Errors* (based on *The Comedy of Errors*). The Globe Theatre Company also takes its productions abroad: 2001's *King Lear* ran at the Tokyo Globe for two weeks; *Macbeth* had performances at the Teatro Olimpico, a contemporary of the original Globe Theatre in Vicenza, Italy; and the acclaimed production of *Cymbeline* was performed in New York in 2002. For the past four years the theatre has also been home to the annual WOMAD (World of Music and Dance) festival, and the Comedy Store Players, who play for one riotous night a year.

The Globe isn't just about performances, there's also Globe Education. The theatre devotes six months of each year exclusively to education, running courses on all aspects of Shakespeare and the experience of performing his works as they were originally intended to be performed, for students and teachers throughout the UK and abroad. There is also a permanent and well-attended Exhibition at the Globe – the largest in the world dedicated to Shakespeare and his workplace.

And construction is still going on! An indoor theatre is being built on the site to a design by Inigo Jones (*c*.1616), and a library and education centre are under construction. This unique centre really is a living, working, passionate tribute to the greatest writer in the English language.

shakespeare's globe theatre
new globe walk = se1

The Strand

Looking at this solid, classical, corner building with its giant columns and pediments, it is difficult to imagine that the Strand was bombed in both World Wars. In each case it continued to function as if nothing had happened. In 1915, during a performance of *The Scarlet Pimpernel*, it suffered a Zeppelin raid. Fred Terry, John Gielgud's great-uncle and an actor-manager in the grand manner, went down among the audience in his Sir Percy Blakeney costume, urging them not to be afraid, before stepping back onto the stage and continuing with the play. During Donald Wolfit's Shakespeare season in October 1940, a German bomb fell on the theatre, damaging the dressing rooms. Having dug out the costumes from the debris, the actors clambered over the ruins to get to the stage. These are two of the most extraordinary examples of the dictum, 'The show must go on.'

Shows have been going on at the Strand non-stop since it opened, in May 1905, with a season of operas alternating with plays given in Italian by the remarkable tragedienne Eleonora Duse and her company. In the same year, a crack in the proscenium arch of his own theatre drove Herbert Beerbohm Tree to bring in *Oliver Twist*, starring himself as Fagin, while it was being repaired. Tree would have found the Waldorf (as the Strand was first called) no less luxurious than His Majesty's. It was built at the same time as and with a facade almost identical to that of the Aldwych Theatre on the opposite corner, separated by the Waldorf Hotel, the architect of both theatres being the renowned W. G. R. Sprague. Although it lacks the delightful oval gallery of its near neighbour, the interior decorations of the Strand are far more impressive.

At the foot of the elegant stairway are twin female figurines holding lamps which throw light upon the highly polished brass

'This mass exhumation of former film stars – British at that – was regarded by the critics as turning the Strand into a disaster area.'

— Michael Denison, 1965

railings and marble walls. In the green and gold 927-seat auditorium are two tiers of boxes, framed in Ionic pilasters and crowned with an ornate sculptural group of cupids. More cupids attend the Sun God in a chariot pulled by four horses, in a vigorous and colourful design above the stage. On the circular ceiling are painted allegorical figures after Le Brun. The Royal Box, used mainly by businessmen wishing to impress their clients or girlfriends, has a large retiring room.

In the years before World War I, apart from Tree and La Duse, many of the great names of the Edwardian theatre appeared at the Strand - H. B. Irving in *Lights Out* (1905), Cyril Maude in *She Stoops to Conquer* (1906) and E. H. Sothem and his wife Julia Marlowe in four Shakespeare plays. Matheson Lang gave the theatre its first long run (403 performances) with *Mr Wu* (1913). So identified did Lang become with the title role that he called his autobiography of 1940 *Mr Wu Looks Back*. During the war, it was the visit of Fred Terry and Julia Neilson in *Henry Of Navarre, Sweet Nell Of Old Drury* and *The Scarlet Pimpernel* that held audiences in rapture.

Arthur Bourchier, whose portrait hangs in the foyer, ran the theatre for eight years from 1919. Among his successes were a dramatisation of *Treasure Island*, presented every Christmas from 1922 to 1926; the first British production of Eugene O'Neill's 1903 play *Anna Christie* (1923) with Pauline Lord in the title role; and another American import, *Broadway* (1926) by Philip Dunning and George Abbott. When Bourchier died while touring South Africa in 1927, George Grossmith took over for a couple of years during which he produced Charles Laughton (a year before his film debut) in *Beauty*, and Miriam Hopkins (three years prior to her Hollywood career) in *Bachelor Father* (both 1927).

While farces were still packing them in a few yards away at the Aldwych, comedian Leslie Henson and Firth Shephard produced a rival series of similar entertainments with titles such as *It's A Boy!* (1930), *It's A Girl!* and *Night Of The Garter* (both 1932). After a year's run of *1066 And All That* (1935), 'a comic history with music', farce returned with Aldwych favourites Robertson 'Oh Calamity' Hare and Alfred Drayton in Vernon Sylvaine's *Aren't Men Beasts* (1936) and *A Spot Of Bother* (1937); and Ben Travers's *Banana Ridge* (1938) and *Spotted Dick* (1939).

For most of the war years from 1942, Joseph Kesselring's black comedy *Arsenic And Old Lace*, with Lilian Braithwaite (created a Dame in 1943 during the run), Mary Jerrold, Frank Pettingell and Naunton Wayne, occupied the large Strand. One night, after the performance, Dame Lilian had to take refuge in the ground floor cloakroom during an air raid that lasted many hours. Asked if she was exhausted by the episode, she replied, 'Certainly not! We were fifty pounds up last night.' Braithwaite, the mother of actress Joyce Carey, had been at the Strand 29 years previously in *Mr Wu*.

If the Strand managed to withstand the bombs of two World Wars, then the booming tones of Peggy Mount as Emma Hornett, the battle-axe mother-in-law-to-be in *Sailor Beware* (1955), shook its very foundations for over three years. The 40-

(above) The renowned Italian tragedienne Eleonora Duse graced the Strand with her acclaimed presence

Felicity Kendal and Roger Rees starred in *The Real Thing* (1982), Tom Stoppard's highly successful play about contemporary marriage

year-old actress, who had spent years in provincial rep, suddenly found herself a West End star. Aside from a satirical revue, *For Adults Only* (1958), and *The Affair* (1961), an adaptation of C. P. Snow's novel, shows came and went with rapidity for a few years. One, *The Princess* (1960), got such bad notices that the management offered free seats for a week. The experiment failed.

the strand

The opening night of *A Funny Thing Happened On The Way To The Forum* in November 1963 coincided with the news of the assassination of John F. Kennedy. The audience was not much in the mood for laughter, but the musical Roman romp, starring Frankie Howerd, and Robertson Hare as a slave called Erronius, overcame the initial resistance, and the show ran nearly two years.

Alastair Sim and Dora Bryan in Shaw's *Too True To Be Good* and Margaret Lockwood and Richard Todd in *An Ideal Husband* (both 1965) breezed through on their way to other theatres. Peggy Mount returned to the scene of her first triumph in J. B. Priestley's *When We Are Married* (1970), before the incredible run – 11 years – of the farce, *No Sex Please, We're British* (1971), by Anthony Marriott and Alistair Foot, featuring a young Michael Crawford. Like *The Mousetrap*, it became virtually a national institution and ran and ran. When it left for the Garrick and then the Duchess, Tom Stoppard's *The Real Thing* (1984) was able to attract the crowds. *Cabaret* (1986) which followed, with dancer Wayne Sleep as the MC, was ended suddenly a year later by a musicians' strike. The next ten years saw some strong drama and fine actors at the Strand – *Lost in Yonkers* with Maureen Lipman, *The Prime of Miss Jean Brodie*, starring Patricia Hodge, *A View From the Bridge* with Joseph Fiennes, and Imogen Stubbs in *St Joan*. Then, in 1996, came the musical *Buddy*, transferred from the Victoria Palace. It was enormously popular, and finally finished its run in March 2002, making it the most successful rock and roll musical ever with an amazing 5,140 performances, and in the process helping this survivor of a theatre to build a solid foundation for the future.

the strand theatre
aldwych = wc2b

The Vaudeville

This refined, discreet, small theatre in the Strand can lay claim to having launched Henry Irving on his way to becoming the dominant actor-manager during the last 30 years of Queen Victoria's reign. The first theatre on the site was built in 1870 by C. J. Phipps for three of the most popular actors of the day: David James, H. J. Montague and Thomas Thorne, known as the Jew, the Gent and the Gentile. They offered the 32-year-old Irving ten pounds a week to join the company and appear in the opening production, *For Love Or Money*. During the run, he was asked by budding playwright James Albery (the same age as Irving) to read the manuscript of his play *Two Roses*, 'a dainty domestic comedy'. Irving, who had been typecast for years as a villain in trashy plays, was worried that David James (the uncle of David Belasco) might claim the comic role for himself. In the event, Irving played the part of Digby Grant for 15 months before the American impresario, the self-styled Colonel Bateman, installed him at his newly bought Lyceum Theatre round the corner. It was there that Irving made theatrical history.

In 1871, Montague (who was to die two years later aged 34) left the Vaudeville in the hands of his partners. They broke all previous records with H. J. Byron's comedy *Our Boys* (1875), which ran four years. Its popularity was so phenomenal that Strand omnibuses would pull up outside the Vaudeville and the conductors would shout, 'Our Boys!' It was immediately followed by the distaff version called *Our Girls* (1879), which failed. Lightweight entertainments were the main fare, and indeed have been throughout most of the theatre's existence, interrupted by Henry Arthur Jones's 'problem play' *Saints And Sinners* (1884), which shocked some people with its 'religious blasphemies'. The charming Cyril Maude, then in his twenties,

'This little jewel-box of a theatre has, unfortunately, over recent years contained more paste than gems.'
— Clive Hirschhorn, 1986

redressed the balance by appearing in a series of comedies from 1888 until the theatre was reconstructed in 1891.

The compact four-storey Portland stone exterior, with its first-level loggia and French casement windows, could well have passed for the private house of a wealthy Victorian merchant. Today, the facade can be appreciated in its entirety because it only has a small sign over the canopy. Thomas Thorne, the remaining member of the original trio, sold the Vaudeville to the brothers Gatti, whose family continued to own it until 1969. From 1900 to 1906, Agostino and Stephano Gatti shared the management with Charles Frohman, who presented a string of successes starring Seymour Hicks and his wife Ellaline Terriss including *Bluebell In Fairyland* (1901) and J. M. Barrie's *Quality Street* (1902). The couple's last appearance at the Vaudeville was in *The Belle Of Mayfair* (1906) before they moved on to the Aldwych built for them and Frohman. Charles Hawtrey (father of the comedian in the 'Carry On' films) carried on the tradition in several comedies.

For ten years from 1915, the Vaudeville was the home of the Charlot revues. André Charlot had made a name for himself previously as a specialist of the genre at the Alhambra, a famous music hall demolished in 1936. (The Odeon Cinema, Leicester Square, now stands on the site.) Most of the Vaudeville revues had one word titles like *Samples* (1915), *Some* (1916), *Cheep* (1917), *Tabs* (1918), *Snap* (1922), and *Yes* (1923), and were instrumental in helping the careers of Beatrice Lillie, Gertrude Lawrence, Binnie Hale and Stanley Lupino (father of film actress-director Ida Lupino).

In 1926, the theatre was given a completely new interior, keeping the 1892 Phipps frontage intact. The proscenium was

Poster for a Charlot revue, 1920s

Left to right: Patricia Hodge, Tim Piggott-Smith, Oliver Cotton and Brenda Blethyn in Michael Frayn's *Benefactors* (1984)

enlarged, new stairways built and the auditorium changed from its horseshoe shape to that of a rectangle with classical ornamentation. It then resumed where it left off – with revues from *Vaudeville Vanities* (1926) to Charlot's *Non-Stop Revue* (1937).

Revue departed, another redecoration ensued, and in came Robert Morley's second play *Goodness, How Sad!* (1938). The wartime successes were three plays by women – *Men In Shadow* (1942) by Mary Hayley Bell, starring her husband John Mills; Enid Bagnold's first play *Lottie Dundass* (1943); and Esther McCracken's *No Medals* (1944), which ran 742 performances.

In 1947, William Douglas Home (brother of future Prime Minister Alec Douglas Home) made a name for himself with the high-life comedy *The Chiltern Hundreds*, which ran for over two years with 78-year-old A. E. Matthews playing a dotty earl. The next long run, in fact the longest in Britain since *Chu Chin Chow*, was a whimsical little English musical by Julian Slade and Dorothy Reynolds called *Salad Days* (1954). Its tinkly but pleasant tunes kept audiences happy for six years. In 1962 the Vaudeville, known mostly for traditional entertainment, had its first whiff of the 'Angry Young Man' school of drama when Arnold Wesker's class-battle air-force play *Chips With Everything* transferred from the Royal Court. But the theatre was soon back to establishment works such as Dorothy Tutin impersonating Victoria in *Portrait Of A Queen* (1965), Sybil Thorndike, Athene Seyler, Richard Briers, Lewis Casson and Julia Lockwood in *Arsenic And Old Lace* (1966) and Leslie Phillips in *The Man Most Likely To...* (1968) which lasted for nearly two years.

In 1969, Peter Saunders bought the theatre from the Gatti family, put in air conditioning and showers in the dressing rooms, and repainted it. The pretty, mirrored entrance with a chandelier leads into the well-preserved auditorium where Moira Lister was seen in boudoir farces *Move Over, Mrs Markham* (1971) and *Key For Two* (1982); Glenda Jackson appeared in tragi-comedies *Stevie* (1977) and *Great And Small* (1983); Michael Frayn's *Benefactors* (1984) was premiered, and the prolific Alan Ayckbourn enjoyed another success with *Woman In Mind* (1986), in which Julia McKenzie won the Society of London Theatres' Best Actress of the Year Award. Other fine performances from women at that time were Pauline Collins in *Shirley Valentine* (1988) and Maureen Lipman in *Re: Joyce* (1989), a tremendous one-woman show based on the life and songs of Joyce Grenfell. The 1990s were a varied decade, with Peter Greenwell's tribute to Noël Coward, *A Talent To Amuse* (1995), the revival of the award-winning David Hare play, *Skylight* (1997), the premiere of the South African musical *Kat And The Kings* (1998) and old favourite *The Chiltern Hundreds* (1999). In 2001 the theatre presented Ray Cooney's sequel to the legendary *Run For Your Wife – Caught in the Net*, starring Eric Sykes and Russ Abbot. And so the Vaudeville continues to supply top-class West End shows in a pleasant setting.

the vaudeville theatre
strand = wc2r

The Victoria Palace

For decades, before air travel became the principal means of transport, most visitors from the Continent would not have had to go far in order to see a supreme example of English theatre architecture. Facing Victoria Station is an imposing and unusual white stone edifice, crowned with giant statues and a Baroque tower and dome. The classical facade, open loggia with Ionic columns high above the entrance and festooned oval windows display the unmistakable touch of master theatre builder Frank Matcham, whose last remaining complete work in London this is.

Two buildings preceded the present Victoria Palace. Moy's Royal Standard Music Hall was demolished in 1886 during the rebuilding of Victoria Station and its environs. A new building on the site continued as a music hall until it, too, was pulled down in 1911. The Victoria Palace, built in the same year for impresario Alfred Butt, must have absorbed the music hall tradition of its antecedents into its very foundation stones for, with large music halls springing up all over the place, this was built to rival them all. The 1,565-seat, richly ornamented auditorium has a domed ceiling (the sliding roof keeps it cool in hot weather) and two tiers of three boxes on either side. Outside, on the pinnacle of the structure, was a gilded metal figure of Pavlova in full flight. It was said that the world's most famous ballerina superstitiously avoided looking at it every time she drove past by drawing the blinds of her car. The statue was taken down to protect it during the Blitz, but its whereabouts today remain a mystery.